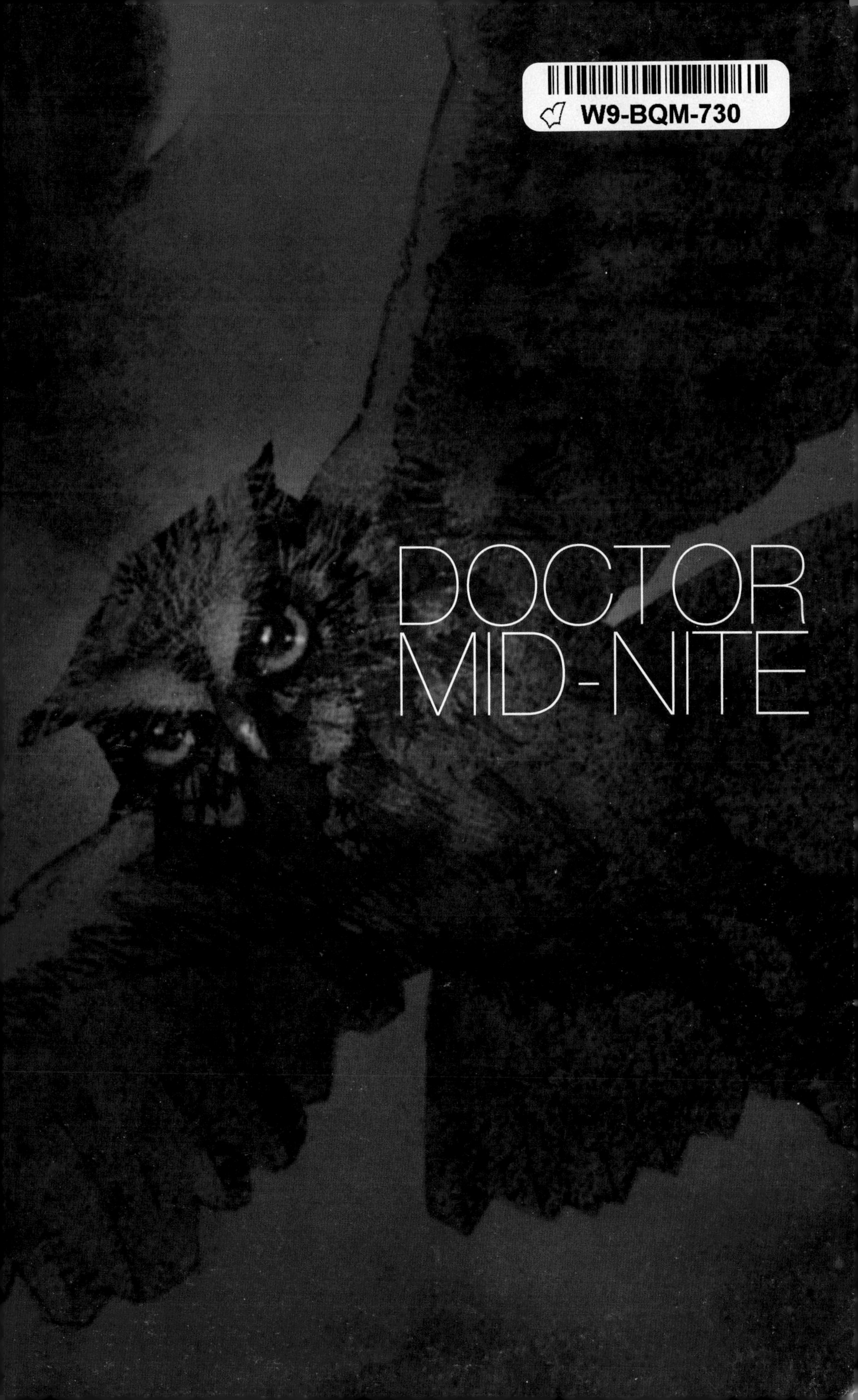
DOCTOR
MID-NITE

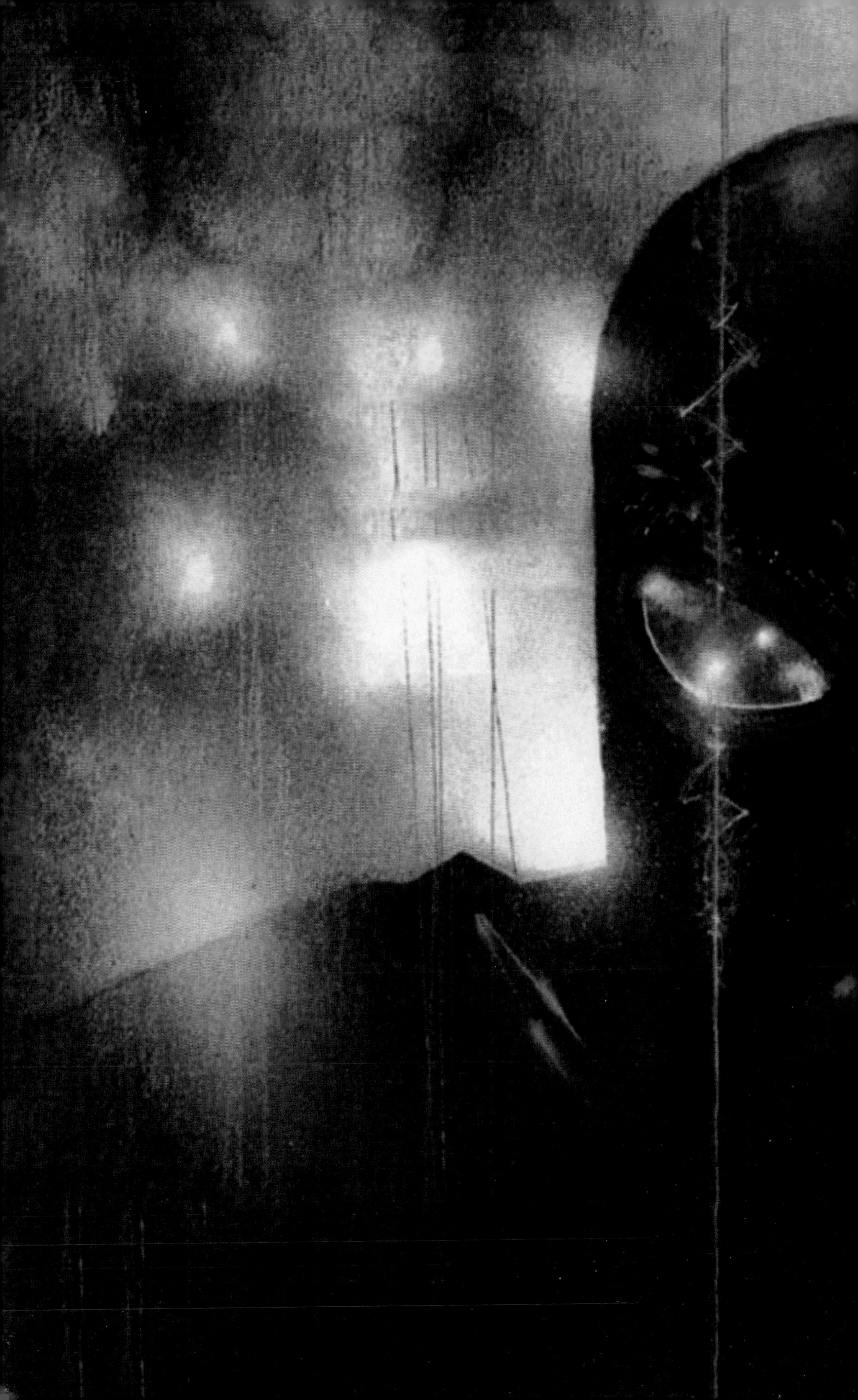

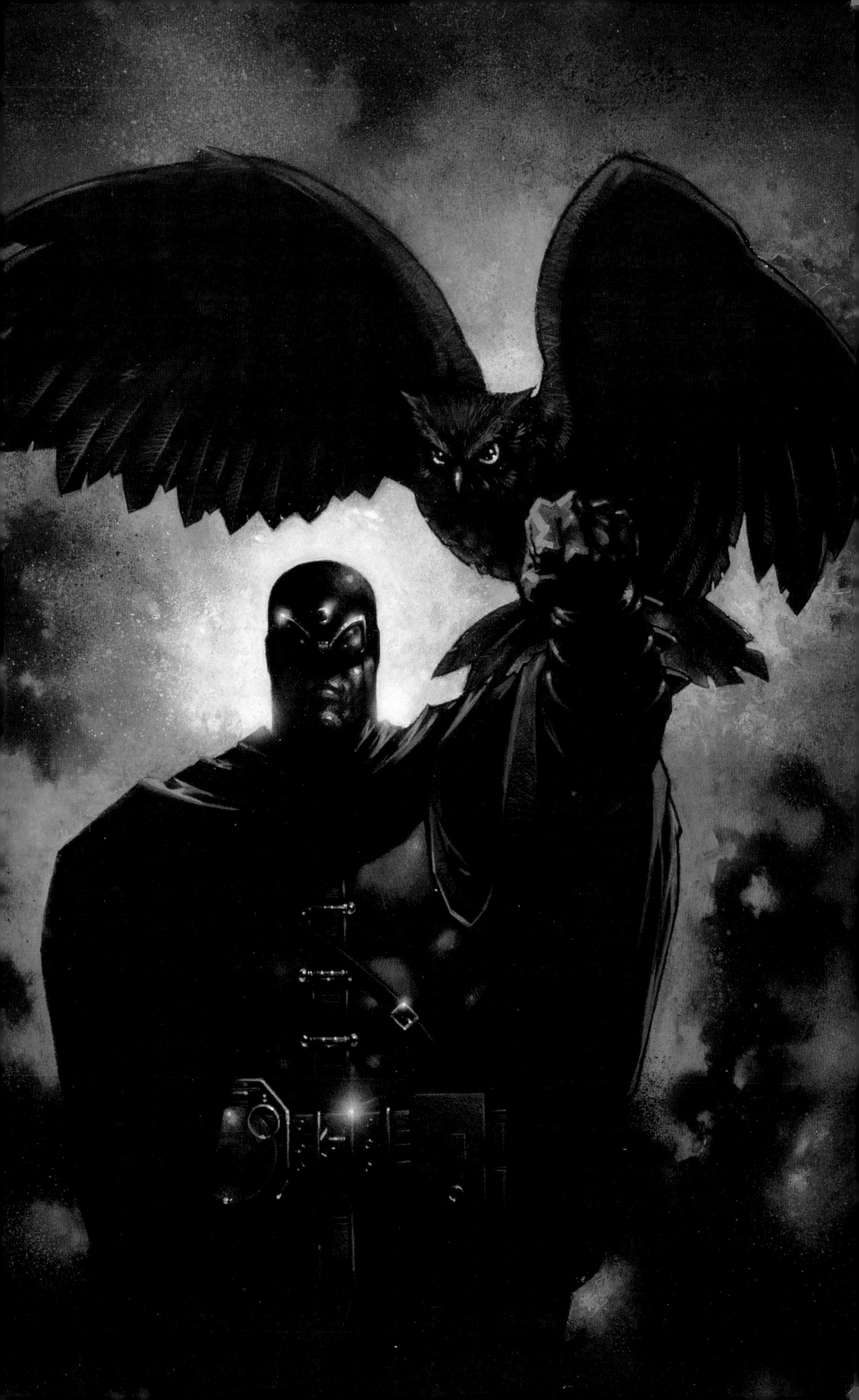

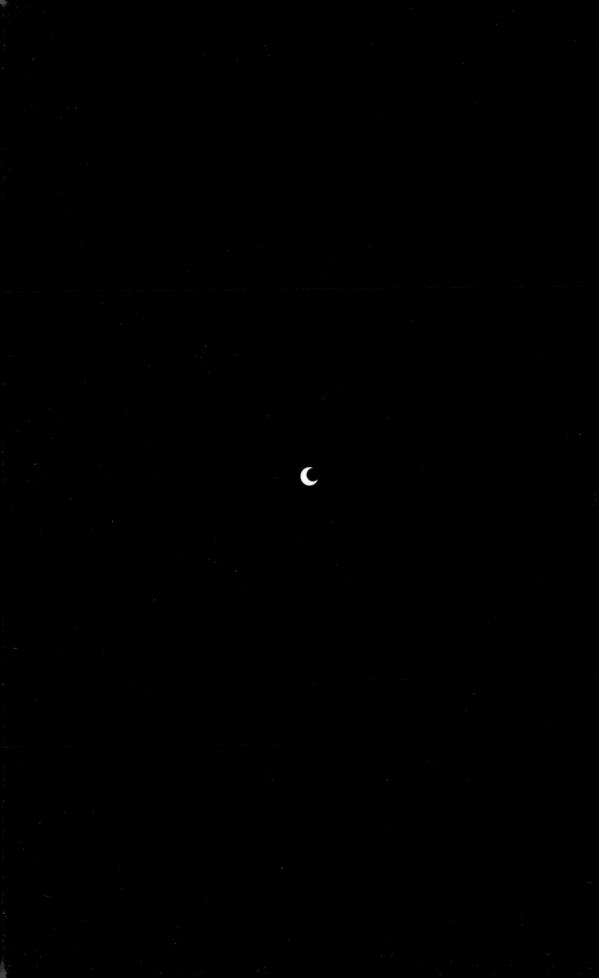

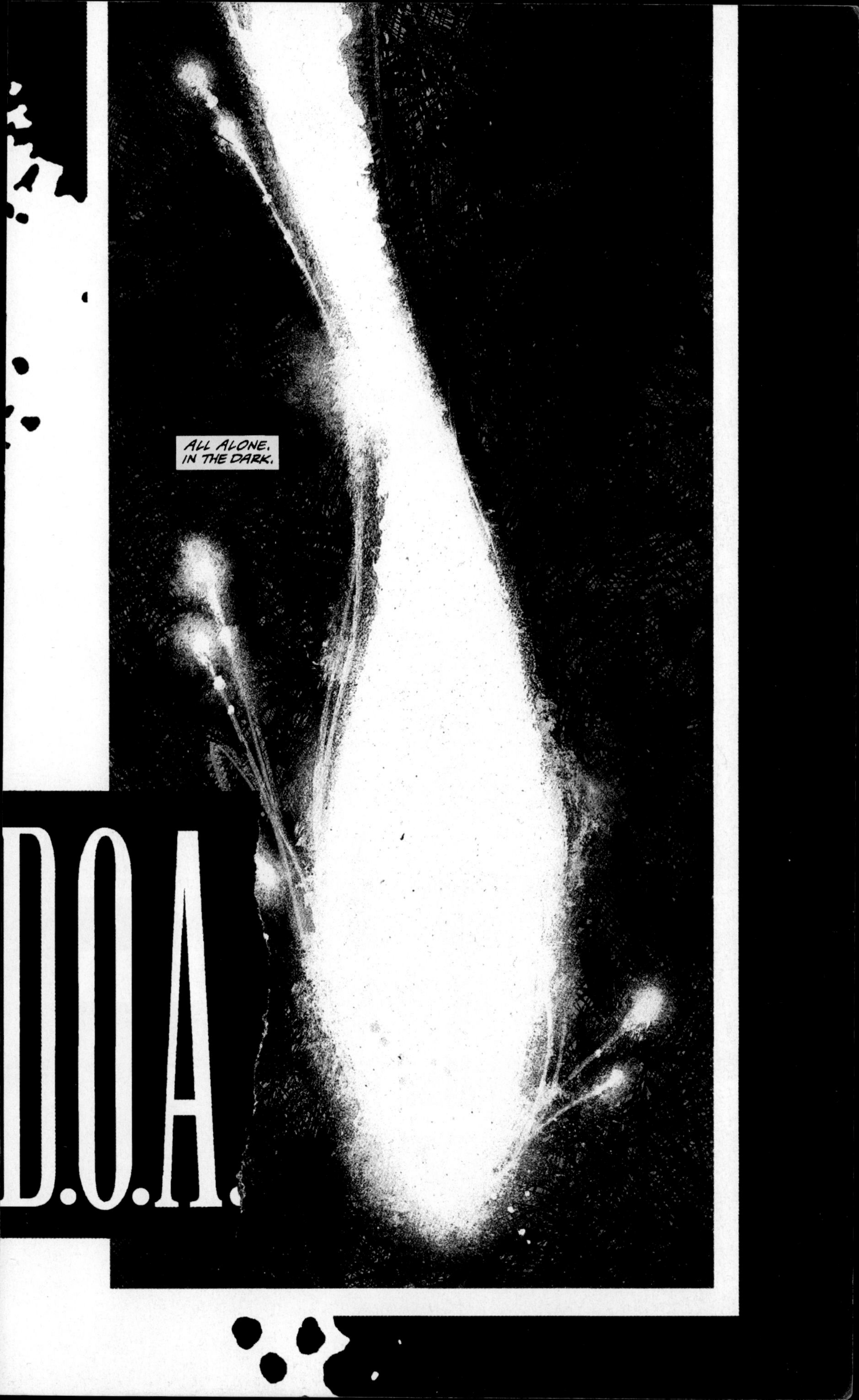
ALL ALONE.
IN THE DARK.
D.O.A.

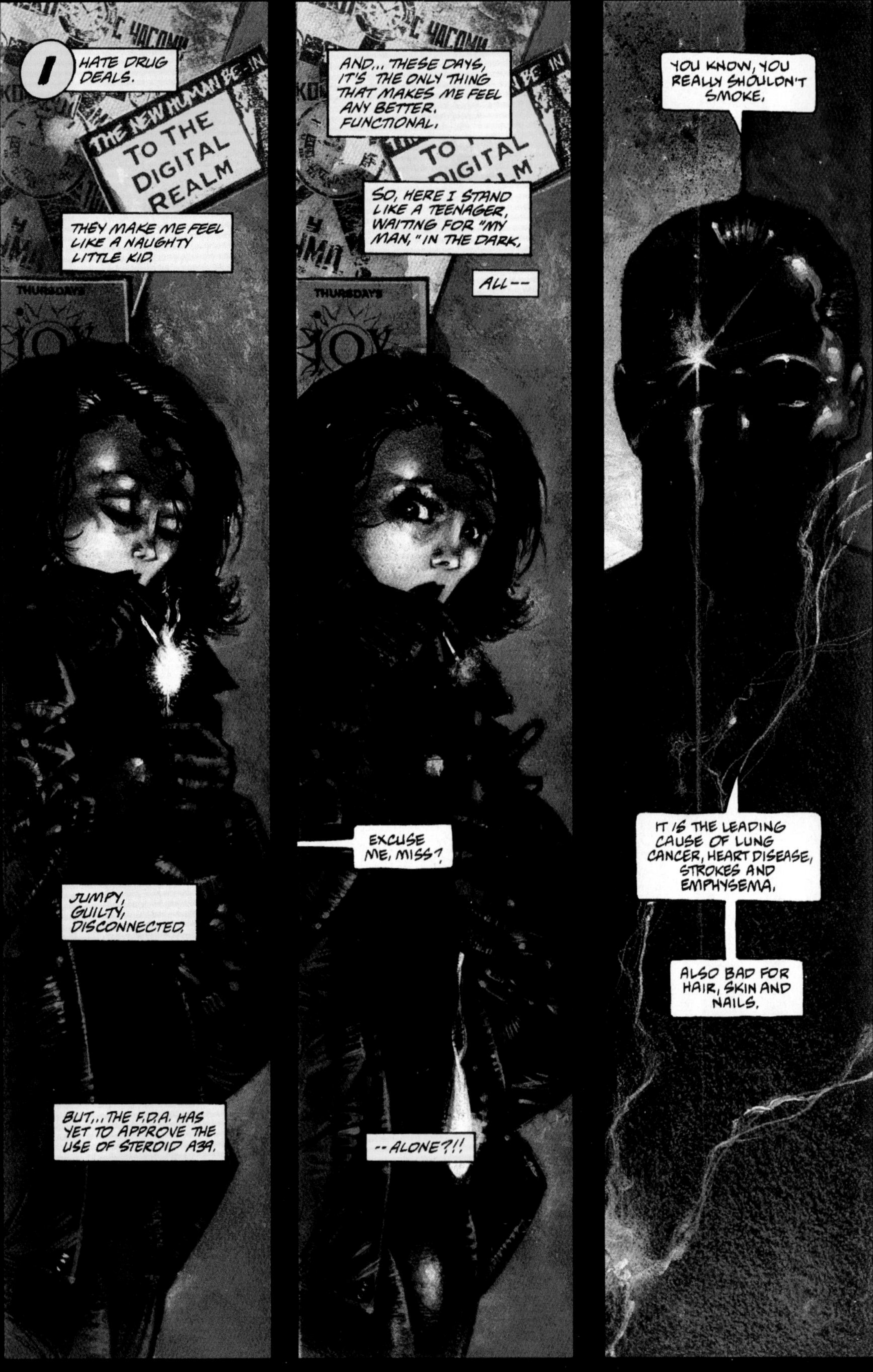

I HATE DRUG DEALS.
THE NEW HUMAN BE-IN
TO THE DIGITAL REALM
THEY MAKE ME FEEL LIKE A NAUGHTY LITTLE KID.
THURSDAYS
JUMPY, GUILTY, DISCONNECTED.
BUT... THE F.D.A. HAS YET TO APPROVE THE USE OF STEROID A39.
AND... THESE DAYS, IT'S THE ONLY THING THAT MAKES ME FEEL ANY BETTER. FUNCTIONAL.
SO, HERE I STAND LIKE A TEENAGER, WAITING FOR "MY MAN," IN THE DARK.
ALL--
EXCUSE ME, MISS?
--ALONE?!!
YOU KNOW, YOU REALLY SHOULDN'T SMOKE.
IT IS THE LEADING CAUSE OF LUNG CANCER, HEART DISEASE, STROKES AND EMPHYSEMA.
ALSO BAD FOR HAIR, SKIN AND NAILS.

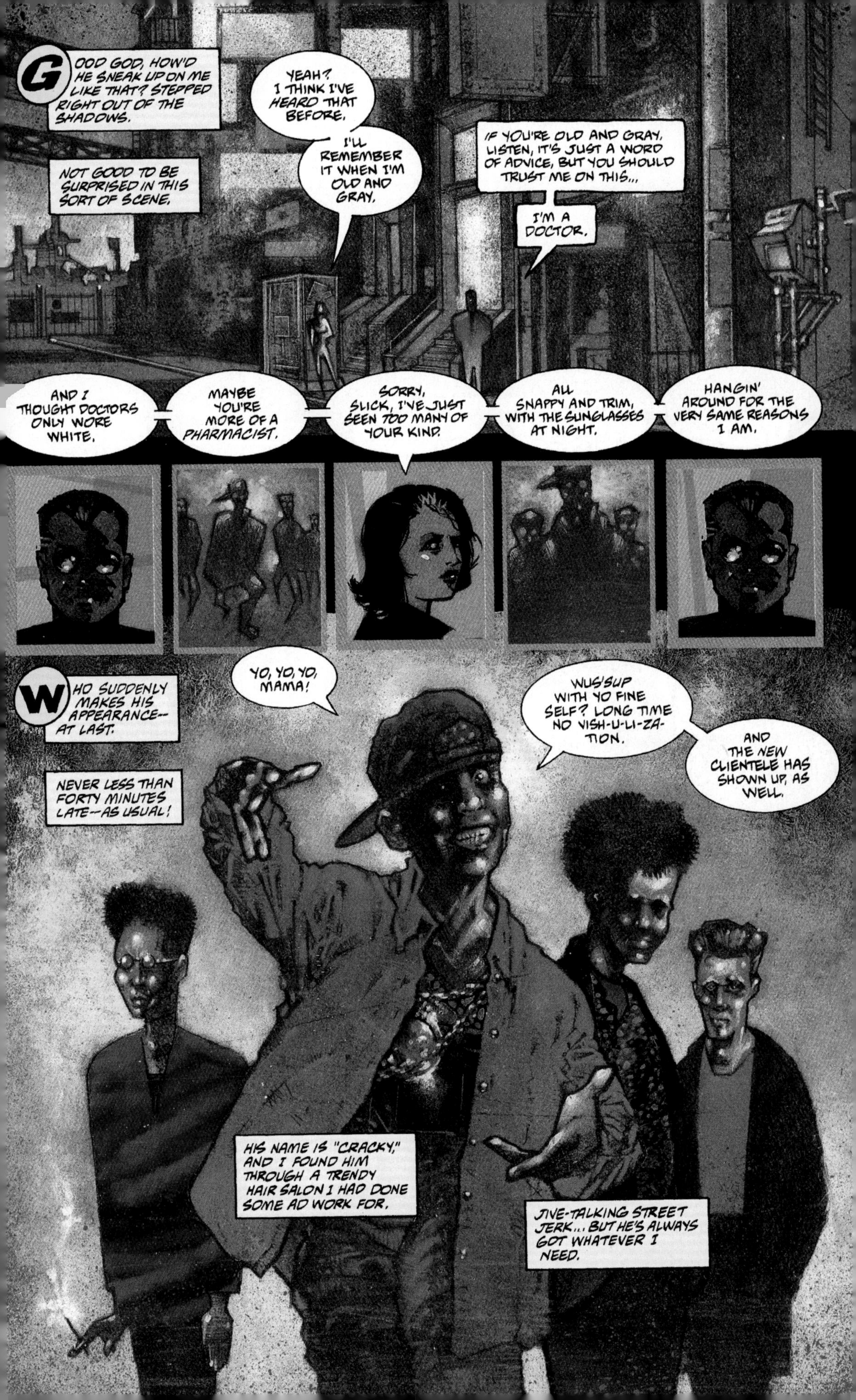
GOOD GOD, HOW'D HE SNEAK UP ON ME LIKE THAT? STEPPED RIGHT OUT OF THE SHADOWS.
NOT GOOD TO BE SURPRISED IN THIS SORT OF SCENE.
YEAH? I THINK I'VE HEARD THAT BEFORE.
I'LL REMEMBER IT WHEN I'M OLD AND GRAY.
IF YOU'RE OLD AND GRAY. LISTEN, IT'S JUST A WORD OF ADVICE, BUT YOU SHOULD TRUST ME ON THIS...
I'M A DOCTOR.
AND I THOUGHT DOCTORS ONLY WORE WHITE.
MAYBE YOU'RE MORE OF A PHARMACIST.
SORRY, SLICK, I'VE JUST SEEN TOO MANY OF YOUR KIND.
ALL SNAPPY AND TRIM, WITH THE SUNGLASSES AT NIGHT.
HANGIN' AROUND FOR THE VERY SAME REASONS I AM.
WHO SUDDENLY MAKES HIS APPEARANCE--AT LAST.
NEVER LESS THAN FORTY MINUTES LATE--AS USUAL!
YO, YO, YO, MAMA!
WUS'SUP WITH YO FINE SELF? LONG TIME NO VISH-U-LI-ZA-TION.
AND THE NEW CLIENTELE HAS SHOWN UP, AS WELL.
HIS NAME IS "CRACKY," AND I FOUND HIM THROUGH A TRENDY HAIR SALON I HAD DONE SOME AD WORK FOR.
JIVE-TALKING STREET JERK... BUT HE'S ALWAYS GOT WHATEVER I NEED.

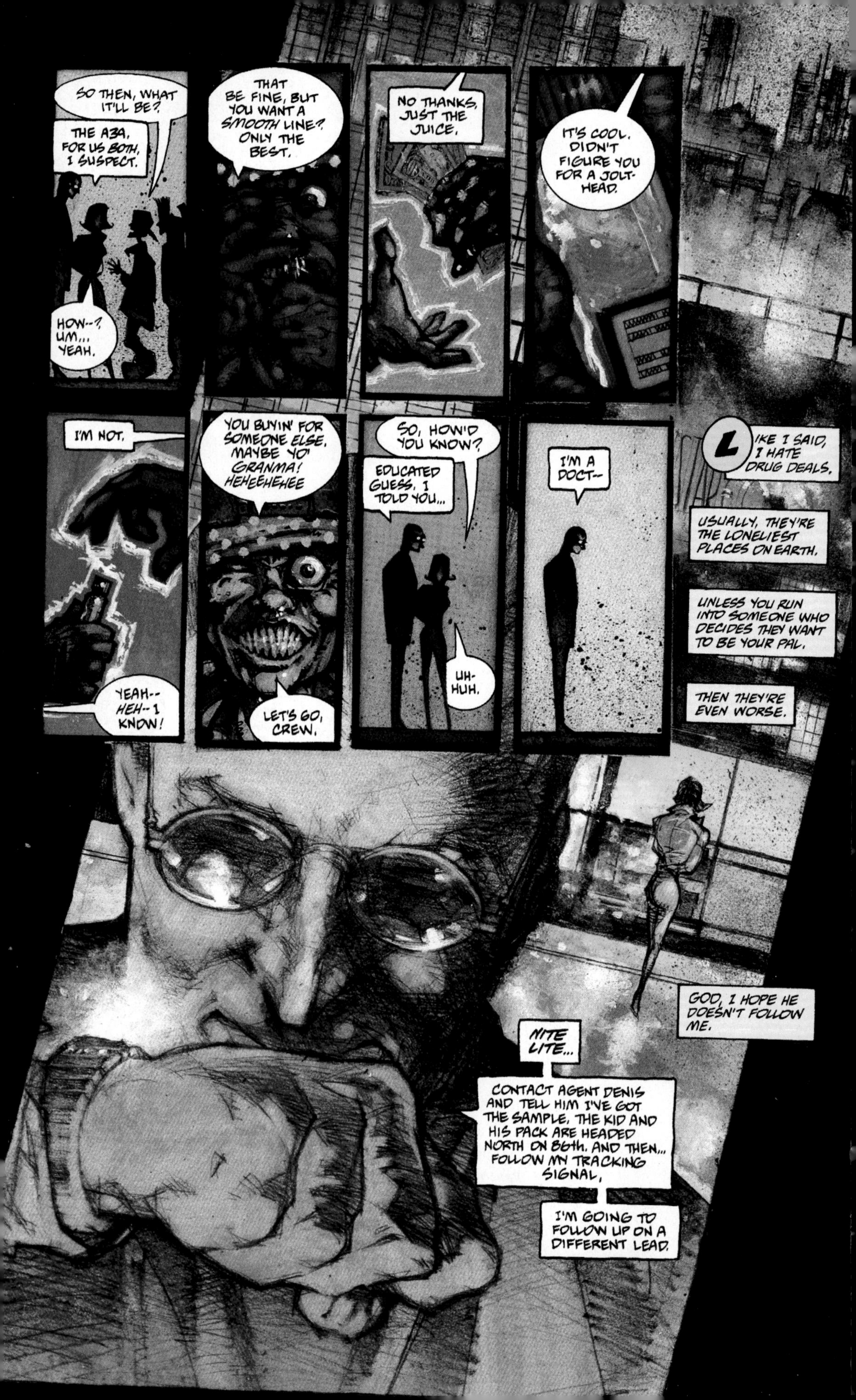
SO THEN, WHAT IT'LL BE?
THE A3A, FOR US BOTH, I SUSPECT.
HOW--? UM... YEAH.
THAT BE FINE, BUT YOU WANT A SMOOTH LINE? ONLY THE BEST.
NO THANKS, JUST THE JUICE.
IT'S COOL. DIDN'T FIGURE YOU FOR A JOLT-HEAD.
I'M NOT.
YEAH--HEH--I KNOW!
YOU BUYIN' FOR SOMEONE ELSE. MAYBE YO' GRANMA! HEHEEHEHEE
LET'S GO, CREW.
SO, HOW'D YOU KNOW?
EDUCATED GUESS. I TOLD YOU...
UH-HUH.
I'M A DOCT--
LIKE I SAID, I HATE DRUG DEALS.
USUALLY, THEY'RE THE LONELIEST PLACES ON EARTH.
UNLESS YOU RUN INTO SOMEONE WHO DECIDES THEY WANT TO BE YOUR PAL.
THEN THEY'RE EVEN WORSE.
GOD, I HOPE HE DOESN'T FOLLOW ME.
NITE LITE...
CONTACT AGENT DENIS AND TELL HIM I'VE GOT THE SAMPLE. THE KID AND HIS PACK ARE HEADED NORTH ON 86th. AND THEN... FOLLOW MY TRACKING SIGNAL.
I'M GOING TO FOLLOW UP ON A DIFFERENT LEAD.

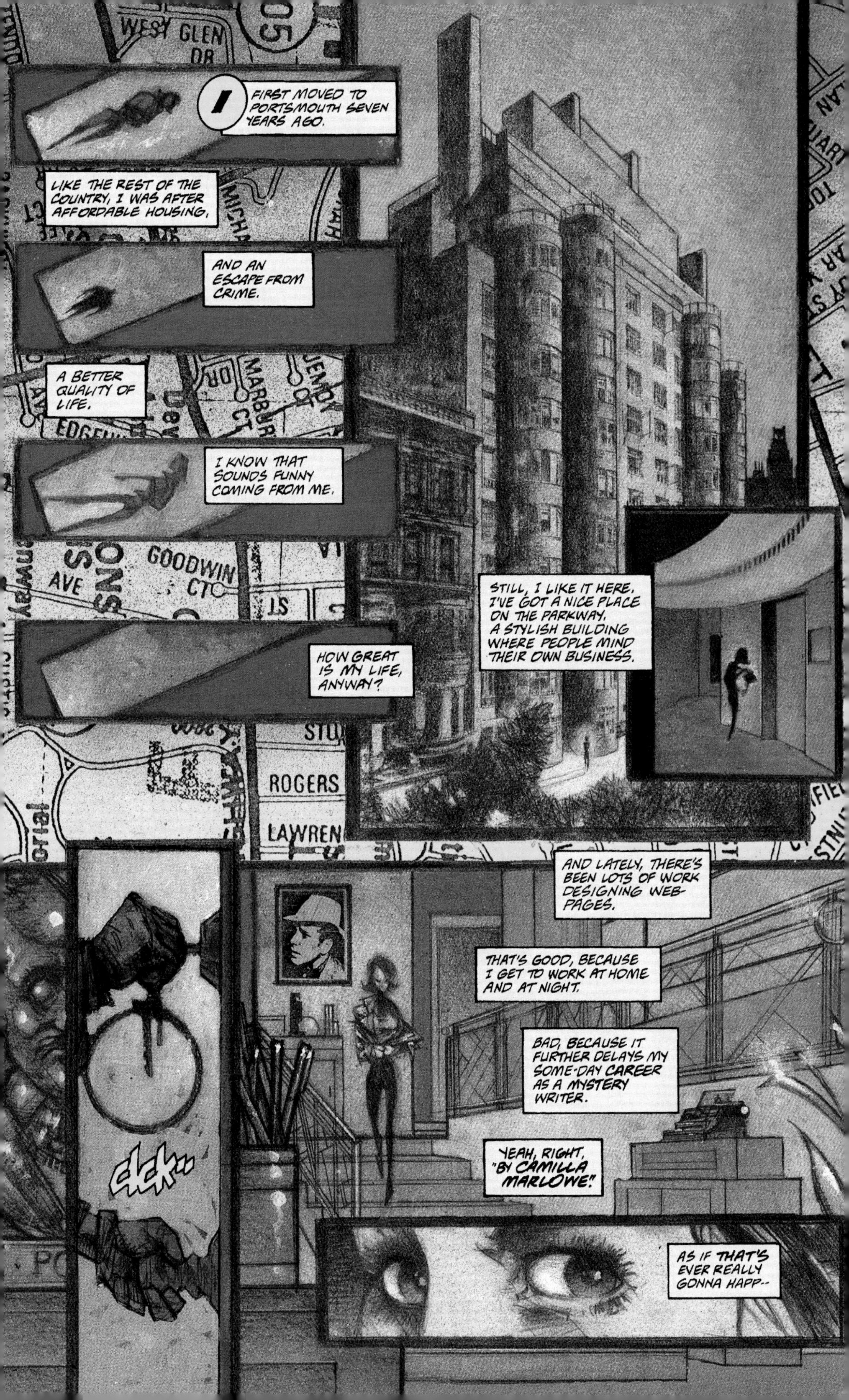
I FIRST MOVED TO PORTSMOUTH SEVEN YEARS AGO.
LIKE THE REST OF THE COUNTRY, I WAS AFTER AFFORDABLE HOUSING,
AND AN ESCAPE FROM CRIME.
A BETTER QUALITY OF LIFE.
I KNOW THAT SOUNDS FUNNY COMING FROM ME.
HOW GREAT IS MY LIFE, ANYWAY?
STILL, I LIKE IT HERE. I'VE GOT A NICE PLACE ON THE PARKWAY, A STYLISH BUILDING WHERE PEOPLE MIND THEIR OWN BUSINESS.
AND LATELY, THERE'S BEEN LOTS OF WORK DESIGNING WEB-PAGES.
THAT'S GOOD, BECAUSE I GET TO WORK AT HOME AND AT NIGHT.
BAD, BECAUSE IT FURTHER DELAYS MY SOME-DAY CAREER AS A MYSTERY WRITER.
YEAH, RIGHT. "BY CAMILLA MARLOWE."
click..
AS IF THAT'S EVER REALLY GONNA HAPP--

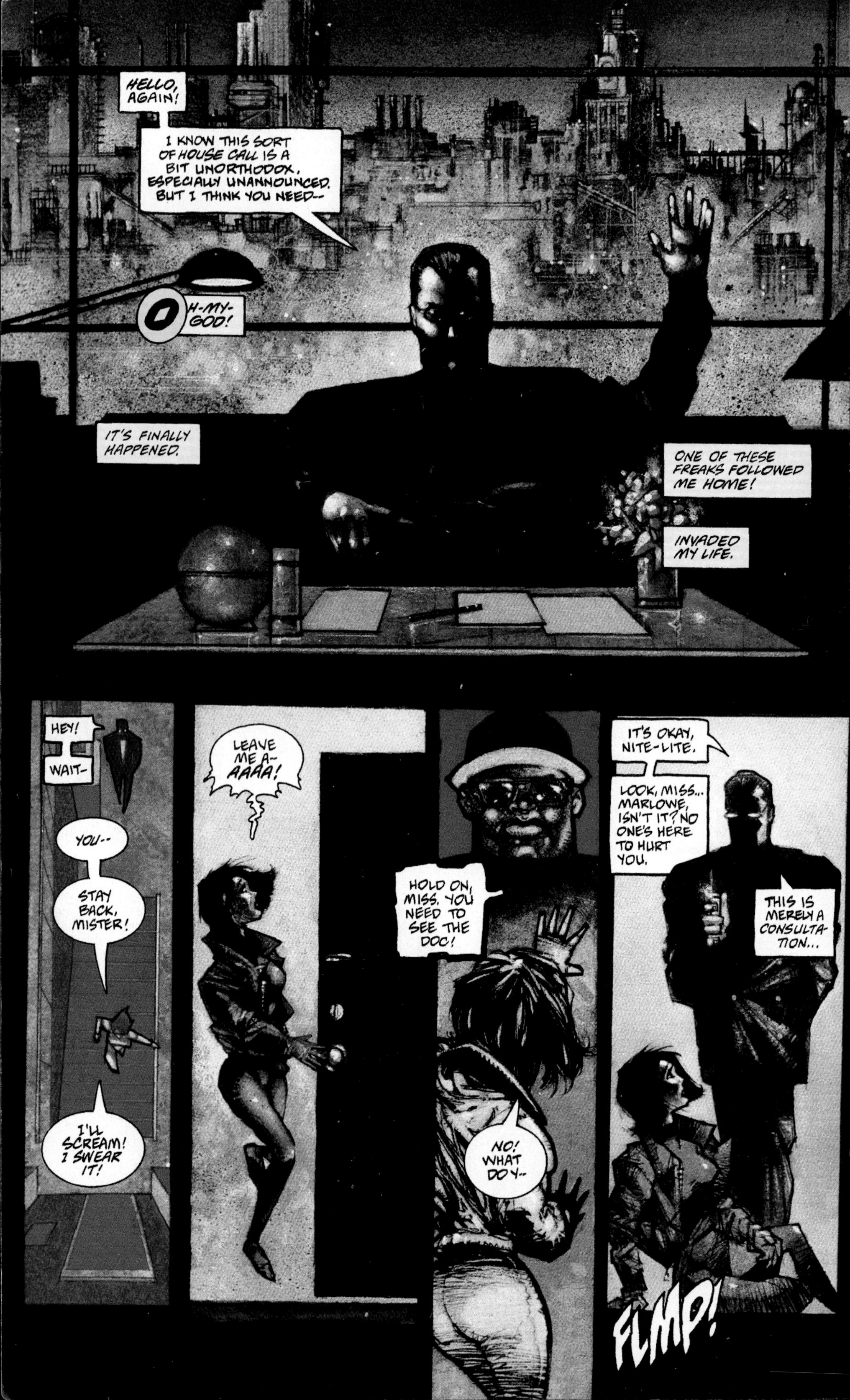
HELLO, AGAIN!
I KNOW THIS SORT OF HOUSE CALL IS A BIT UNORTHODOX, ESPECIALLY UNANNOUNCED. BUT I THINK YOU NEED--
OH-MY-GOD!
IT'S FINALLY HAPPENED.
ONE OF THESE FREAKS FOLLOWED ME HOME!
INVADED MY LIFE.
HEY!
WAIT-
YOU--
STAY BACK, MISTER!
I'LL SCREAM! I SWEAR IT!
LEAVE ME A--AAAA!
HOLD ON, MISS. YOU NEED TO SEE THE DOC!
NO! WHAT DO Y--
IT'S OKAY, NITE-LITE.
LOOK, MISS... MARLOWE, ISN'T IT? NO ONE'S HERE TO HURT YOU.
THIS IS MERELY A CONSULTATION...
FLMP!

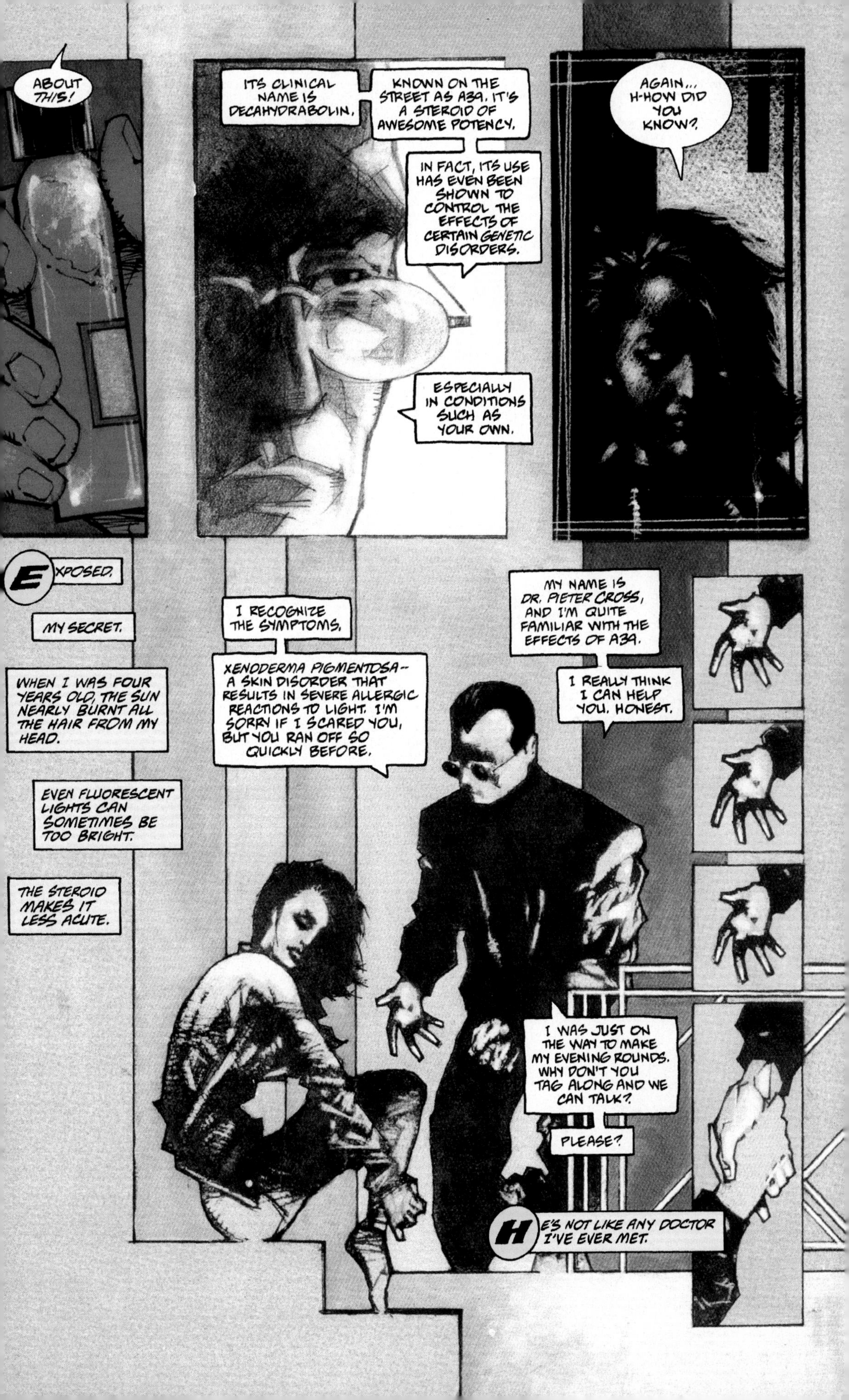
ABOUT THIS!
ITS CLINICAL NAME IS DECAHYDRABOLIN.
KNOWN ON THE STREET AS A39. IT'S A STEROID OF AWESOME POTENCY.
IN FACT, ITS USE HAS EVEN BEEN SHOWN TO CONTROL THE EFFECTS OF CERTAIN GENETIC DISORDERS.
ESPECIALLY IN CONDITIONS SUCH AS YOUR OWN.
AGAIN... H-HOW DID YOU KNOW?
EXPOSED.
MY SECRET.
WHEN I WAS FOUR YEARS OLD, THE SUN NEARLY BURNT ALL THE HAIR FROM MY HEAD.
EVEN FLUORESCENT LIGHTS CAN SOMETIMES BE TOO BRIGHT.
THE STEROID MAKES IT LESS ACUTE.
I RECOGNIZE THE SYMPTOMS.
XENODERMA PIGMENTOSA-- A SKIN DISORDER THAT RESULTS IN SEVERE ALLERGIC REACTIONS TO LIGHT. I'M SORRY IF I SCARED YOU, BUT YOU RAN OFF SO QUICKLY BEFORE.
MY NAME IS DR. PIETER CROSS, AND I'M QUITE FAMILIAR WITH THE EFFECTS OF A39.
I REALLY THINK I CAN HELP YOU. HONEST.
I WAS JUST ON THE WAY TO MAKE MY EVENING ROUNDS. WHY DON'T YOU TAG ALONG AND WE CAN TALK?
PLEASE?
HE'S NOT LIKE ANY DOCTOR I'VE EVER MET.

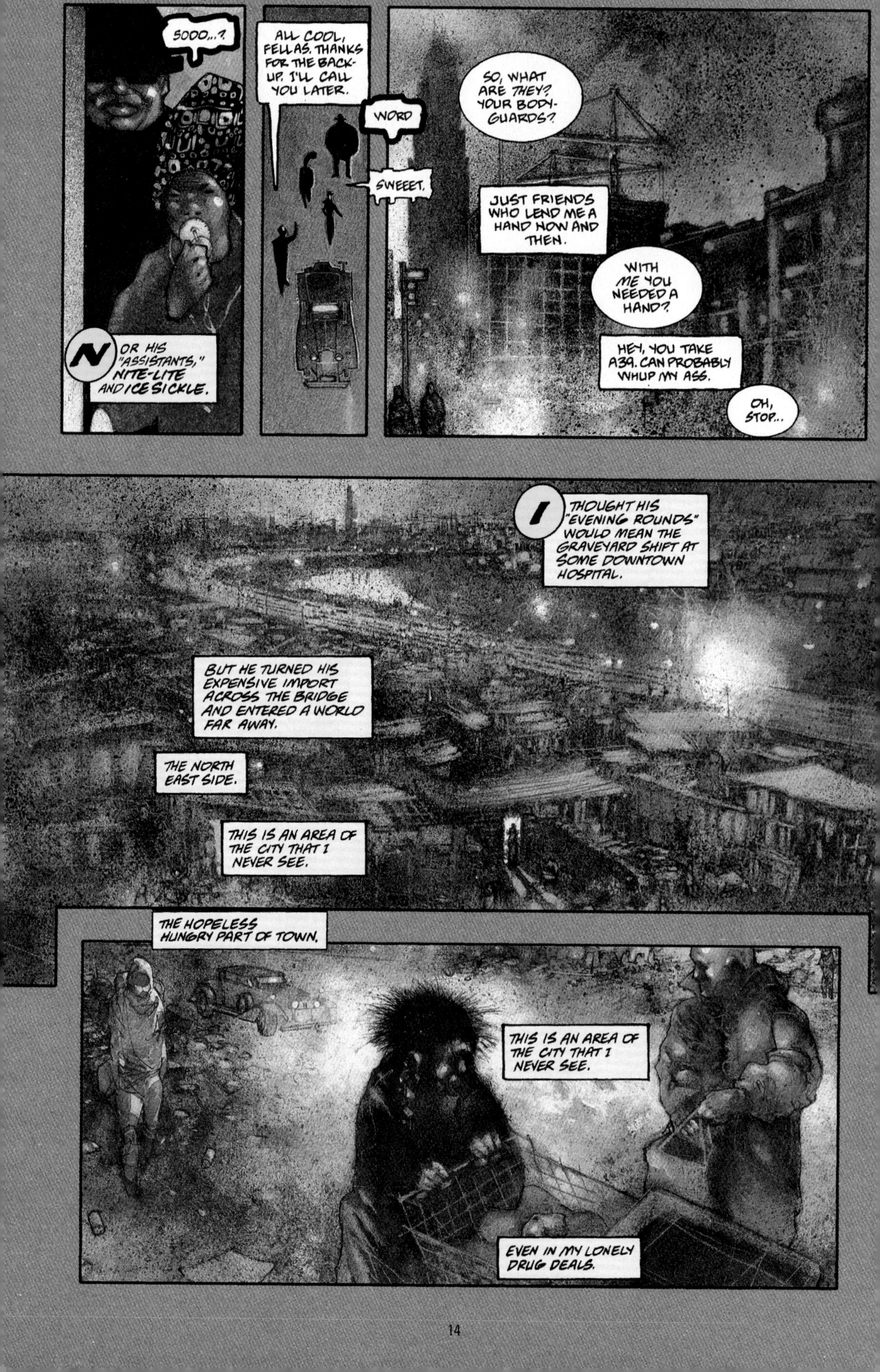
SOOO...?
NOR HIS "ASSISTANTS," NITE-LITE AND ICE SICKLE.
ALL COOL, FELLAS. THANKS FOR THE BACK-UP. I'LL CALL YOU LATER.
WORD
SWEEET.
SO, WHAT ARE THEY? YOUR BODY-GUARDS?
JUST FRIENDS WHO LEND ME A HAND NOW AND THEN.
WITH ME YOU NEEDED A HAND?
HEY, YOU TAKE A39. CAN PROBABLY WHUP MY ASS.
OH, STOP...
I THOUGHT HIS "EVENING ROUNDS" WOULD MEAN THE GRAVEYARD SHIFT AT SOME DOWNTOWN HOSPITAL.
BUT HE TURNED HIS EXPENSIVE IMPORT ACROSS THE BRIDGE AND ENTERED A WORLD FAR AWAY.
THE NORTH EAST SIDE.
THIS IS AN AREA OF THE CITY THAT I NEVER SEE.
THE HOPELESS HUNGRY PART OF TOWN.
THIS IS AN AREA OF THE CITY THAT I NEVER SEE.
EVEN IN MY LONELY DRUG DEALS.

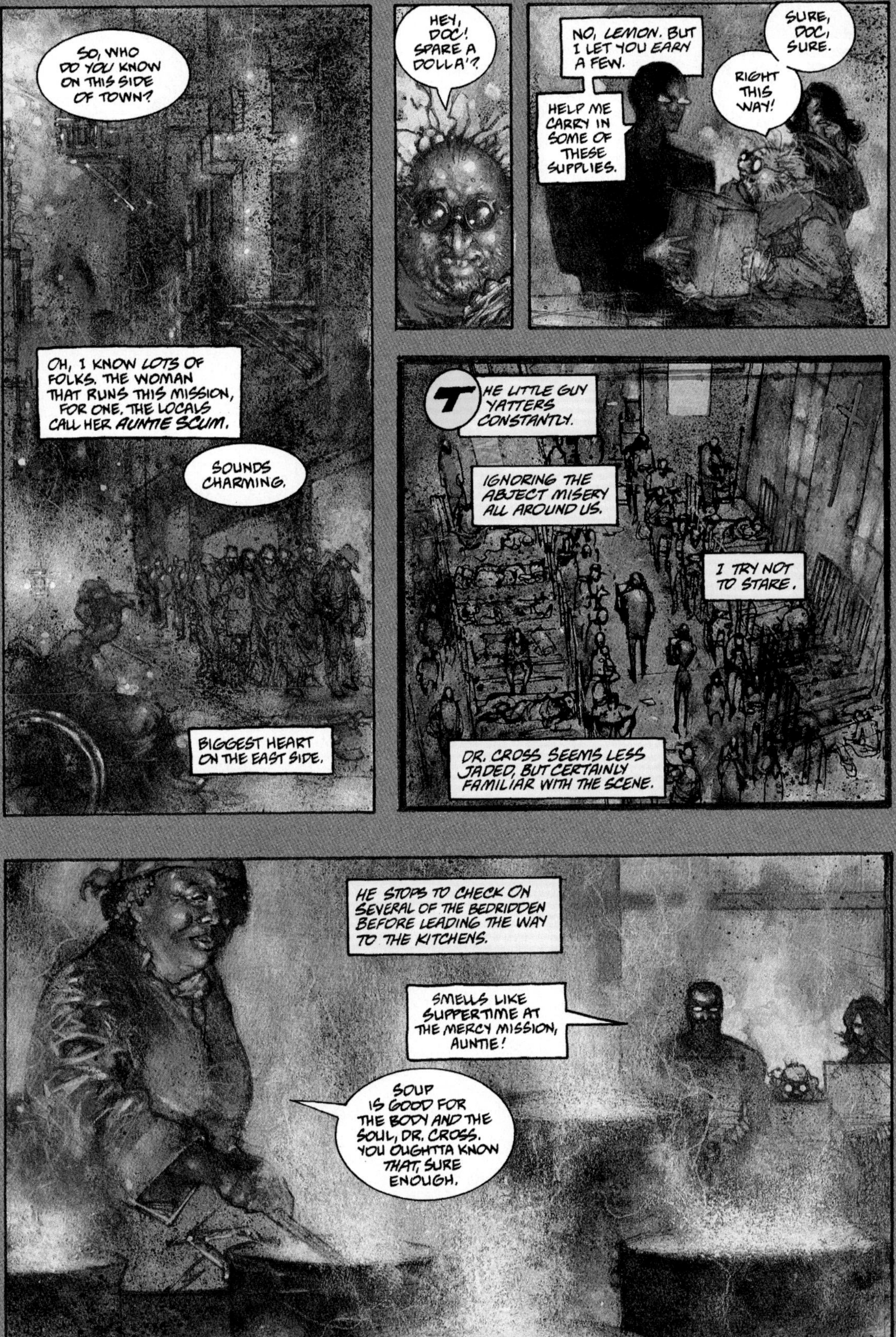

SO, WHO DO YOU KNOW ON THIS SIDE OF TOWN?
OH, I KNOW LOTS OF FOLKS. THE WOMAN THAT RUNS THIS MISSION, FOR ONE. THE LOCALS CALL HER AUNTIE SCUM.
SOUNDS CHARMING.
BIGGEST HEART ON THE EAST SIDE.
HEY, DOC! SPARE A DOLLA'?
NO, LEMON. BUT I LET YOU EARN A FEW.
HELP ME CARRY IN SOME OF THESE SUPPLIES.
SURE, DOC, SURE.
RIGHT THIS WAY!
THE LITTLE GUY YATTERS CONSTANTLY.
IGNORING THE ABJECT MISERY ALL AROUND US.
I TRY NOT TO STARE.
DR. CROSS SEEMS LESS JADED, BUT CERTAINLY FAMILIAR WITH THE SCENE.
HE STOPS TO CHECK ON SEVERAL OF THE BEDRIDDEN BEFORE LEADING THE WAY TO THE KITCHENS.
SMELLS LIKE SUPPERTIME AT THE MERCY MISSION, AUNTIE!
SOUP IS GOOD FOR THE BODY AND THE SOUL, DR. CROSS. YOU OUGHTTA KNOW THAT, SURE ENOUGH.

BROUGHT SOME MORE AMMO, AUNTIE. OVER THERE, LEMON.

THE "SUPPLIES" TURN OUT TO BE FRESH SPIKES AND GALLONS OF BLEACH FOR THE MISSION'S NEEDLE EXCHANGE PROGRAM.

LIKE I SAID, HE'S NOT LIKE ANY DOCTOR I'VE EVER MET.

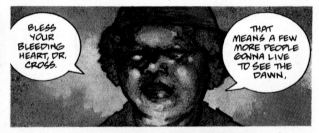

BLESS YOUR BLEEDING HEART, DR. CROSS.

THAT MEANS A FEW MORE PEOPLE GONNA LIVE TO SEE THE DAWN.

HERE, LEMON. THANKS FOR YOUR HELP.

NO BOOZE, OKAY?

SURE, DOC. SURE.

'SIDES...

I HEARD ABOUT A SURE THING ON THE NASDAQ!

JUST LIKE THE LAST "SURE THING"?

AHHH... DOC!

WHO IS THIS GUY?

WHAT'S HIS STORY?

HE DRIVES AND DRESSES LIKE SOME RICH NIGHT OWL.

BUT HE'S REALLY SOME KIND OF GHETTO MISSIONARY UNDERNEATH?

IT DOESN'T ADD UP.

WHAT HAPPENED TO THE LITTLE GUY'S FINGERS?

WHO... LEMON? HE USED TO BE A JUNK BOND TRADER.

ONE OF HIS MOST EXTREME INVESTORS LOST A BUNDLE ON A DEAL THAT LEMON HAD ARRANGED.

COST LEMON A DIGIT FOR EVERY TWENTY GRAND. AT LEAST HE'S STILL GOT HIS THUMBS.

UGH.

SO, WHERE'S OUR NEXT STOP ON THIS TRAGIC CARPET RIDE?

RIGHT OVER HERE.

I NEED TO SEE MY LAWYER.

16

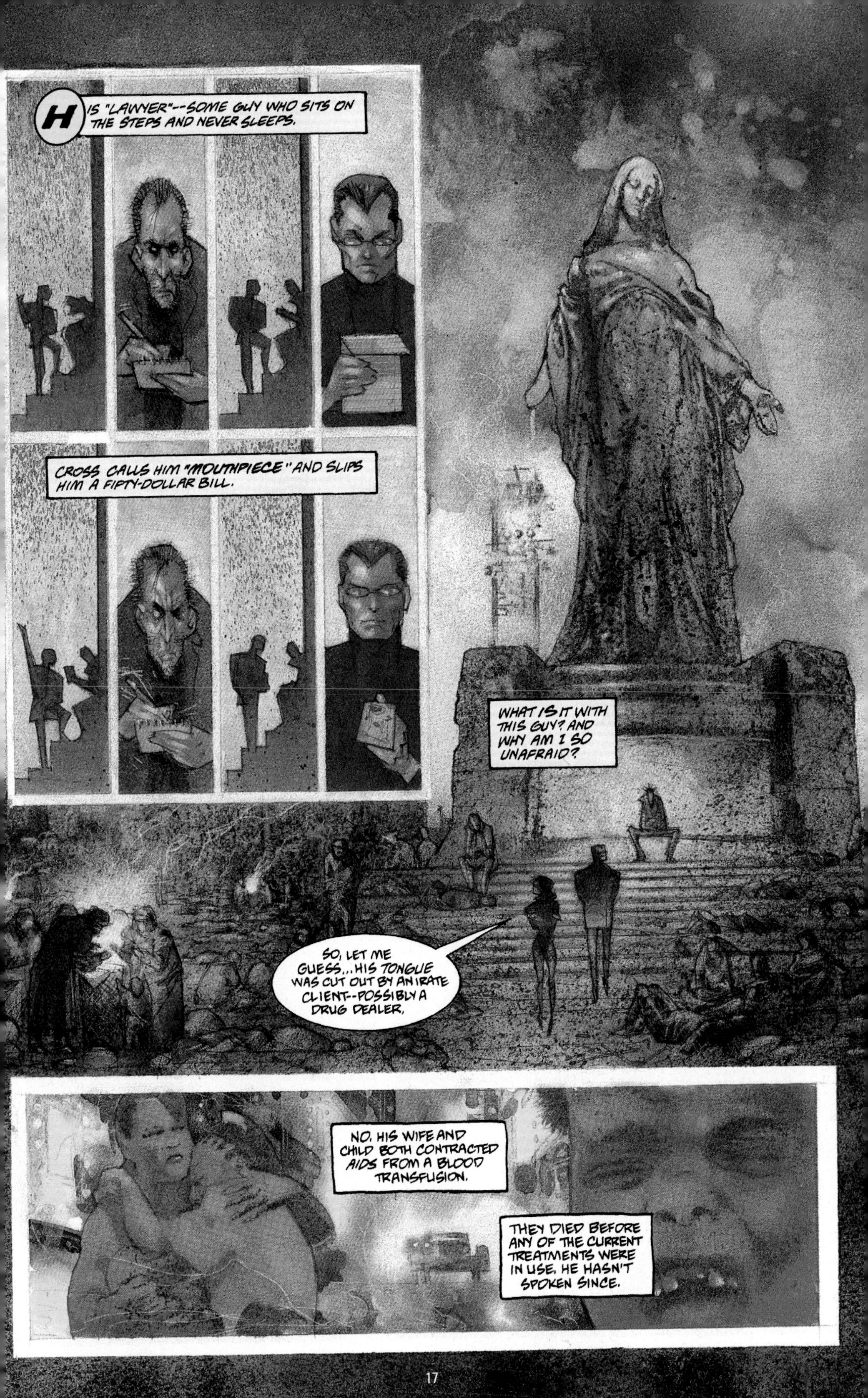
HIS "LAWYER"--SOME GUY WHO SITS ON THE STEPS AND NEVER SLEEPS.
CROSS CALLS HIM "MOUTHPIECE" AND SLIPS HIM A FIFTY-DOLLAR BILL.
WHAT IS IT WITH THIS GUY? AND WHY AM I SO UNAFRAID?
SO, LET ME GUESS... HIS TONGUE WAS CUT OUT BY AN IRATE CLIENT--POSSIBLY A DRUG DEALER.
NO. HIS WIFE AND CHILD BOTH CONTRACTED AIDS FROM A BLOOD TRANSFUSION.
THEY DIED BEFORE ANY OF THE CURRENT TREATMENTS WERE IN USE. HE HASN'T SPOKEN SINCE.

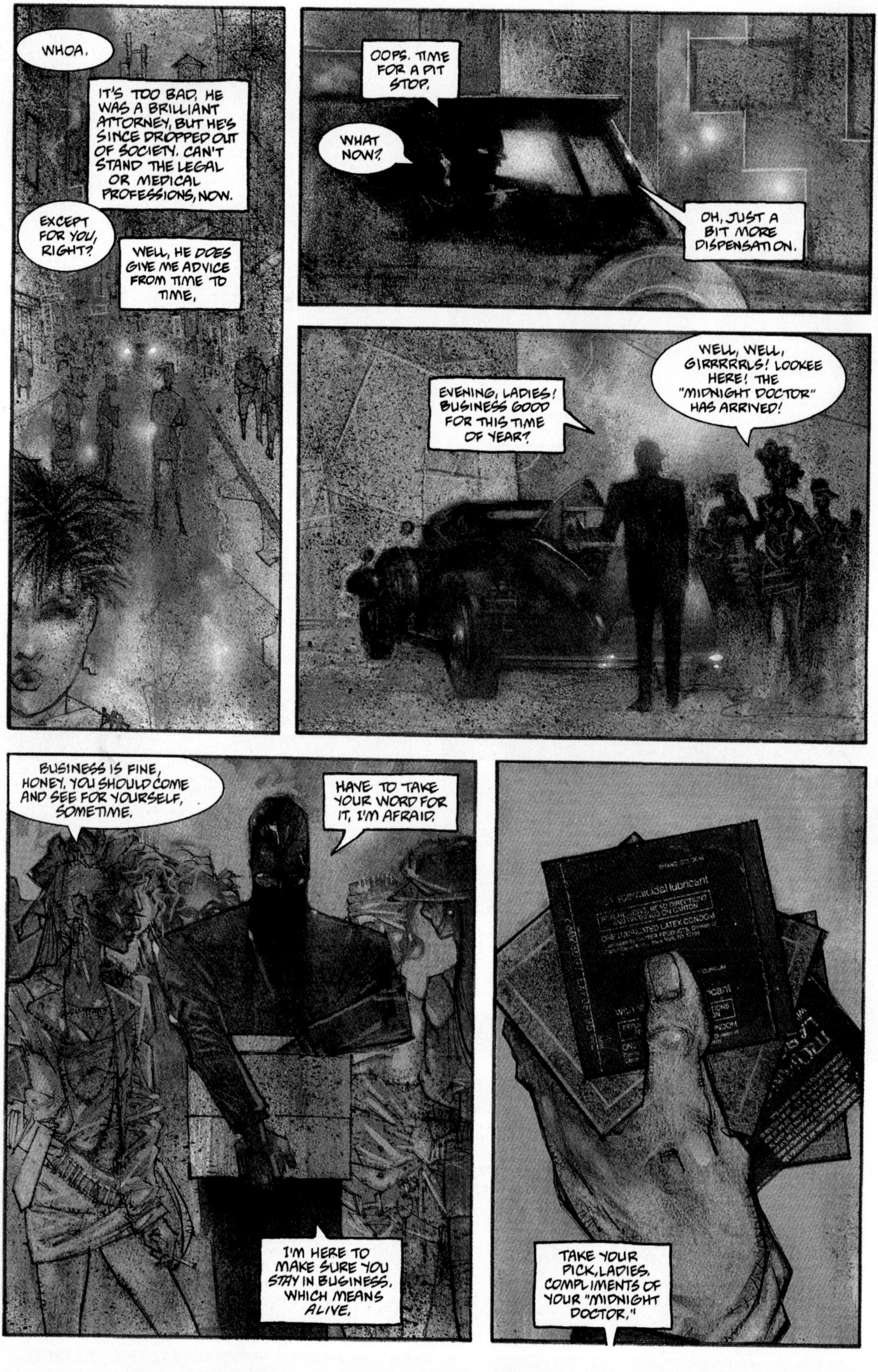
WHOA.
IT'S TOO BAD. HE WAS A BRILLIANT ATTORNEY, BUT HE'S SINCE DROPPED OUT OF SOCIETY. CAN'T STAND THE LEGAL OR MEDICAL PROFESSIONS, NOW.
EXCEPT FOR YOU, RIGHT?
WELL, HE DOES GIVE ME ADVICE FROM TIME TO TIME.
OOPS. TIME FOR A PIT STOP.
WHAT NOW?
OH, JUST A BIT MORE DISPENSATION.
EVENING, LADIES! BUSINESS GOOD FOR THIS TIME OF YEAR?
WELL, WELL, GIRRRRRLS! LOOKEE HERE! THE "MIDNIGHT DOCTOR" HAS ARRIVED!
BUSINESS IS FINE, HONEY. YOU SHOULD COME AND SEE FOR YOURSELF, SOMETIME.
HAVE TO TAKE YOUR WORD FOR IT, I'M AFRAID.
I'M HERE TO MAKE SURE YOU STAY IN BUSINESS. WHICH MEANS ALIVE.
TAKE YOUR PICK, LADIES. COMPLIMENTS OF YOUR "MIDNIGHT DOCTOR."

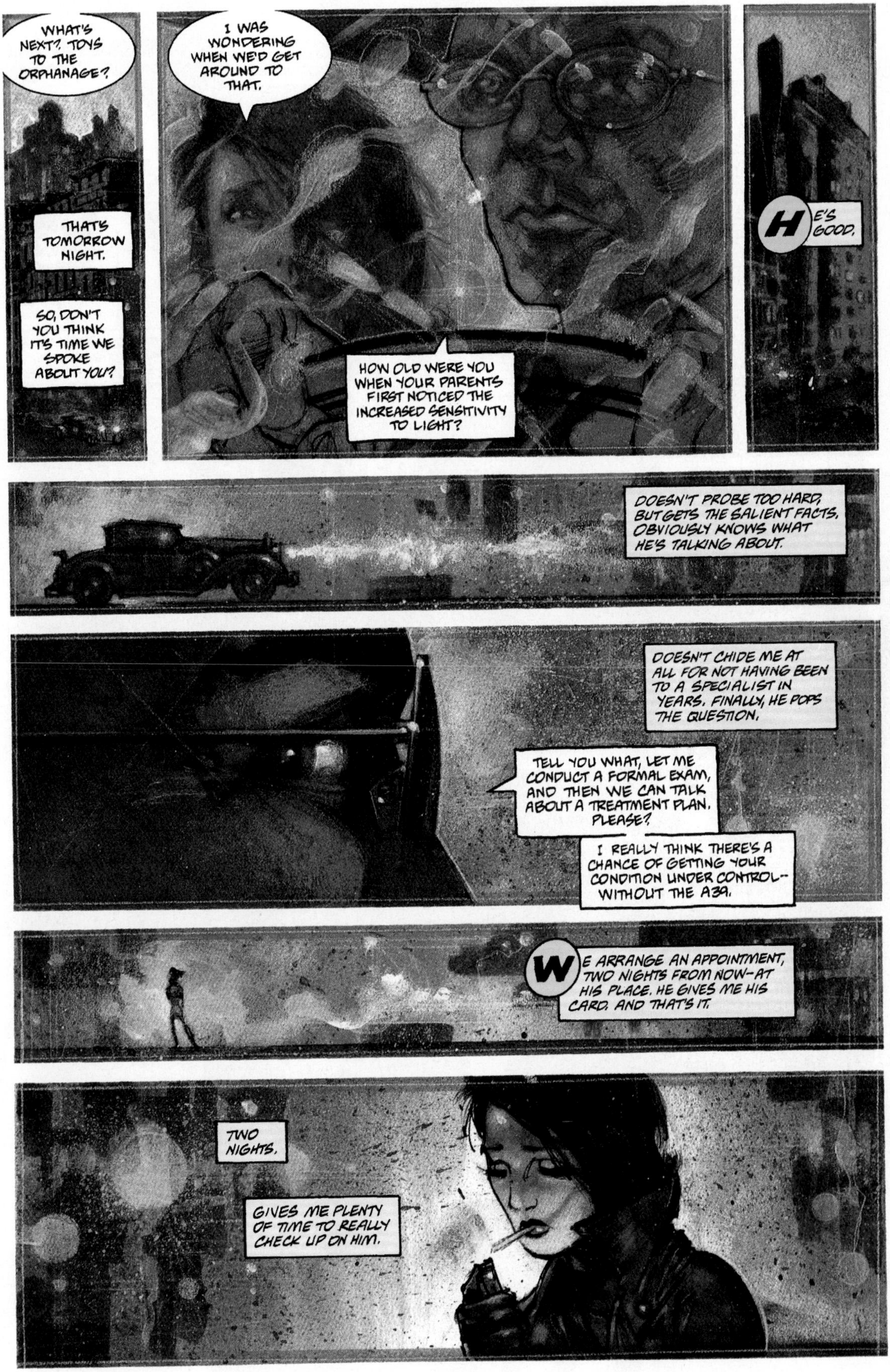
WHAT'S NEXT? TOYS TO THE ORPHANAGE?
I WAS WONDERING WHEN WE'D GET AROUND TO THAT.
THAT'S TOMORROW NIGHT.
SO, DON'T YOU THINK IT'S TIME WE SPOKE ABOUT YOU?
HOW OLD WERE YOU WHEN YOUR PARENTS FIRST NOTICED THE INCREASED SENSITIVITY TO LIGHT?
HE'S GOOD.
DOESN'T PROBE TOO HARD, BUT GETS THE SALIENT FACTS. OBVIOUSLY KNOWS WHAT HE'S TALKING ABOUT.
DOESN'T CHIDE ME AT ALL FOR NOT HAVING BEEN TO A SPECIALIST IN YEARS. FINALLY, HE POPS THE QUESTION.
TELL YOU WHAT, LET ME CONDUCT A FORMAL EXAM, AND THEN WE CAN TALK ABOUT A TREATMENT PLAN. PLEASE?
I REALLY THINK THERE'S A CHANCE OF GETTING YOUR CONDITION UNDER CONTROL-- WITHOUT THE A39.
WE ARRANGE AN APPOINTMENT, TWO NIGHTS FROM NOW--AT HIS PLACE. HE GIVES ME HIS CARD. AND THAT'S IT.
TWO NIGHTS.
GIVES ME PLENTY OF TIME TO REALLY CHECK UP ON HIM.

S O, IT'S PIETER ANTON CROSS, BORN IN NORWAY, 4/5/62.

A YOUNG HOTSHOT, GENIUS--GRADUATED FROM HARVARD MEDICAL SCHOOL AT AGE NINETEEN.

HIS FATHER WAS DR. THEODORIC CROSS, A COLLEAGUE OF ALFRED NOBEL.

s Resignation

THE SON BECAME A GIFTED SURGEON, DEVELOPING ADVANCED TECHNIQUES IN LIMB GRAFTING.

e critical first   Thus, Hunter

AND THEN, SCANDAL.

A WELL-PUBLICIZED BATTLE OVER INSURANCE FRAUD LEADS TO PIETER'S LOSS OF RESIDENCY.

LAWSUITS ARE THREATENED, NEVER FILED.

AFTER THAT, HARDLY ANYTHING IN THE PAPERS OR JOURNALS.

DR. PIETER CROSS GOES UNDERGROUND.

OUTSIDE THE REALM OF THE ESTABLISHED MEDICAL COMMUNITY.

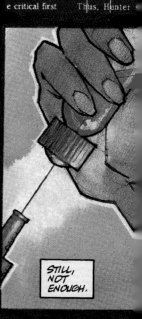

STILL, NOT ENOUGH.

HOW DOES ONE BECOME A "MIDNIGHT DOCTOR"?

AND WHY SHOULD I TRUST HIM?

SO, THE FACTS TELL ME LITTLE OF THIS RENEGADE PHYSICIAN.

HAVE TO DIG A LITTLE HARDER.

TOMORROW NIGHT.

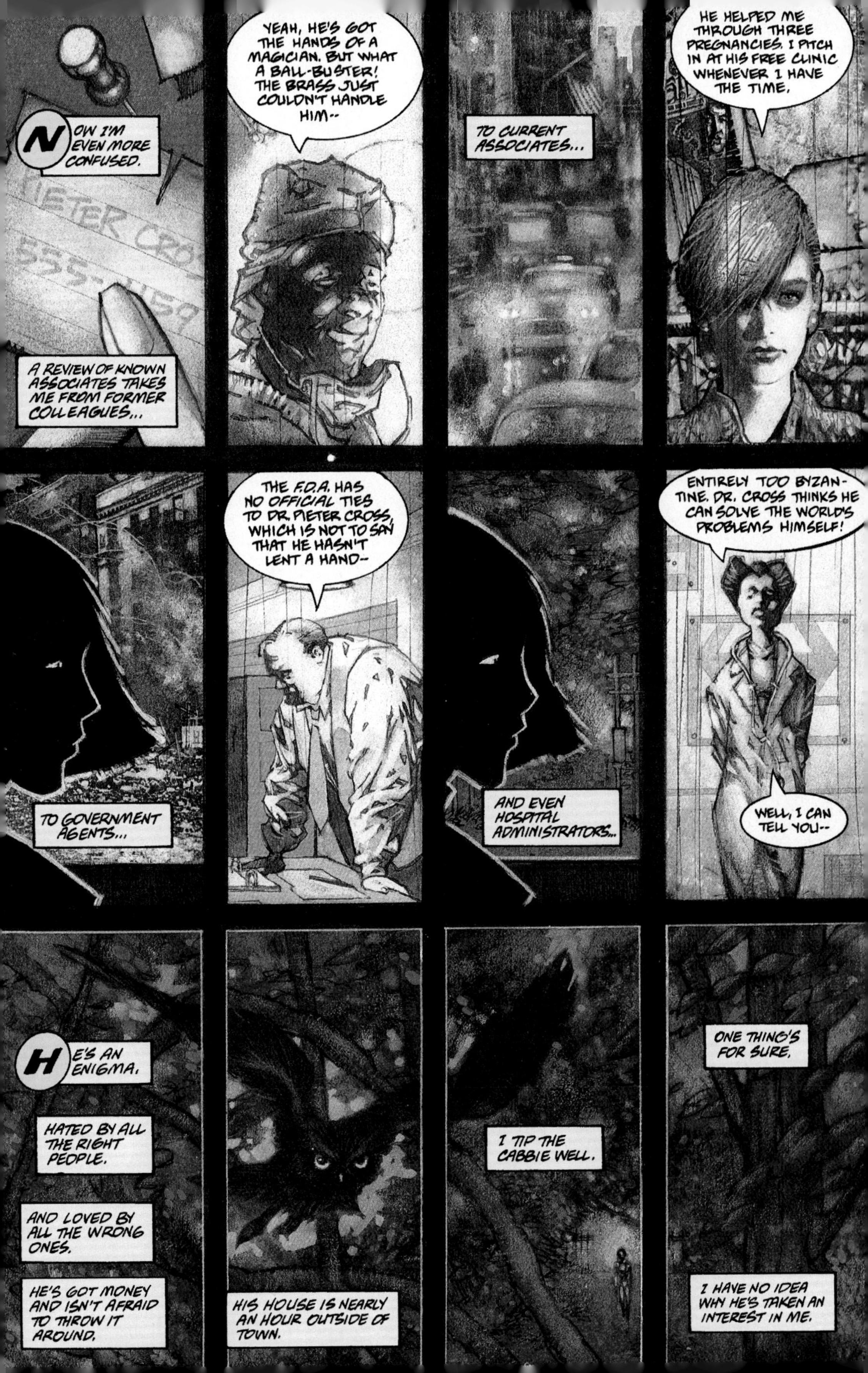
NOW I'M EVEN MORE CONFUSED.
PIETER CROSS
555-1159
A REVIEW OF KNOWN ASSOCIATES TAKES ME FROM FORMER COLLEAGUES...
YEAH, HE'S GOT THE HANDS OF A MAGICIAN. BUT WHAT A BALL-BUSTER! THE BRASS JUST COULDN'T HANDLE HIM--
TO CURRENT ASSOCIATES...
HE HELPED ME THROUGH THREE PREGNANCIES. I PITCH IN AT HIS FREE CLINIC WHENEVER I HAVE THE TIME.
TO GOVERNMENT AGENTS...
THE F.D.A. HAS NO OFFICIAL TIES TO DR. PIETER CROSS, WHICH IS NOT TO SAY THAT HE HASN'T LENT A HAND--
AND EVEN HOSPITAL ADMINISTRATORS...
ENTIRELY TOO BYZANTINE. DR. CROSS THINKS HE CAN SOLVE THE WORLD'S PROBLEMS HIMSELF!
WELL, I CAN TELL YOU--
HE'S AN ENIGMA.
HATED BY ALL THE RIGHT PEOPLE.
AND LOVED BY ALL THE WRONG ONES.
HE'S GOT MONEY AND ISN'T AFRAID TO THROW IT AROUND.
HIS HOUSE IS NEARLY AN HOUR OUTSIDE OF TOWN.
I TIP THE CABBIE WELL.
ONE THING'S FOR SURE.
I HAVE NO IDEA WHY HE'S TAKEN AN INTEREST IN ME.

WHAT HAVE I GOTTEN MYSELF INTO?

THIS PLACE LOOKS LIKE IT FELL OFF THE MOON!

FOR SUCH A SOCIAL CRUSADER, HE'S SURE GOT AN OSTENTATIOUS SENSE OF HOME.

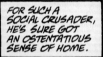

AND THEN THE DOOR SPEAKS TO ME!

GOOD EVENING, MS. MARLOWE. WELCOME TO THE CROSS HOUSE.

YOU WILL FIND YOUR HOST ON THE LOWER LEVEL OF THE EAST WING. PLEASE FOLLOW MY SIGNAL.

ting ting ting

UM... THANKS.

THIS WAY, PLEASE.

ting ting

THAT'S OKAY.

I THINK I'VE GOT IT.

ting ting ting tin

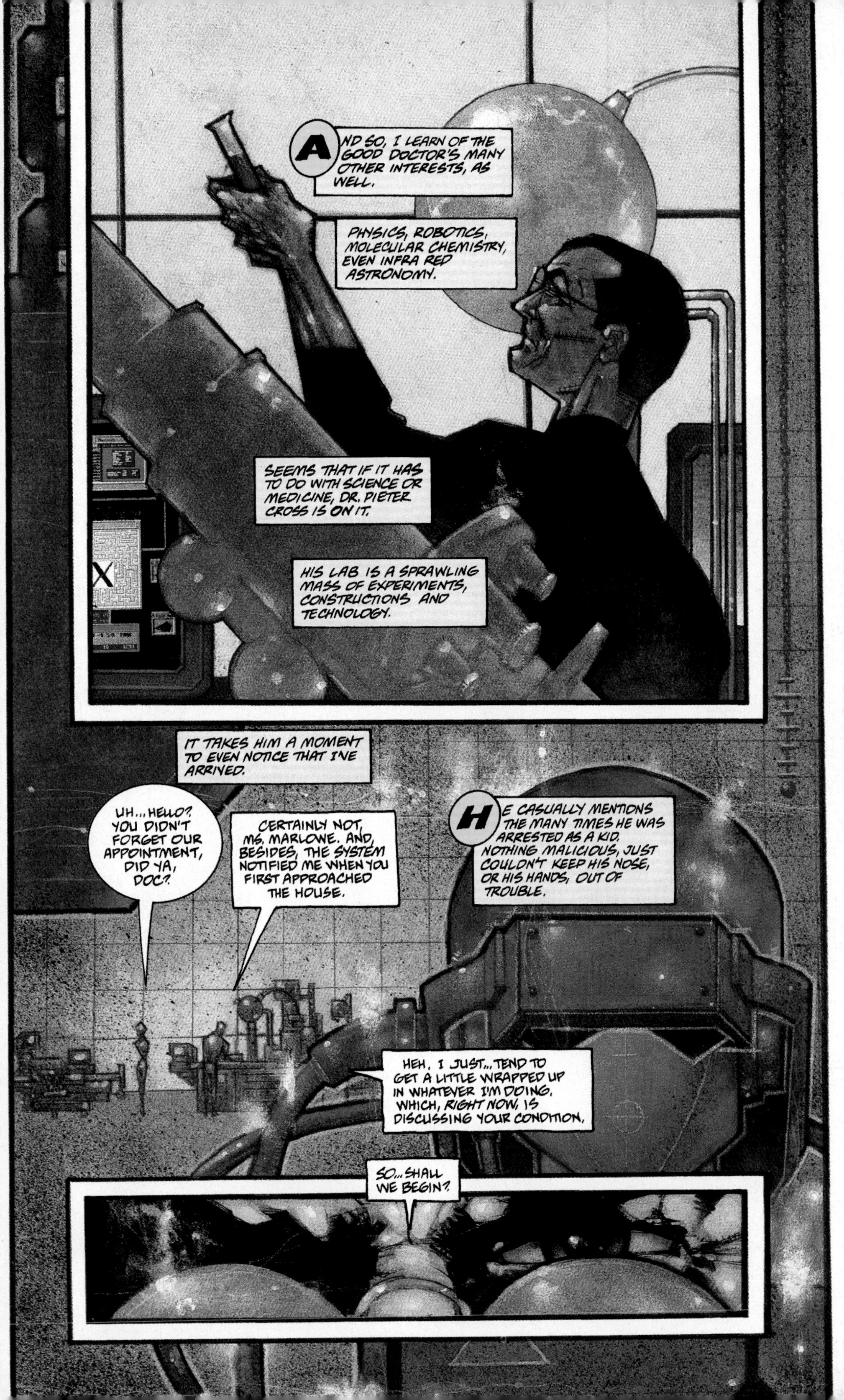
AND SO, I LEARN OF THE GOOD DOCTOR'S MANY OTHER INTERESTS, AS WELL.
PHYSICS, ROBOTICS, MOLECULAR CHEMISTRY, EVEN INFRA RED ASTRONOMY.
SEEMS THAT IF IT HAS TO DO WITH SCIENCE OR MEDICINE, DR. PIETER CROSS IS ON IT.
HIS LAB IS A SPRAWLING MASS OF EXPERIMENTS, CONSTRUCTIONS AND TECHNOLOGY.
IT TAKES HIM A MOMENT TO EVEN NOTICE THAT I'VE ARRIVED.
UH... HELLO? YOU DIDN'T FORGET OUR APPOINTMENT, DID YA, DOC?
CERTAINLY NOT, MS. MARLOWE. AND, BESIDES, THE SYSTEM NOTIFIED ME WHEN YOU FIRST APPROACHED THE HOUSE.
HE CASUALLY MENTIONS THE MANY TIMES HE WAS ARRESTED AS A KID. NOTHING MALICIOUS, JUST COULDN'T KEEP HIS NOSE, OR HIS HANDS, OUT OF TROUBLE.
HEH, I JUST... TEND TO GET A LITTLE WRAPPED UP IN WHATEVER I'M DOING. WHICH, RIGHT NOW, IS DISCUSSING YOUR CONDITION.
SO... SHALL WE BEGIN?

BROWNSTEIN, YOUR LAWYER'S HERE TO SEE YOU.
LAWYER?! I AIN'T GOT NO--
HELLO, CRACKY. SORRY TO SEE YOU HAVING TROUBLES OF THIS SORT.
I JUST STOPPED BY TO MAKE SURE OF YOUR ...LOYALTY.
OH, HI, MR. LARGO. THIS IS ALL SOME JIVE SETUP WITH THE FEDS, MAN! THEY DON'T HAVE NOTHIN' ON ME BUT SOME BLOW. CHUMP CHANGE!
IS THAT A FACT?
I SWEAR, MR. LARGO, THIS WHOLE THING WAS A SETUP. THEY'S GOT SOME MOLE POSIN' AS A DOCTOR! DR. CRISS CROSS... SOMETHIN' LIKE THAT.
VERY GOOD, CRACKY.
I KNOW INCARCER-ATION CAN BE... TRYING.
WOO HOO! AIN'T NOTHIN' LIKE THE REAL THING, MR. LARGO! THANK YOU, SIR!!
MY PLEASURE, OH, AND ONE OTHER THING.
YOU'RE SURE THE FEDS DIDN'T OBTAIN A SAMPLE OF THE OTHER KIND?
SNNNRRRRRRTTTTT

WELL...⟨sniff-sniff⟩ YEAH, THEY MIGHTA, LIKE I SAID. THEY'S WORKIN' THIS DECOY DOCTOR. ⟨sniff.⟩

AHH... I SEE.

S-SO, MR. LARGO ⟨sniff⟩ WOW, THIS STUFF'S GOOD ⟨sniff⟩ YOU GUYS GONNA, LIKE, GET ME SPRUNG? HEHEEHEEHEEHEE

HEE HEE-HEH-HEE HEH-HE-H-H...

OH, YES, MY FRIEND. YOU JUST SIT TIGHT FOR NOW.

MY ASSOCIATES AND I WILL SECURE YOUR RELEASE.

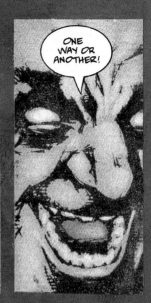

ONE WAY OR ANOTHER!

HEEEEEE-- urgh!!

WUNK!

SURPRISINGLY, I TELL HIM EVERYTHING.

ABOUT THE EARLY YEARS SPENT IN PRIVATE TUTORIALS. THE SEASONAL BOUTS WITH DEPRESSION. EVEN ABOUT THE MANY DRUGS.

THROUGH IT ALL, HE DOESN'T JUDGE. NEVER FLINCHES. LETS ME TALK AND ASKS QUESTIONS WHEN HE ISN'T CLEAR ON SOMETHING.

OKAY, YOU CAN GET DRESSED NOW, MS. MARLOWE.

PLEASE... CAMILLA.

CALL IT A DOCTOR'S TRUST.

25

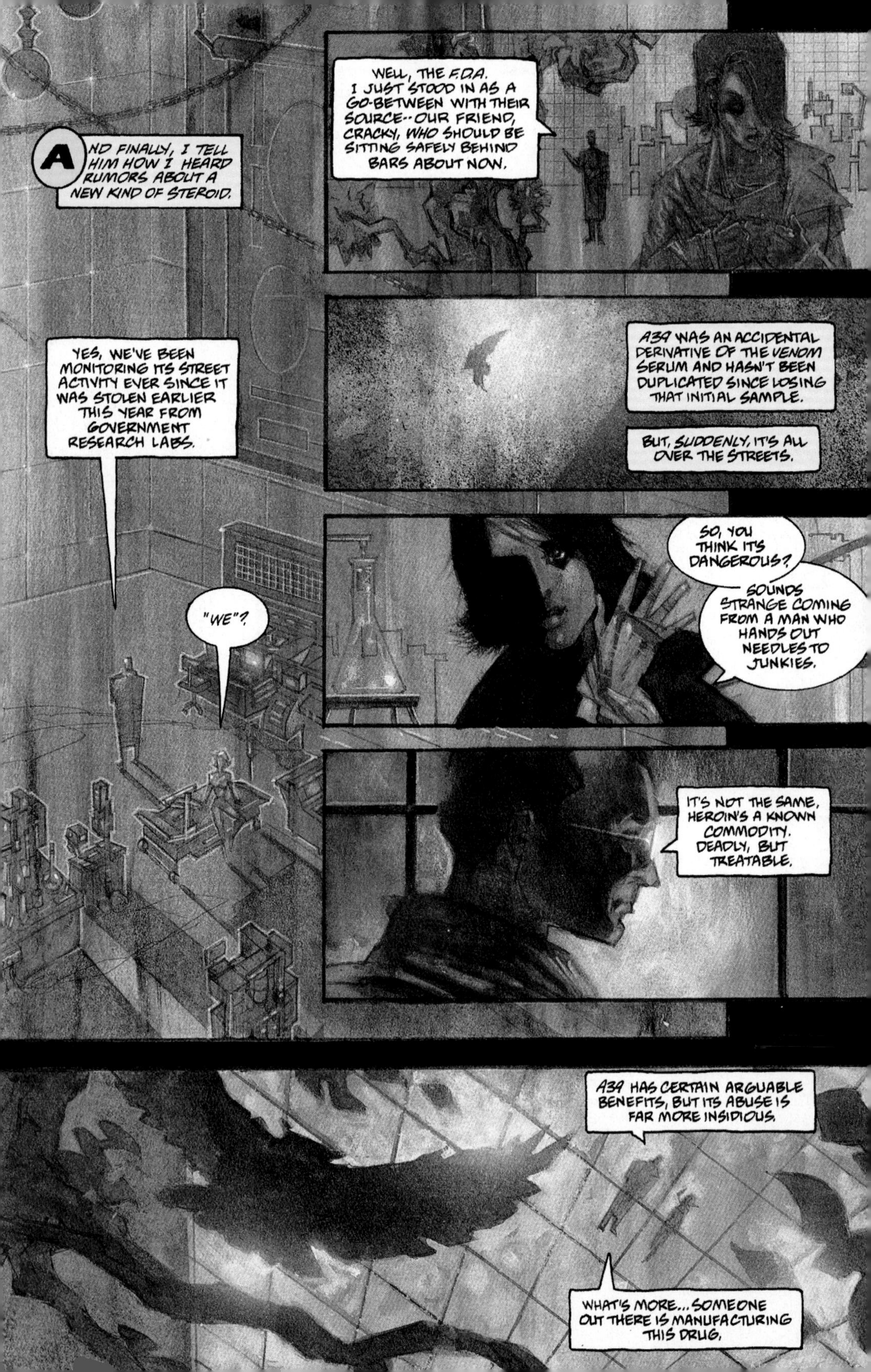
AND FINALLY, I TELL HIM HOW I HEARD RUMORS ABOUT A NEW KIND OF STEROID.
WELL, THE F.D.A. I JUST STOOD IN AS A GO-BETWEEN WITH THEIR SOURCE-- OUR FRIEND, CRACKY, WHO SHOULD BE SITTING SAFELY BEHIND BARS ABOUT NOW.
YES, WE'VE BEEN MONITORING ITS STREET ACTIVITY EVER SINCE IT WAS STOLEN EARLIER THIS YEAR FROM GOVERNMENT RESEARCH LABS.
A39 WAS AN ACCIDENTAL DERIVATIVE OF THE VENOM SERUM AND HASN'T BEEN DUPLICATED SINCE LOSING THAT INITIAL SAMPLE.
BUT, SUDDENLY, IT'S ALL OVER THE STREETS.
"WE"?
SO, YOU THINK IT'S DANGEROUS?
SOUNDS STRANGE COMING FROM A MAN WHO HANDS OUT NEEDLES TO JUNKIES.
IT'S NOT THE SAME, HEROIN'S A KNOWN COMMODITY. DEADLY, BUT TREATABLE.
A39 HAS CERTAIN ARGUABLE BENEFITS, BUT ITS ABUSE IS FAR MORE INSIDIOUS.
WHAT'S MORE... SOMEONE OUT THERE IS MANUFACTURING THIS DRUG.

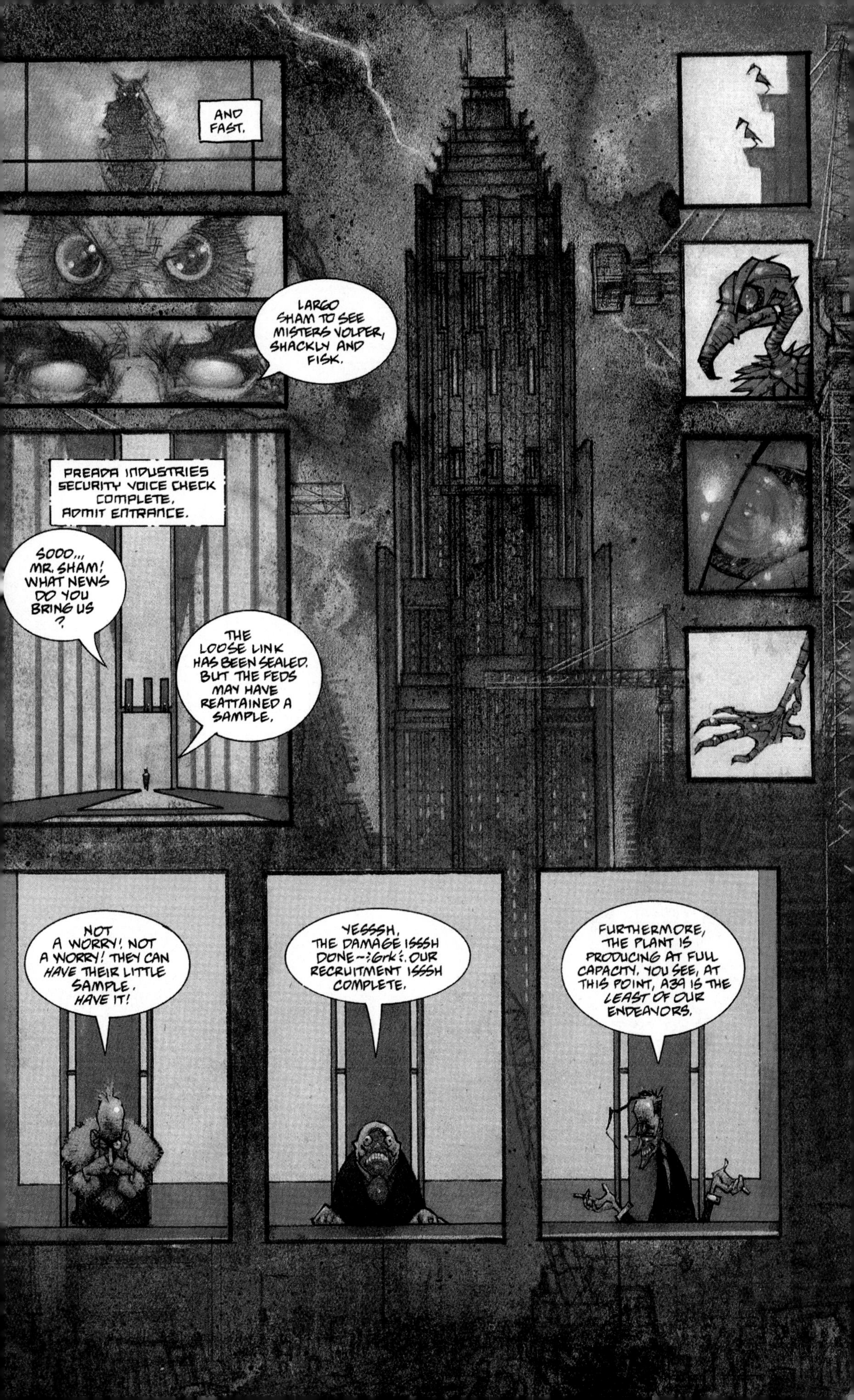
AND FAST.
LARGO SHAM TO SEE MISTERS VOLPER, SHACKLY AND FISK.
PREADA INDUSTRIES SECURITY VOICE CHECK COMPLETE. ADMIT ENTRANCE.
SOOO... MR. SHAM! WHAT NEWS DO YOU BRING US ?
THE LOOSE LINK HAS BEEN SEALED. BUT THE FEDS MAY HAVE REATTAINED A SAMPLE.
NOT A WORRY! NOT A WORRY! THEY CAN HAVE THEIR LITTLE SAMPLE. HAVE IT!
YESSSH, THE DAMAGE ISSSH DONE--;Grk;. OUR RECRUITMENT ISSSH COMPLETE.
FURTHERMORE, THE PLANT IS PRODUCING AT FULL CAPACITY. YOU SEE, AT THIS POINT, A39 IS THE LEAST OF OUR ENDEAVORS.

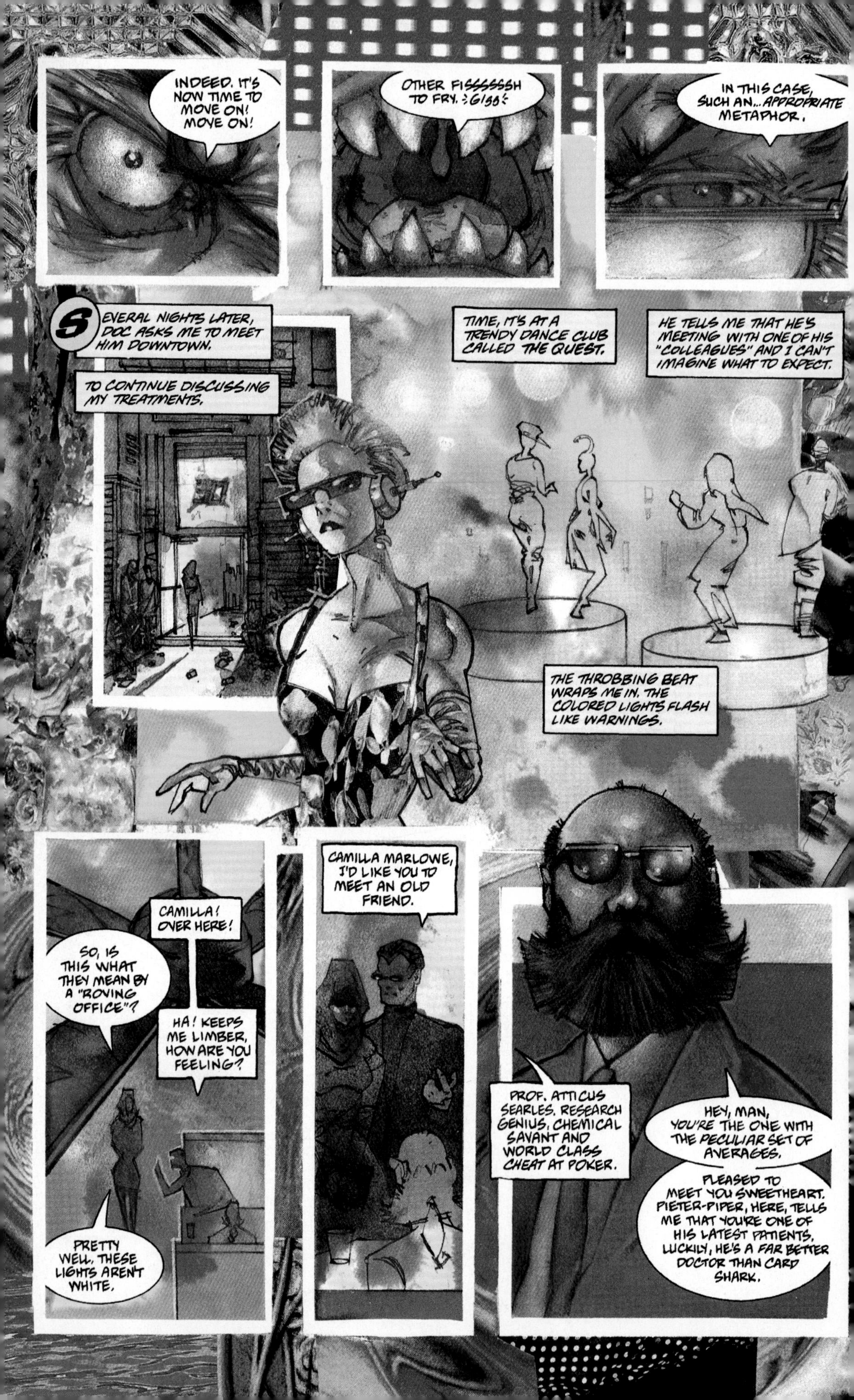
INDEED. IT'S NOW TIME TO MOVE ON! MOVE ON!
OTHER FISSSSSSH TO FRY. ✧Gigg✧
IN THIS CASE, SUCH AN... APPROPRIATE METAPHOR.
SEVERAL NIGHTS LATER, DOC ASKS ME TO MEET HIM DOWNTOWN.
TO CONTINUE DISCUSSING MY TREATMENTS.
TIME, IT'S AT A TRENDY DANCE CLUB CALLED THE QUEST.
HE TELLS ME THAT HE'S MEETING WITH ONE OF HIS "COLLEAGUES" AND I CAN'T IMAGINE WHAT TO EXPECT.
THE THROBBING BEAT WRAPS ME IN. THE COLORED LIGHTS FLASH LIKE WARNINGS.
CAMILLA! OVER HERE!
SO, IS THIS WHAT THEY MEAN BY A "ROVING OFFICE"?
HA! KEEPS ME LIMBER, HOW ARE YOU FEELING?
PRETTY WELL. THESE LIGHTS AREN'T WHITE.
CAMILLA MARLOWE, I'D LIKE YOU TO MEET AN OLD FRIEND.
PROF. ATTICUS SEARLES. RESEARCH GENIUS. CHEMICAL SAVANT AND WORLD CLASS CHEAT AT POKER.
HEY, MAN, YOU'RE THE ONE WITH THE PECULIAR SET OF AVERAGES.
PLEASED TO MEET YOU SWEETHEART. PIETER-PIPER, HERE, TELLS ME THAT YOU'RE ONE OF HIS LATEST PATIENTS. LUCKILY, HE'S A FAR BETTER DOCTOR THAN CARD SHARK.

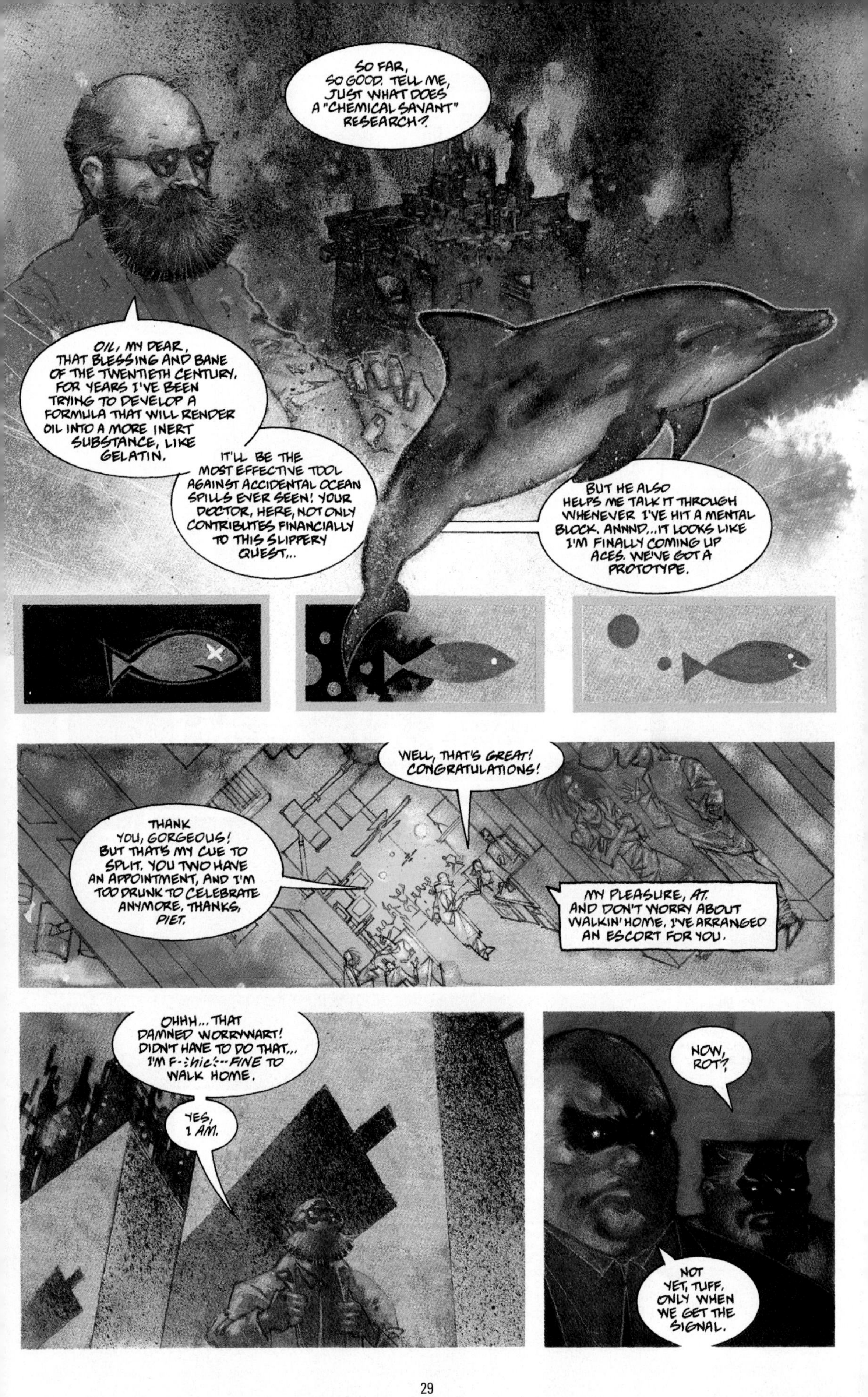
SO FAR, SO GOOD. TELL ME, JUST WHAT DOES A "CHEMICAL SAVANT" RESEARCH?
OIL, MY DEAR, THAT BLESSING AND BANE OF THE TWENTIETH CENTURY. FOR YEARS I'VE BEEN TRYING TO DEVELOP A FORMULA THAT WILL RENDER OIL INTO A MORE INERT SUBSTANCE, LIKE GELATIN.
IT'LL BE THE MOST EFFECTIVE TOOL AGAINST ACCIDENTAL OCEAN SPILLS EVER SEEN! YOUR DOCTOR, HERE, NOT ONLY CONTRIBUTES FINANCIALLY TO THIS SLIPPERY QUEST...
BUT HE ALSO HELPS ME TALK IT THROUGH WHENEVER I'VE HIT A MENTAL BLOCK. ANNND...IT LOOKS LIKE I'M FINALLY COMING UP ACES. WE'VE GOT A PROTOTYPE.
WELL, THAT'S GREAT! CONGRATULATIONS!
THANK YOU, GORGEOUS! BUT THAT'S MY CUE TO SPLIT. YOU TWO HAVE AN APPOINTMENT, AND I'M TOO DRUNK TO CELEBRATE ANYMORE. THANKS, PIET.
MY PLEASURE, AT. AND DON'T WORRY ABOUT WALKIN' HOME. I'VE ARRANGED AN ESCORT FOR YOU.
OHHH... THAT DAMNED WORRYWART! DIDN'T HAVE TO DO THAT... I'M F--hic--FINE TO WALK HOME.
YES, I AM.
NOW, ROT?
NOT YET, TUFF, ONLY WHEN WE GET THE SIGNAL.

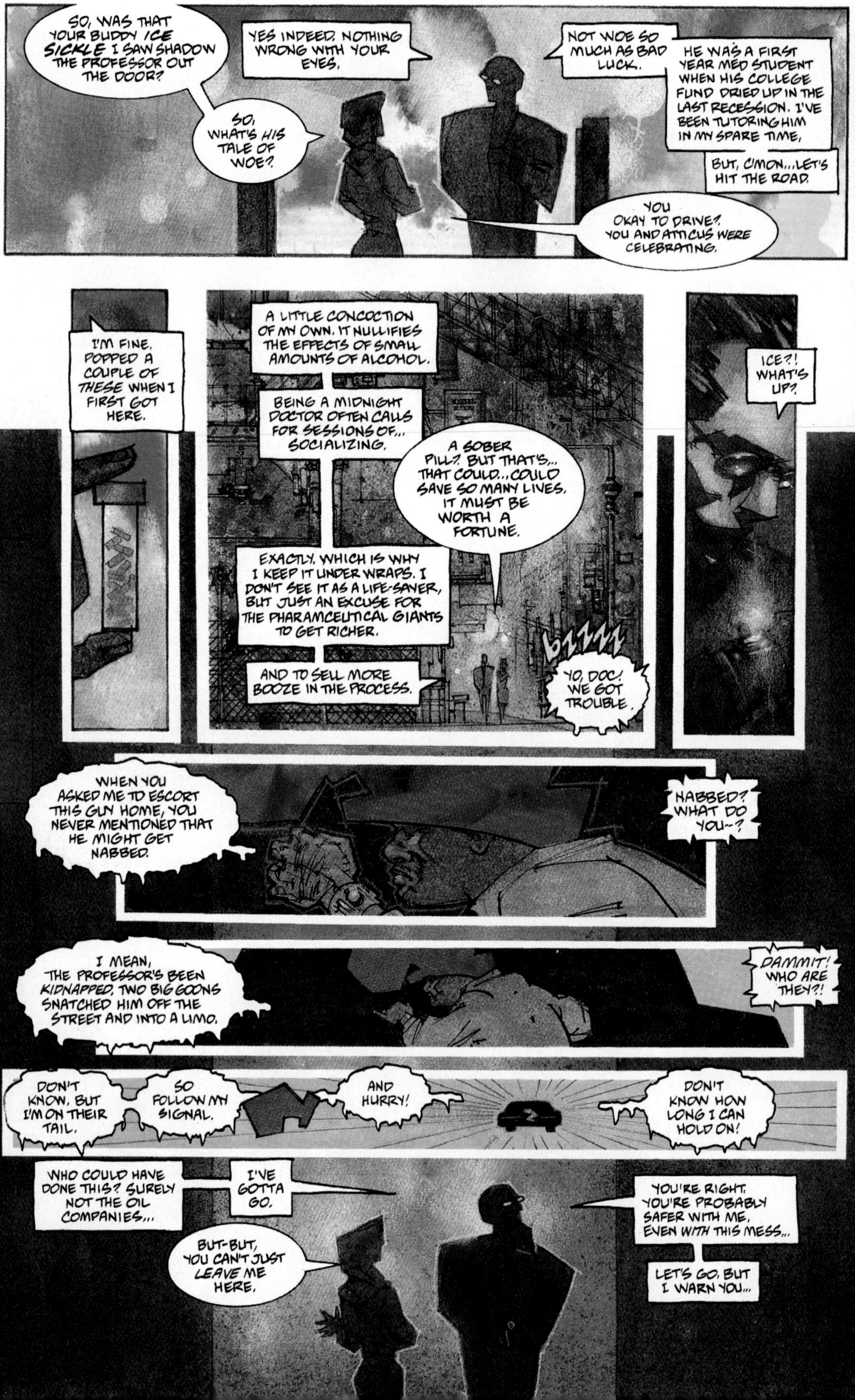
SO, WAS THAT YOUR BUDDY *ICE SICKLE* I SAW SHADOW THE PROFESSOR OUT THE DOOR?
YES INDEED. NOTHING WRONG WITH YOUR EYES.
SO, WHAT'S *HIS* TALE OF WOE?
NOT WOE SO MUCH AS BAD LUCK.
HE WAS A FIRST YEAR MED STUDENT WHEN HIS COLLEGE FUND DRIED UP IN THE LAST RECESSION. I'VE BEEN TUTORING HIM IN MY SPARE TIME.
BUT, C'MON... LET'S HIT THE ROAD.
YOU OKAY TO DRIVE? YOU AND ATTICUS WERE CELEBRATING.
I'M FINE. POPPED A COUPLE OF *THESE* WHEN I FIRST GOT HERE.
A LITTLE CONCOCTION OF MY OWN. IT NULLIFIES THE EFFECTS OF SMALL AMOUNTS OF ALCOHOL.
BEING A MIDNIGHT DOCTOR OFTEN CALLS FOR SESSIONS OF... SOCIALIZING.
A SOBER PILL? BUT THAT'S... THAT COULD... COULD SAVE SO MANY LIVES. IT MUST BE WORTH A FORTUNE.
EXACTLY. WHICH IS WHY I KEEP IT UNDER WRAPS. I DON'T SEE IT AS A LIFE-SAVER, BUT JUST AN EXCUSE FOR THE PHARAMCEUTICAL GIANTS TO GET RICHER.
AND TO SELL MORE BOOZE IN THE PROCESS.
bzzzz
YO, DOC! WE GOT TROUBLE.
ICE?! WHAT'S UP?
WHEN YOU ASKED ME TO ESCORT THIS GUY HOME, YOU NEVER MENTIONED THAT HE MIGHT GET NABBED.
NABBED? WHAT DO YOU--?
I MEAN, THE PROFESSOR'S BEEN *KIDNAPPED*. TWO BIG GOONS SNATCHED HIM OFF THE STREET AND INTO A LIMO.
DAMMIT! WHO ARE THEY?!
DON'T KNOW, BUT I'M ON THEIR TAIL.
SO FOLLOW MY SIGNAL.
AND HURRY!
DON'T KNOW HOW LONG I CAN HOLD ON!
WHO COULD HAVE DONE THIS? SURELY NOT THE OIL COMPANIES...
I'VE GOTTA GO.
BUT-BUT, YOU CAN'T JUST *LEAVE* ME HERE.
YOU'RE RIGHT. YOU'RE PROBABLY SAFER WITH ME, EVEN *WITH* THIS MESS...
LET'S GO, BUT I WARN YOU...

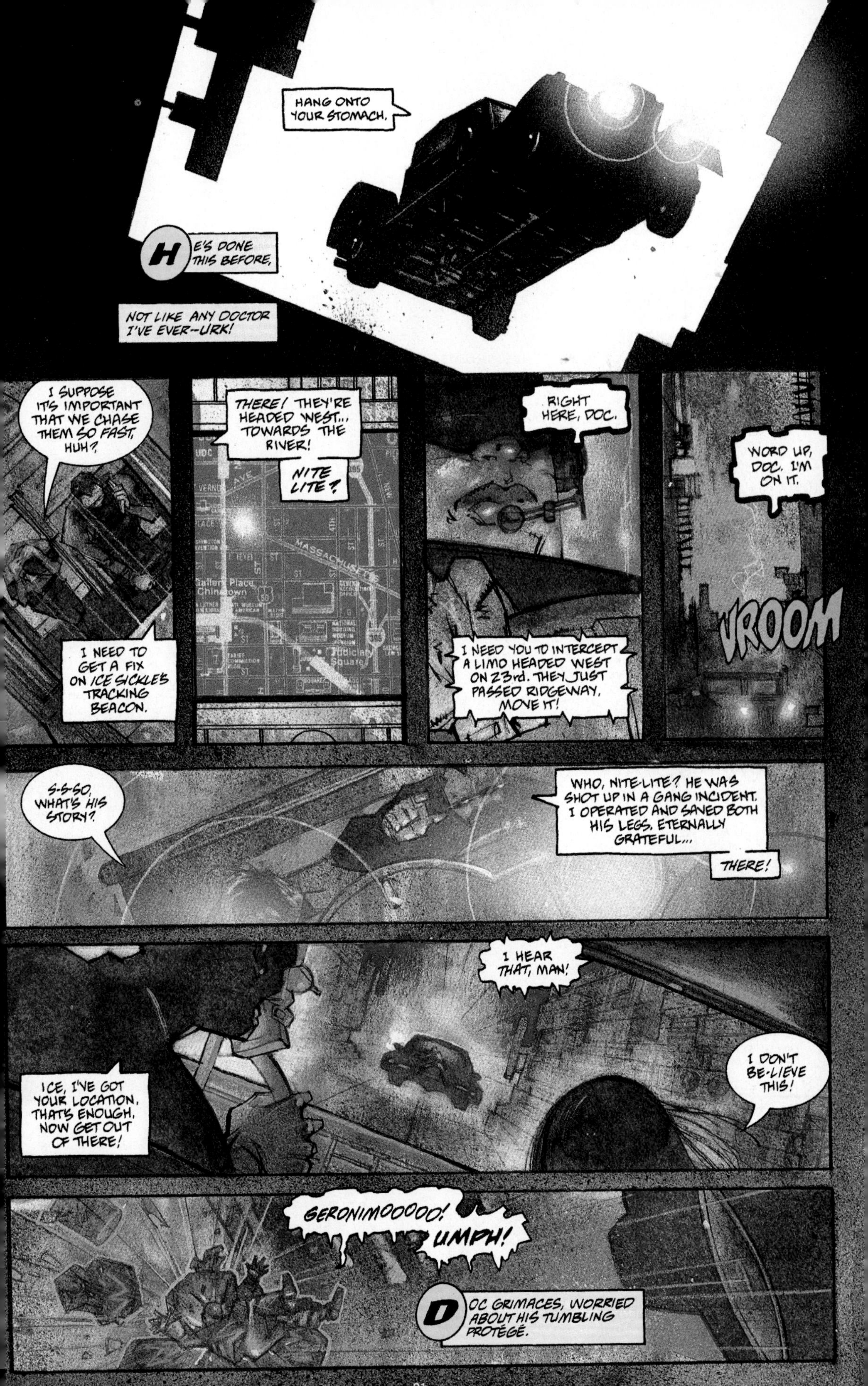
HANG ONTO YOUR STOMACH.
HE'S DONE THIS BEFORE.
NOT LIKE ANY DOCTOR I'VE EVER--URK!
I SUPPOSE IT'S IMPORTANT THAT WE CHASE THEM SO FAST, HUH?
I NEED TO GET A FIX ON ICE SICKLE'S TRACKING BEACON.
THERE! THEY'RE HEADED WEST... TOWARDS THE RIVER!
NITE LITE?
RIGHT HERE, DOC.
I NEED YOU TO INTERCEPT A LIMO HEADED WEST ON 23rd. THEY JUST PASSED RIDGEWAY. MOVE IT!
WORD UP, DOC. I'M ON IT.
VROOM
S-S-SO, WHAT'S HIS STORY?
WHO, NITE-LITE? HE WAS SHOT UP IN A GANG INCIDENT. I OPERATED AND SAVED BOTH HIS LEGS. ETERNALLY GRATEFUL...
THERE!
I HEAR THAT, MAN!
ICE, I'VE GOT YOUR LOCATION. THAT'S ENOUGH. NOW GET OUT OF THERE!
I DON'T BE-LIEVE THIS!
GERONIMOOOOOO!
UMPH!
DOC GRIMACES, WORRIED ABOUT HIS TUMBLING PROTÉGÉ.

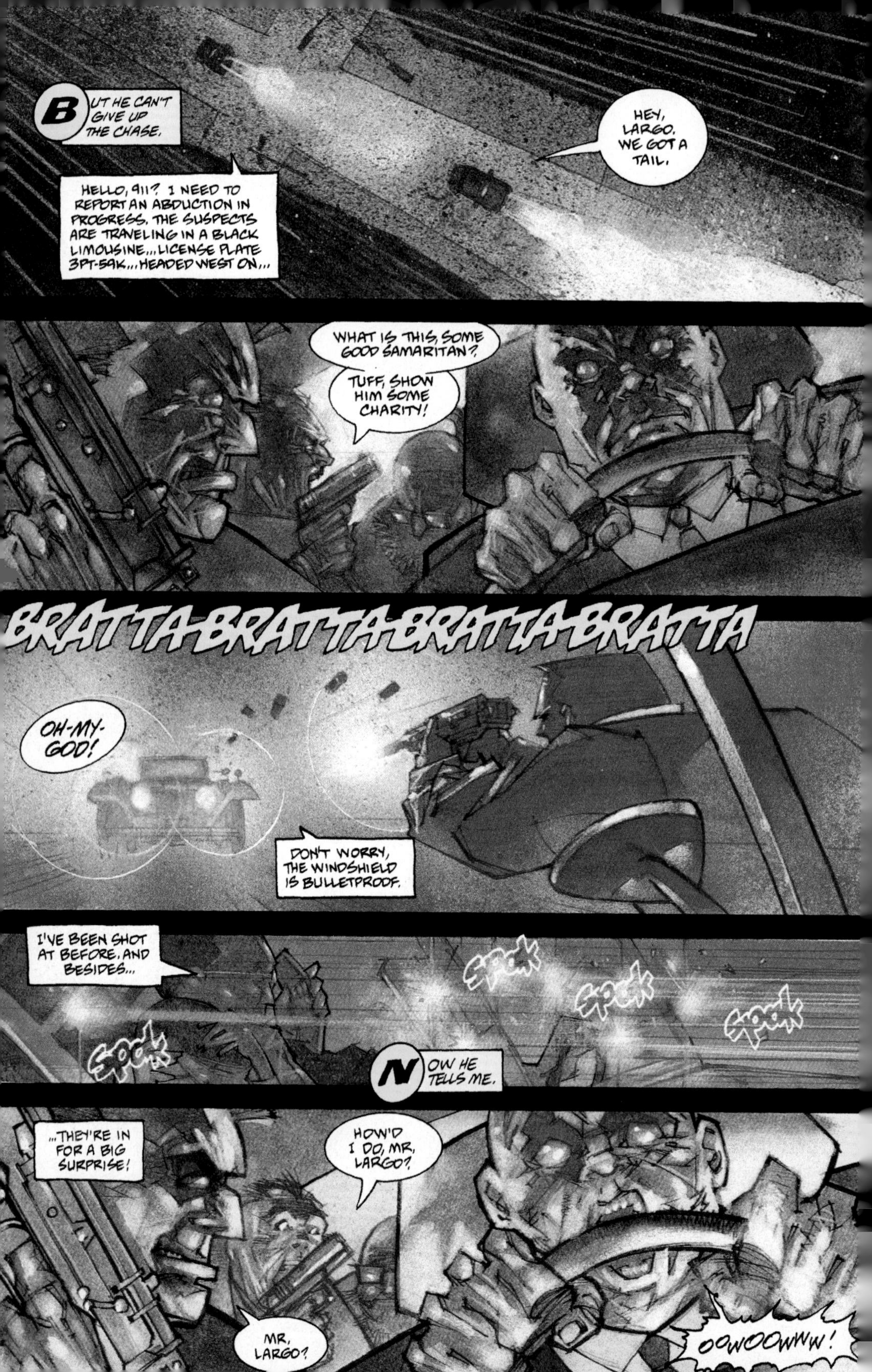
BUT HE CAN'T GIVE UP THE CHASE.
HEY, LARGO, WE GOT A TAIL.
HELLO, 911? I NEED TO REPORT AN ABDUCTION IN PROGRESS. THE SUSPECTS ARE TRAVELING IN A BLACK LIMOUSINE... LICENSE PLATE 3PT-59K... HEADED WEST ON...
WHAT IS THIS, SOME GOOD SAMARITAN?
TUFF, SHOW HIM SOME CHARITY!
BRATTA-BRATTA-BRATTA-BRATTA
OH-MY-GOD!
DON'T WORRY, THE WINDSHIELD IS BULLETPROOF.
I'VE BEEN SHOT AT BEFORE, AND BESIDES...
SPAK
SPAK
SPAK
SPAK
NOW HE TELLS ME.
...THEY'RE IN FOR A BIG SURPRISE!
HOW'D I DO, MR. LARGO?
MR. LARGO?
OOWOOWWW!

MAKE WAY, BOYS! TIME FOR NITE-LITE'S **MONSTER** **TRUCK RALLY!**

THE SHRIEK OF RENDING METAL IS DEAFENING.

HONK

AND FINALLY, THE REST OF THE TRAFFIC CATCHES UP WITH US.

HONK HONK

CHAOS CONTINUES AS FENDER BENDERS STACK UP LIKE DOMINOES.

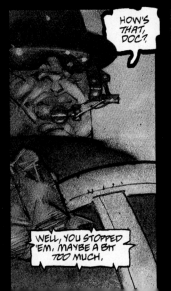

HOW'S THAT, DOC?

WELL, YOU STOPPED 'EM, MAYBE A BIT TOO MUCH.

LET'S HOPE THEY SURVIVED!

Uuh-?!

AAARGH! YOU TWO ARE USELESS! WHO THE HELL WAS THAT?

LET ME THROUGH! I'M A **DOCTOR!**

CHANGE OF PLANS, PROFESSOR!

ACK--!

PIETER CROSS! HELP MEEEE!

AAAND OF TRANSPORTATION!

BANG BANG BANG

BUT YOU'RE STILL COMING WITH ME!!

T HE CABBY NARROWLY AVOIDS ANY INJURY.

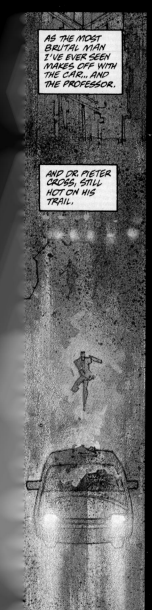

AS THE MOST BRUTAL MAN I'VE EVER SEEN MAKES OFF WITH THE CAR... AND THE PROFESSOR.

AND DR. PIETER CROSS, STILL HOT ON HIS TRAIL.

DAMMIT!

HE'S LIKE A FRUSTRATED PANTHER, SEEING HIS QUARRY SLIP AWAY INTO THE NIGHT.

STILL, THERE ARE INJURIES TO TEND.

GROWLING, HE RELENTS.

NITE-LITE! SEE IF YOU CAN PICK UP THEIR TRAIL!

DO MY BEST, DOC, BUT THAT'LL MAKE THIS "HIT AND RUN."

I'LL HANDLE THE COPS ...GO!

T HIS IS UNLIKE ANYTHING THAT'S EVER HAPPENED TO ME.

I'M NOT INJURED, BUT MY HEART IS RACING LIKE AN ENGINE.

WHAT HAVE I GOTTEN MYSELF INTO?

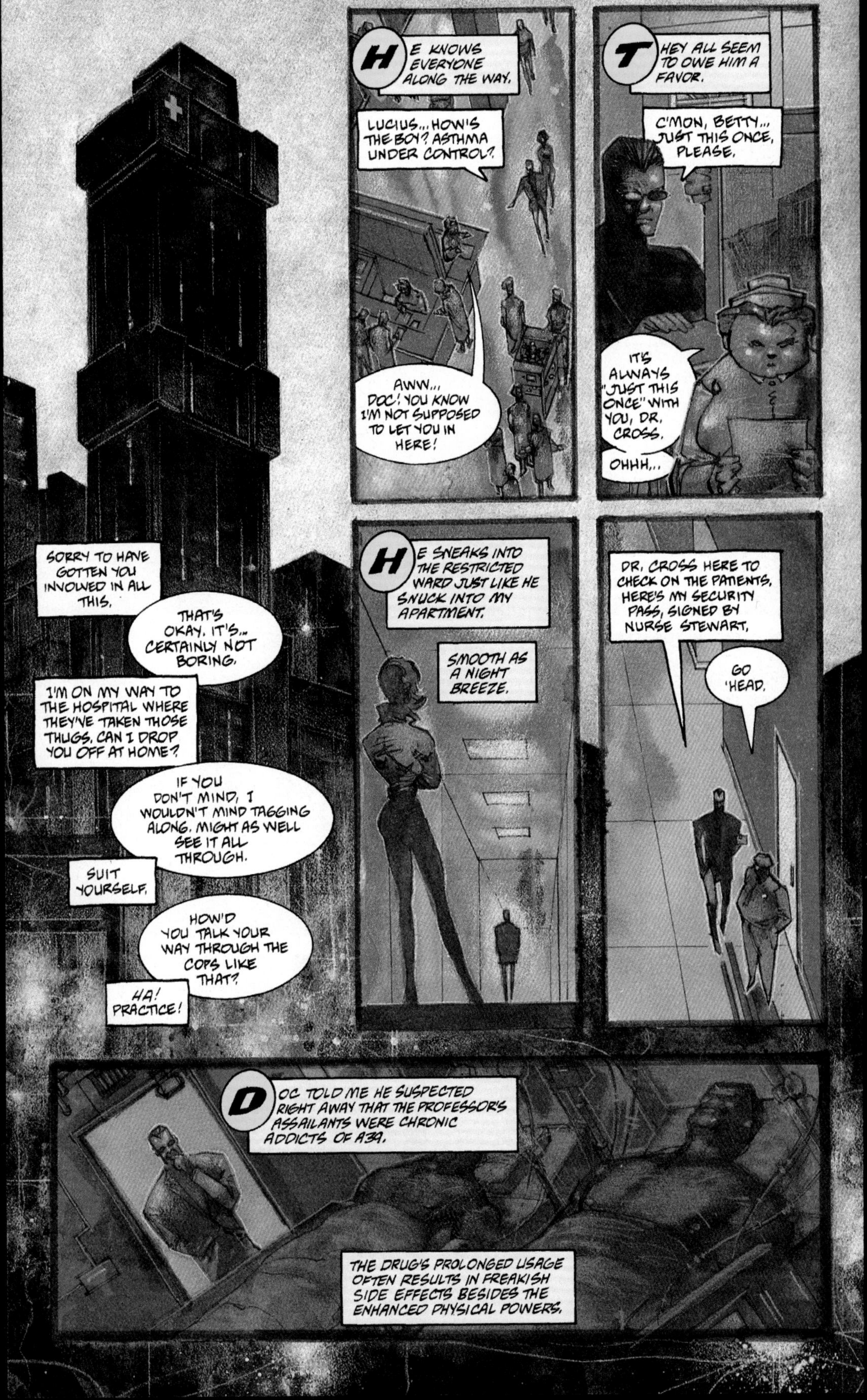
SORRY TO HAVE GOTTEN YOU INVOLVED IN ALL THIS.
THAT'S OKAY. IT'S... CERTAINLY NOT BORING.
I'M ON MY WAY TO THE HOSPITAL WHERE THEY'VE TAKEN THOSE THUGS. CAN I DROP YOU OFF AT HOME?
IF YOU DON'T MIND, I WOULDN'T MIND TAGGING ALONG. MIGHT AS WELL SEE IT ALL THROUGH.
SUIT YOURSELF.
HOW'D YOU TALK YOUR WAY THROUGH THE COPS LIKE THAT?
HA! PRACTICE!
HE KNOWS EVERYONE ALONG THE WAY.
LUCIUS... HOW'S THE BOY? ASTHMA UNDER CONTROL?
AWW... DOC! YOU KNOW I'M NOT SUPPOSED TO LET YOU IN HERE!
THEY ALL SEEM TO OWE HIM A FAVOR.
C'MON, BETTY... JUST THIS ONCE, PLEASE.
IT'S ALWAYS "JUST THIS ONCE" WITH YOU, DR. CROSS.
OHHH...
HE SNEAKS INTO THE RESTRICTED WARD JUST LIKE HE SNUCK INTO MY APARTMENT.
SMOOTH AS A NIGHT BREEZE.
DR. CROSS HERE TO CHECK ON THE PATIENTS. HERE'S MY SECURITY PASS, SIGNED BY NURSE STEWART.
GO 'HEAD.
DOC TOLD ME HE SUSPECTED RIGHT AWAY THAT THE PROFESSOR'S ASSAILANTS WERE CHRONIC ADDICTS OF A39.
THE DRUG'S PROLONGED USAGE OFTEN RESULTS IN FREAKISH SIDE EFFECTS BESIDES THE ENHANCED PHYSICAL POWERS.

A CURIOUS ANEMIA THAT STRIKES THE PIGMENTS IN THE IRIS AND PUPILS.

PITUITARY ATRIFICATION.

AND RECURRING RASHES OF HIVES, MOST OFTEN ON THE CHEST, BACK AND SHOULDERS.

QUITE A PRICE TO PAY JUST TO BE SO BIG AND SURLY/TOUGH.

DOC, OF COURSE, HAD KEPT A PORTION OF THE A39 SAMPLE HE'D OBTAINED FROM THE FEDS.

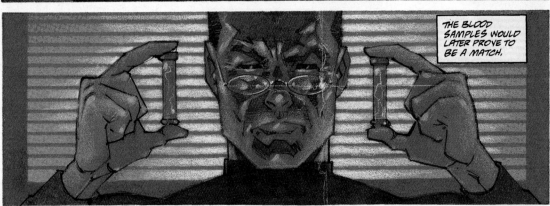

THE BLOOD SAMPLES WOULD LATER PROVE TO BE A MATCH.

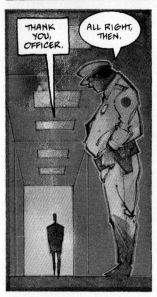

THANK YOU, OFFICER.

ALL RIGHT, THEN.

IT'S A39, I'M SURE, SO I CAN'T BELIEVE THIS IS ALL JUST A COINCIDENCE, BUT WHY KIDNAP ATTICUS?

HE'S NOT CONNECTED TO YOUR... UNDERCOVER ACTIVITIES?

ABSOLUTELY NOT. HE LIVES FOR HIS OIL GOOP.

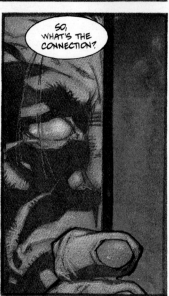

SO, WHAT'S THE CONNECTION?

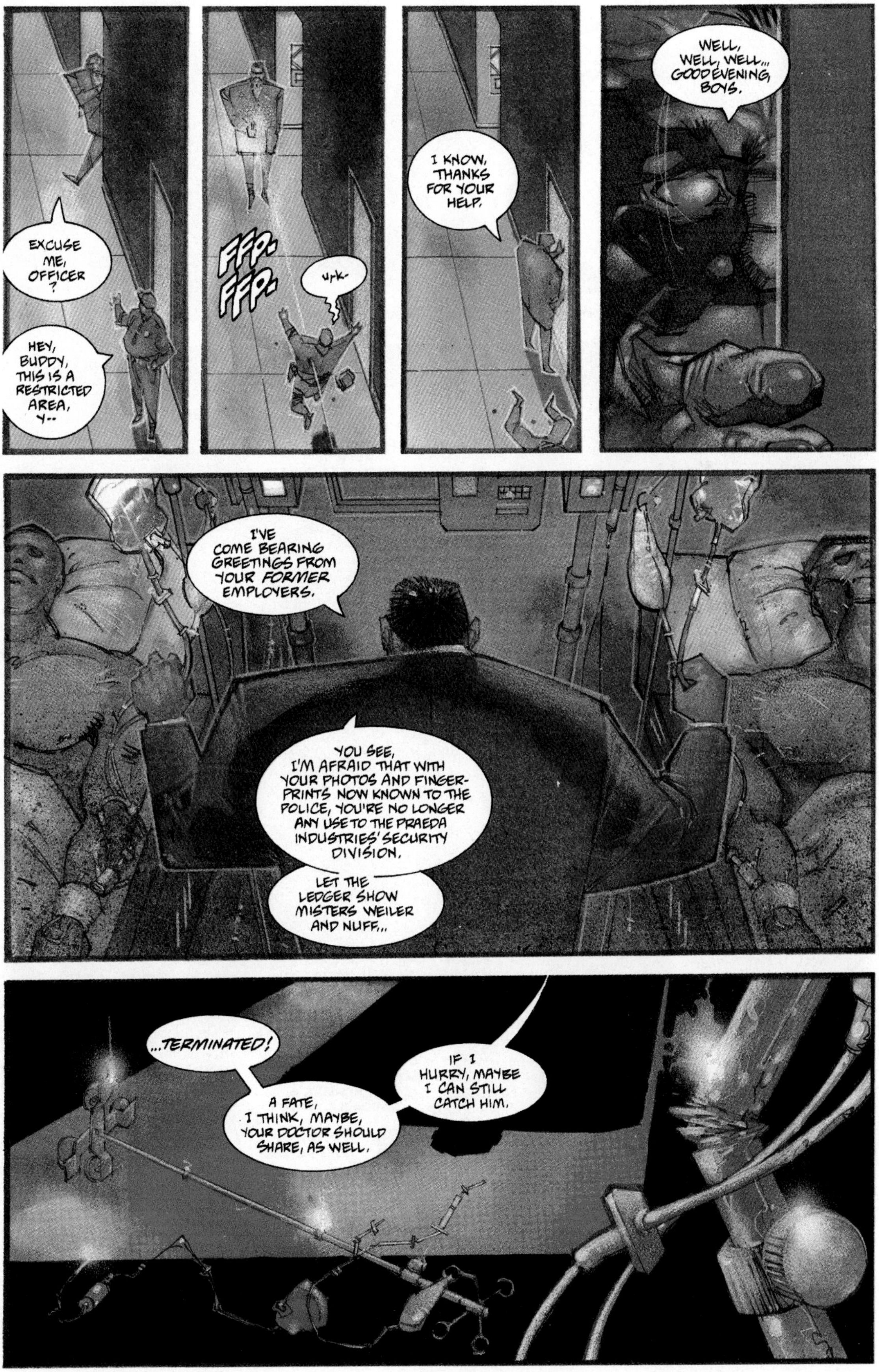
EXCUSE ME, OFFICER?
HEY, BUDDY, THIS IS A RESTRICTED AREA, Y--
FFP. FFP.
URK-
I KNOW, THANKS FOR YOUR HELP.
WELL, WELL, WELL... GOOD EVENING, BOYS.
I'VE COME BEARING GREETINGS FROM YOUR FORMER EMPLOYERS.
YOU SEE, I'M AFRAID THAT WITH YOUR PHOTOS AND FINGER-PRINTS NOW KNOWN TO THE POLICE, YOU'RE NO LONGER ANY USE TO THE PRAEDA INDUSTRIES' SECURITY DIVISION.
LET THE LEDGER SHOW MISTERS WEILER AND NUFF...
...TERMINATED!
A FATE, I THINK, MAYBE, YOUR DOCTOR SHOULD SHARE, AS WELL.
IF I HURRY, MAYBE I CAN STILL CATCH HIM.

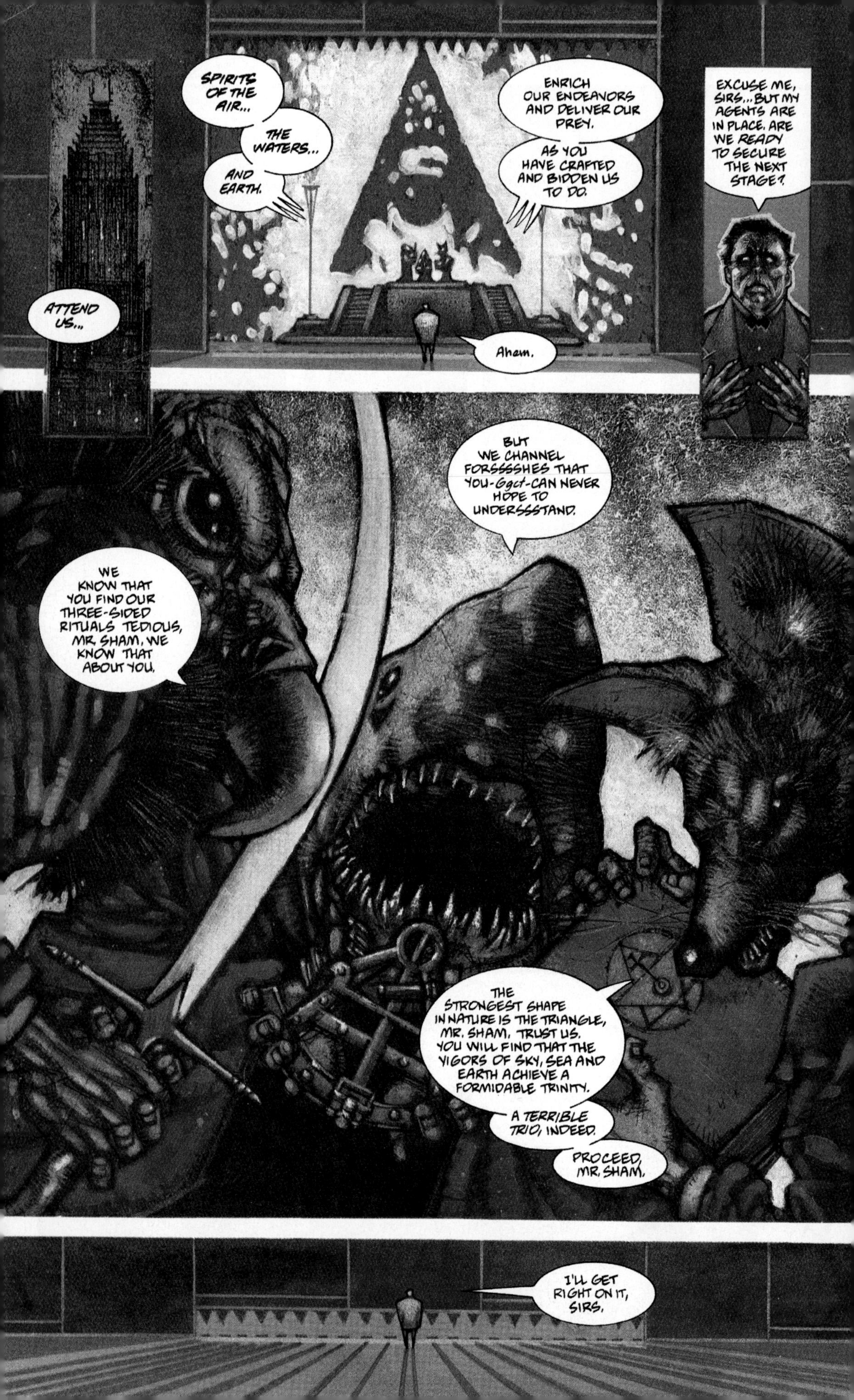
SPIRITS OF THE AIR...
THE WATERS...
AND EARTH.
ENRICH OUR ENDEAVORS AND DELIVER OUR PREY.
AS YOU HAVE CRAFTED AND BIDDEN US TO DO.
ATTEND US...
Ahem.
EXCUSE ME, SIRS... BUT MY AGENTS ARE IN PLACE. ARE WE READY TO SECURE THE NEXT STAGE?
WE KNOW THAT YOU FIND OUR THREE-SIDED RITUALS TEDIOUS, MR. SHAM. WE KNOW THAT ABOUT YOU.
BUT WE CHANNEL FORSSSSHES THAT YOU-Ggct-CAN NEVER HOPE TO UNDERSSSTAND.
THE STRONGEST SHAPE IN NATURE IS THE TRIANGLE, MR. SHAM. TRUST US. YOU WILL FIND THAT THE VIGORS OF SKY, SEA AND EARTH ACHIEVE A FORMIDABLE TRINITY.
A TERRIBLE TRIO, INDEED.
PROCEED, MR. SHAM.
I'LL GET RIGHT ON IT, SIRS.

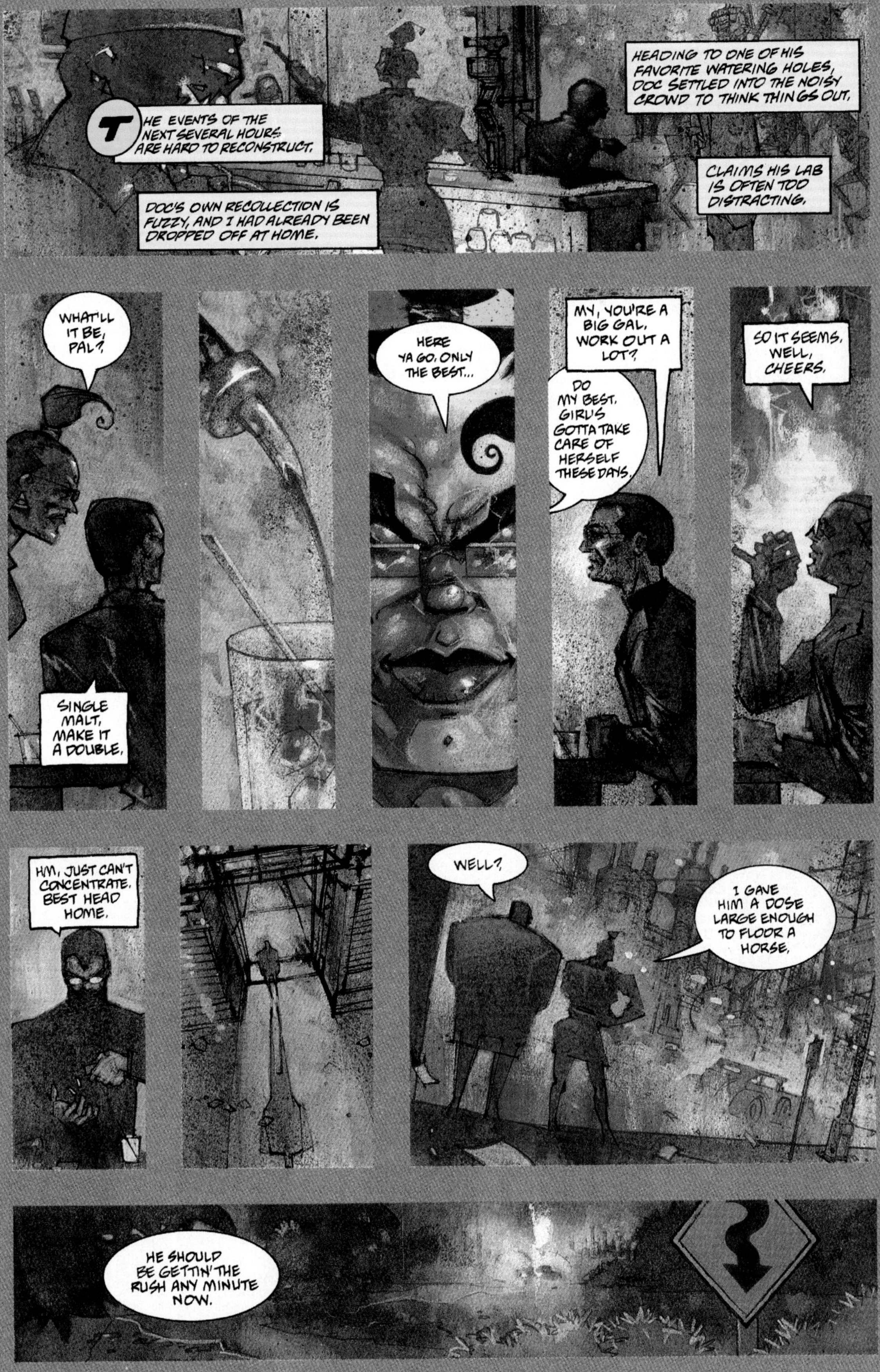
THE EVENTS OF THE NEXT SEVERAL HOURS ARE HARD TO RECONSTRUCT.
DOC'S OWN RECOLLECTION IS FUZZY, AND I HAD ALREADY BEEN DROPPED OFF AT HOME.
HEADING TO ONE OF HIS FAVORITE WATERING HOLES, DOC SETTLED INTO THE NOISY CROWD TO THINK THINGS OUT.
CLAIMS HIS LAB IS OFTEN TOO DISTRACTING.
WHAT'LL IT BE, PAL?
SINGLE MALT, MAKE IT A DOUBLE.
HERE YA GO, ONLY THE BEST...
MY, YOU'RE A BIG GAL, WORK OUT A LOT?
DO MY BEST, GIRL'S GOTTA TAKE CARE OF HERSELF THESE DAYS.
SO IT SEEMS. WELL, CHEERS.
HM, JUST CAN'T CONCENTRATE. BEST HEAD HOME.
WELL?
I GAVE HIM A DOSE LARGE ENOUGH TO FLOOR A HORSE.
HE SHOULD BE GETTIN' THE RUSH ANY MINUTE NOW.

SOMETIME LATER, ON THE WINDING DRIVE HOME, DOC EXPERIENCED A SUDDEN SURGE OF ADRENAL FLUID.

HIS HEART BEGAN RAPID PALPITATIONS, AND MUSCLE SPASMS RACKED HIS ENTIRE BODY.

DESPITE HIS AGGRAVATED STATE, DOC MANAGED TO PULL HIMSELF FREE OF THE WRECK, AND FRANTICALLY BEGAN TO DRAG THE OTHER VICTIMS TO SAFETY,

IN THE DARK, HE WAS UNSURE OF THE OTHER CAR'S PASSENGERS AND WENT BACK TO CHECK FOR MORE SURVIVORS.

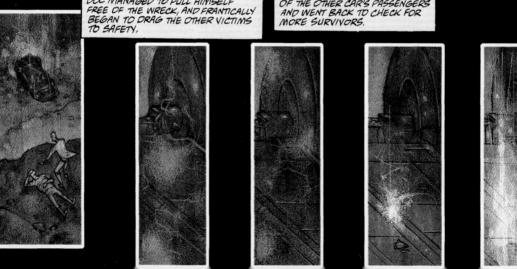

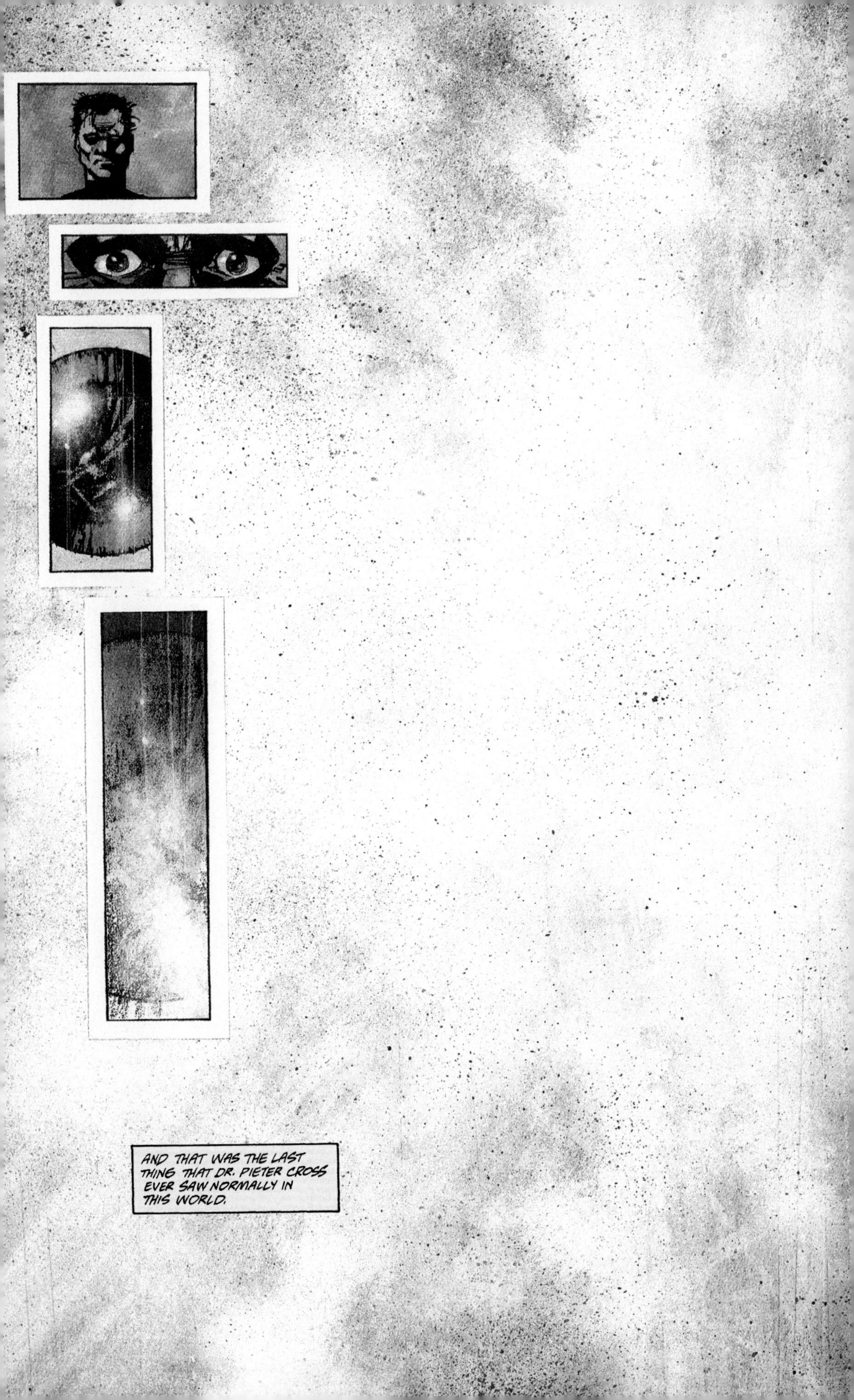
AND THAT WAS THE LAST THING THAT DR. PIETER CROSS EVER SAW NORMALLY IN THIS WORLD.

DR. CROSS...?

DR. CROSS...?

DR. CROSS...?

DR. CROSS...?

DR. CROSS...?

DR. CROSS...?

DR. CROSS...?

DR. CROSS...?

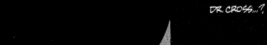

DR. CROSS...?

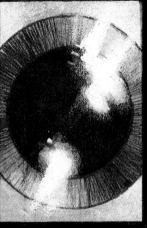

DR. CROSS...?

DR. CROSS, I KNOW YOU CAN HEAR ME, IT ISN'T YOUR HEARING THAT'S BEEN AFFECTED.

YOUR EYE-SIGHT, ON THE OTHER HAND...

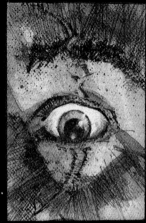

YOU ARE A PATIENT AT EMMANUEL HOSPITAL, WHERE YOU WERE BROUGHT FOLLOWING A CAR CRASH.

THE TRAUMA HAS RESULTED IN A NEARLY TOTAL LOSS OF YOUR PRIMARY VISION.

YOU DO STILL EXHIBIT CERTAIN OPTICAL RESPONSE TO LOWER-RANGE SPECTRUMS.

YOUR BLOOD, FOLLOWING THE ACCIDENT, WAS SHOWN TO CONTAIN A VARIETY OF CHEMICAL STIMULANTS.

AS A PHYSICIAN, I KNOW YOU UNDERSTAND THE IMPLICATIONS OF THIS SITUATION. A PASSENGER DIED IN THAT EXPLOSION.

THE A.M.A. HAS REVOKED YOUR LICENSE TO PRACTICE MEDICINE.

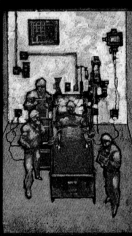

REST ASSURED THAT WE RETAIN SOME OF THE VERY FINEST COUNSELORS FOR THE BLIND IN THE STATE.

YOU...WERE A SURGEON, YOU SHOULD QUICKLY BE ABLE TO MASTER THE TACTILE SUBTLETIES OF BRAILLE.

YOU'RE YOUNG AND IN SHAPE, YOUR EQUILIBRIUM SHOULD EASILY ADAPT TO A SIGHTING CANE.

THERE'S NO REASON YOU CAN'T CONTINUE TO FUNCTION, BOTH IN SOCIETY, JUST... NOT IN YOUR CHOSEN PROFESSION.

YOU REALLY DO HAVE TO LOOK...UH, CONSIDER THE BRIGHT SIDE OF THIS.

DR. CROSS...?

POOR BASTARD. WELL, THAT'S WHAT YOU GET FOR ALWAYS DASHING INTO TROUBLE.

DR. CROSS...?

HOW ARE YOU FEELING?

DR. CROSS...?

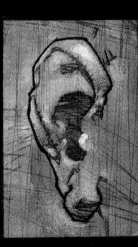

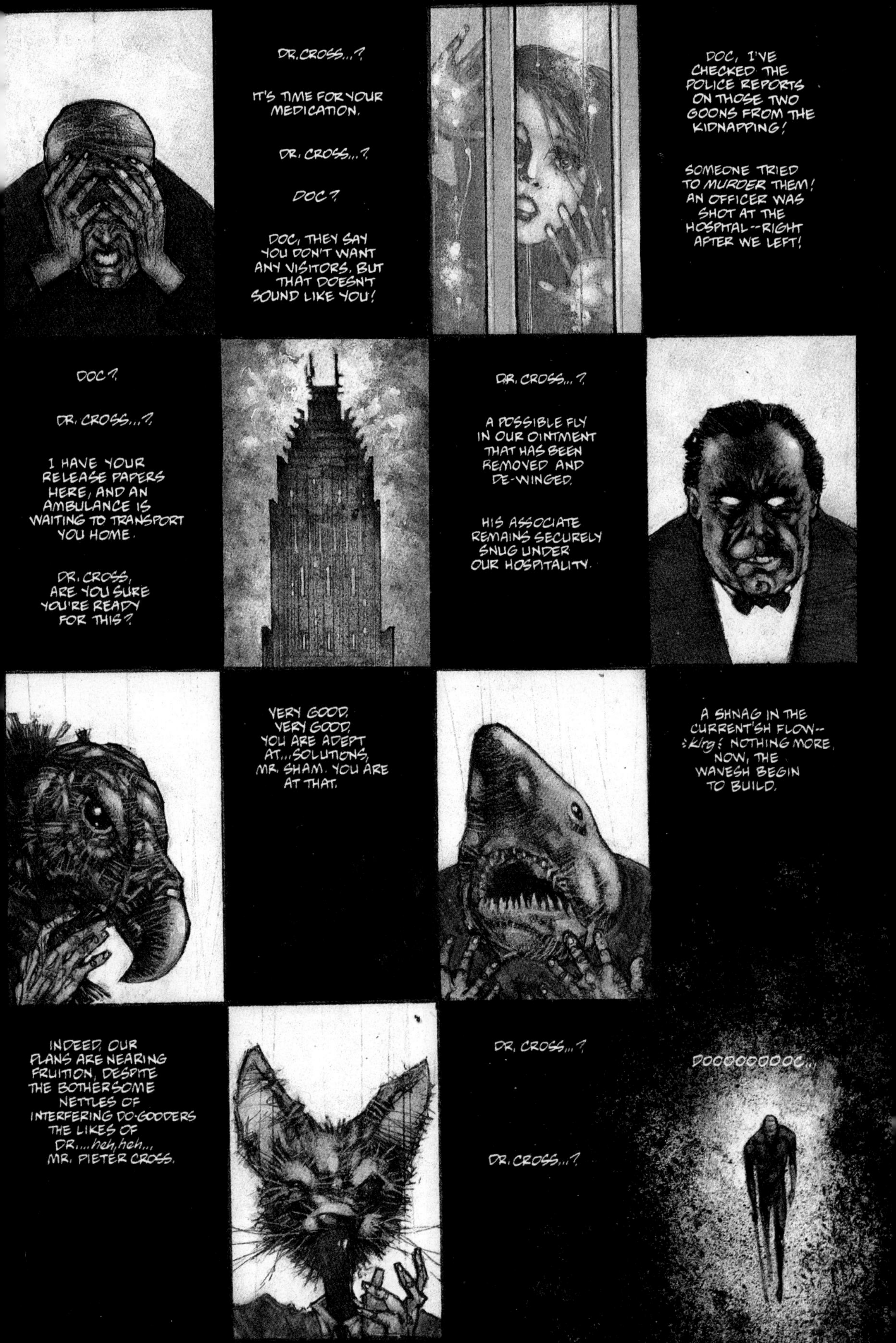
DR. CROSS...?
IT'S TIME FOR YOUR MEDICATION.
DR. CROSS...?
DOC?
DOC, THEY SAY YOU DON'T WANT ANY VISITORS. BUT THAT DOESN'T SOUND LIKE YOU!
DOC, I'VE CHECKED THE POLICE REPORTS ON THOSE TWO GOONS FROM THE KIDNAPPING!
SOMEONE TRIED TO MURDER THEM! AN OFFICER WAS SHOT AT THE HOSPITAL--RIGHT AFTER WE LEFT!
DOC?
DR. CROSS...?
I HAVE YOUR RELEASE PAPERS HERE, AND AN AMBULANCE IS WAITING TO TRANSPORT YOU HOME.
DR. CROSS, ARE YOU SURE YOU'RE READY FOR THIS?
DR. CROSS...?
A POSSIBLE FLY IN OUR OINTMENT THAT HAS BEEN REMOVED AND DE-WINGED.
HIS ASSOCIATE REMAINS SECURELY SNUG UNDER OUR HOSPITALITY.
VERY GOOD. VERY GOOD. YOU ARE ADEPT AT...SOLUTIONS, MR. SHAM. YOU ARE AT THAT.
A SHNAG IN THE CURRENT'SH FLOW-- *kirg!* NOTHING MORE. NOW, THE WAVESH BEGIN TO BUILD.
INDEED. OUR PLANS ARE NEARING FRUITION, DESPITE THE BOTHERSOME NETTLES OF INTERFERING DO-GOODERS THE LIKES OF DR. ...heh, heh... MR. PIETER CROSS.
DR. CROSS...?
DR. CROSS...?
DOOOOOOOOC...

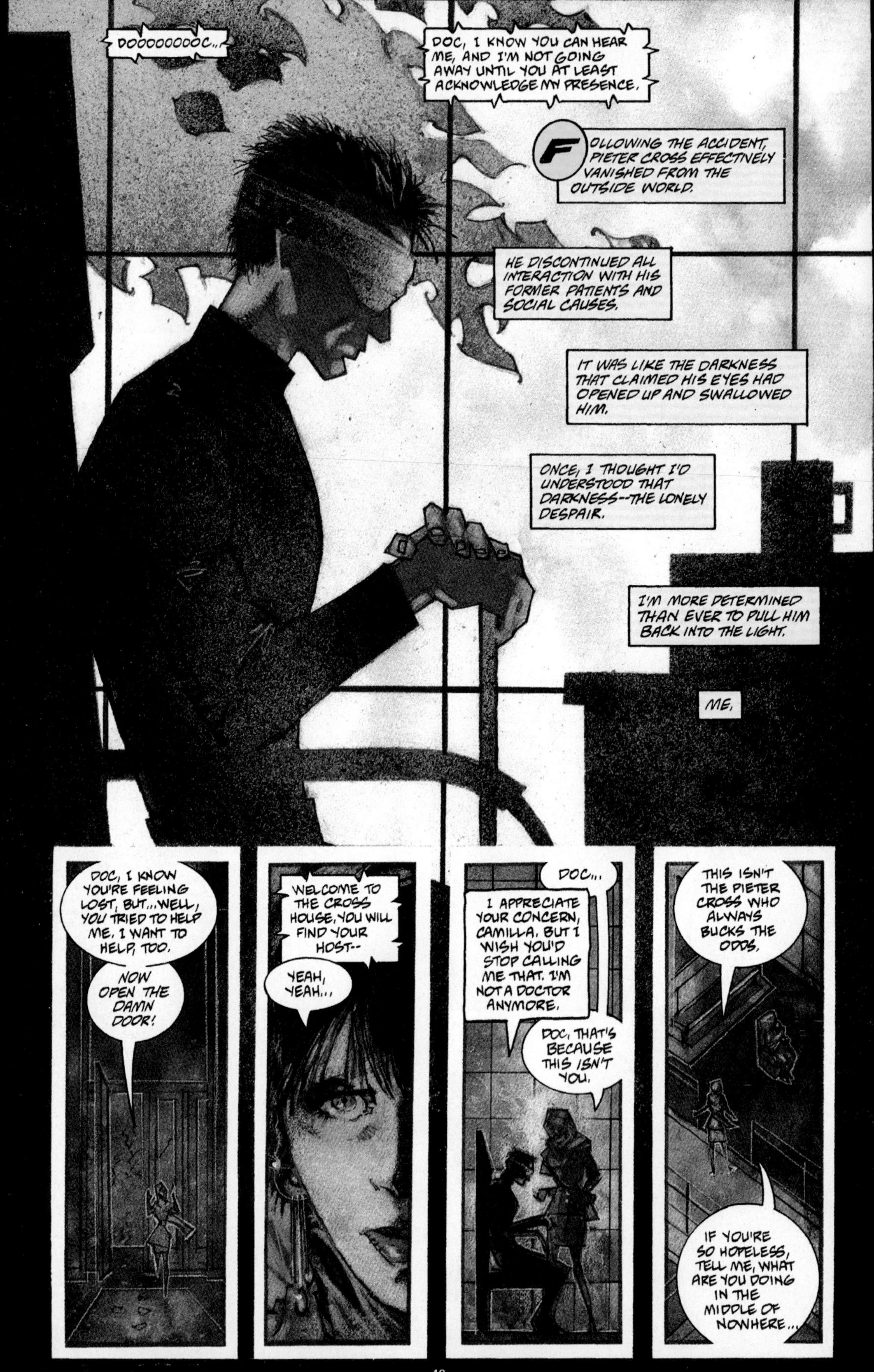
DOOOOOOOOC...
DOC, I KNOW YOU CAN HEAR ME, AND I'M NOT GOING AWAY UNTIL YOU AT LEAST ACKNOWLEDGE MY PRESENCE.
FOLLOWING THE ACCIDENT, PIETER CROSS EFFECTIVELY VANISHED FROM THE OUTSIDE WORLD.
HE DISCONTINUED ALL INTERACTION WITH HIS FORMER PATIENTS AND SOCIAL CAUSES.
IT WAS LIKE THE DARKNESS THAT CLAIMED HIS EYES HAD OPENED UP AND SWALLOWED HIM.
ONCE, I THOUGHT I'D UNDERSTOOD THAT DARKNESS--THE LONELY DESPAIR.
I'M MORE DETERMINED THAN EVER TO PULL HIM BACK INTO THE LIGHT.
ME.
DOC, I KNOW YOU'RE FEELING LOST, BUT... WELL, YOU TRIED TO HELP ME. I WANT TO HELP, TOO.
NOW OPEN THE DAMN DOOR!
WELCOME TO THE CROSS HOUSE. YOU WILL FIND YOUR HOST--
YEAH, YEAH...
DOC...
I APPRECIATE YOUR CONCERN, CAMILLA. BUT I WISH YOU'D STOP CALLING ME THAT. I'M NOT A DOCTOR ANYMORE.
DOC, THAT'S BECAUSE THIS ISN'T YOU.
THIS ISN'T THE PIETER CROSS WHO ALWAYS BUCKS THE ODDS.
IF YOU'RE SO HOPELESS, TELL ME, WHAT ARE YOU DOING IN THE MIDDLE OF NOWHERE...

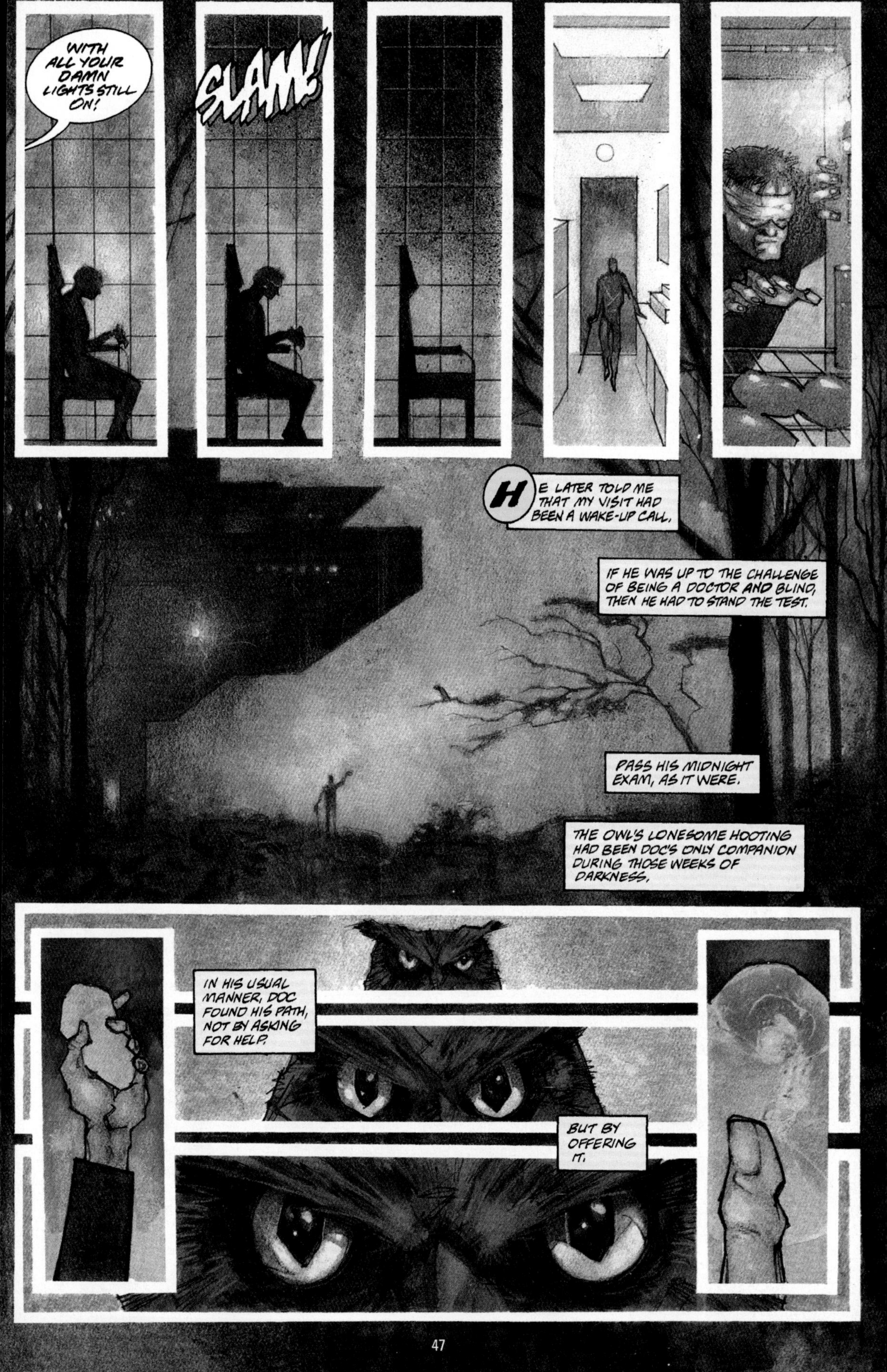
WITH ALL YOUR DAMN LIGHTS STILL ON!
SLAM!
HE LATER TOLD ME THAT MY VISIT HAD BEEN A WAKE-UP CALL.
IF HE WAS UP TO THE CHALLENGE OF BEING A DOCTOR AND BLIND, THEN HE HAD TO STAND THE TEST.
PASS HIS MIDNIGHT EXAM, AS IT WERE.
THE OWL'S LONESOME HOOTING HAD BEEN DOC'S ONLY COMPANION DURING THOSE WEEKS OF DARKNESS.
IN HIS USUAL MANNER, DOC FOUND HIS PATH, NOT BY ASKING FOR HELP.
BUT BY OFFERING IT.

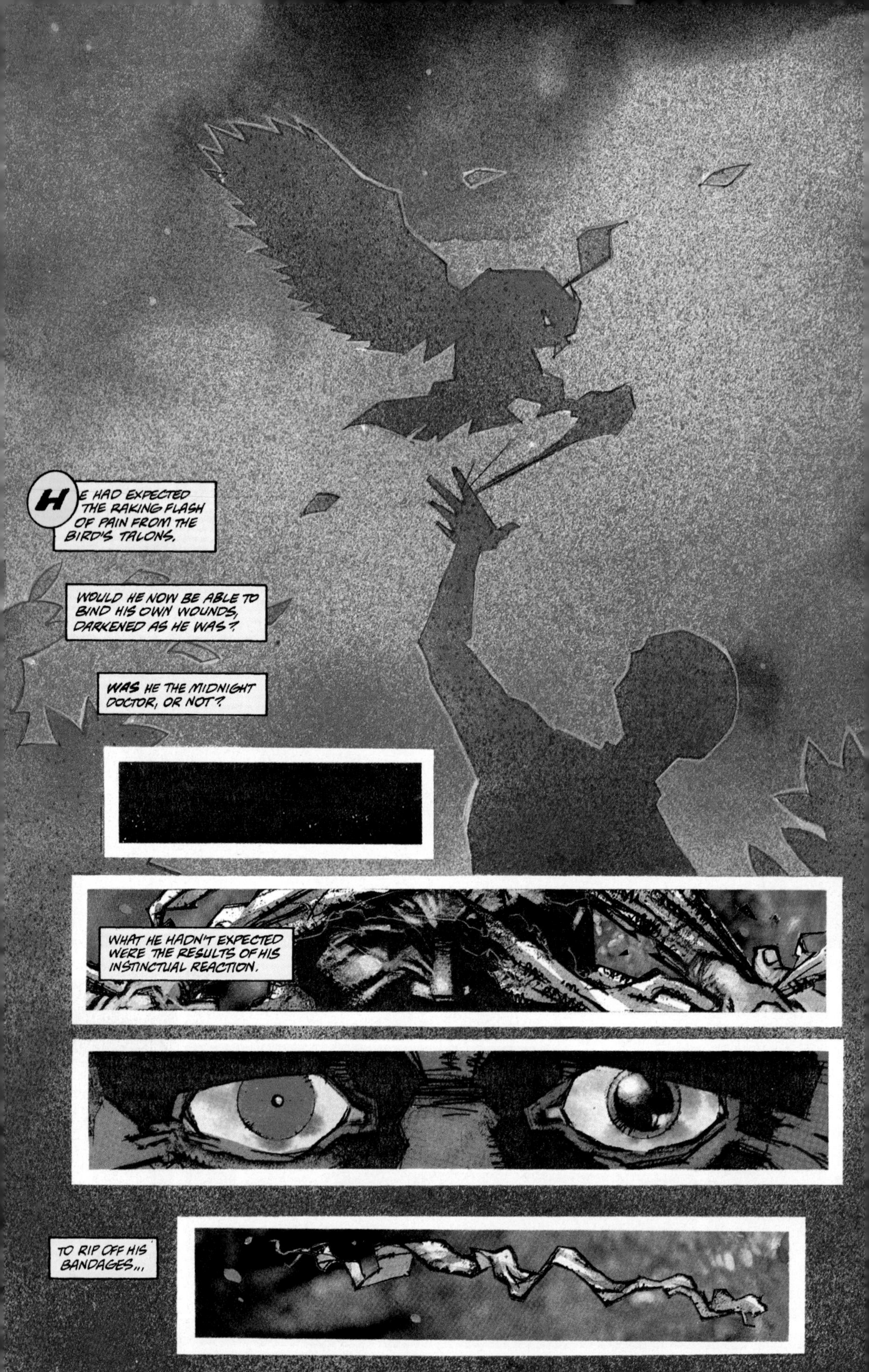
HE HAD EXPECTED THE RAKING FLASH OF PAIN FROM THE BIRD'S TALONS.
WOULD HE NOW BE ABLE TO BIND HIS OWN WOUNDS, DARKENED AS HE WAS?
WAS HE THE MIDNIGHT DOCTOR, OR NOT?
WHAT HE HADN'T EXPECTED WERE THE RESULTS OF HIS INSTINCTUAL REACTION.
TO RIP OFF HIS BANDAGES...

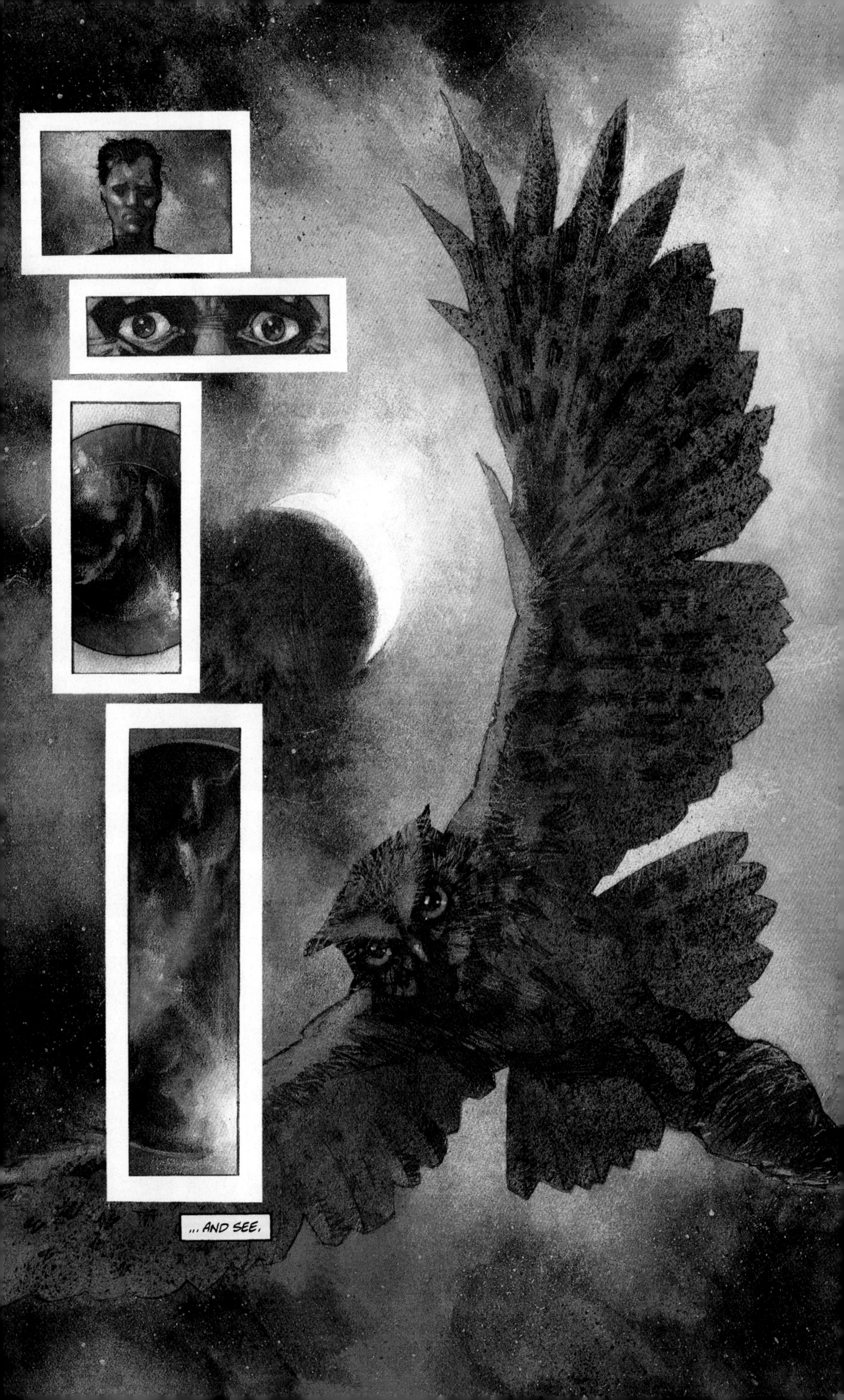
...AND SEE.

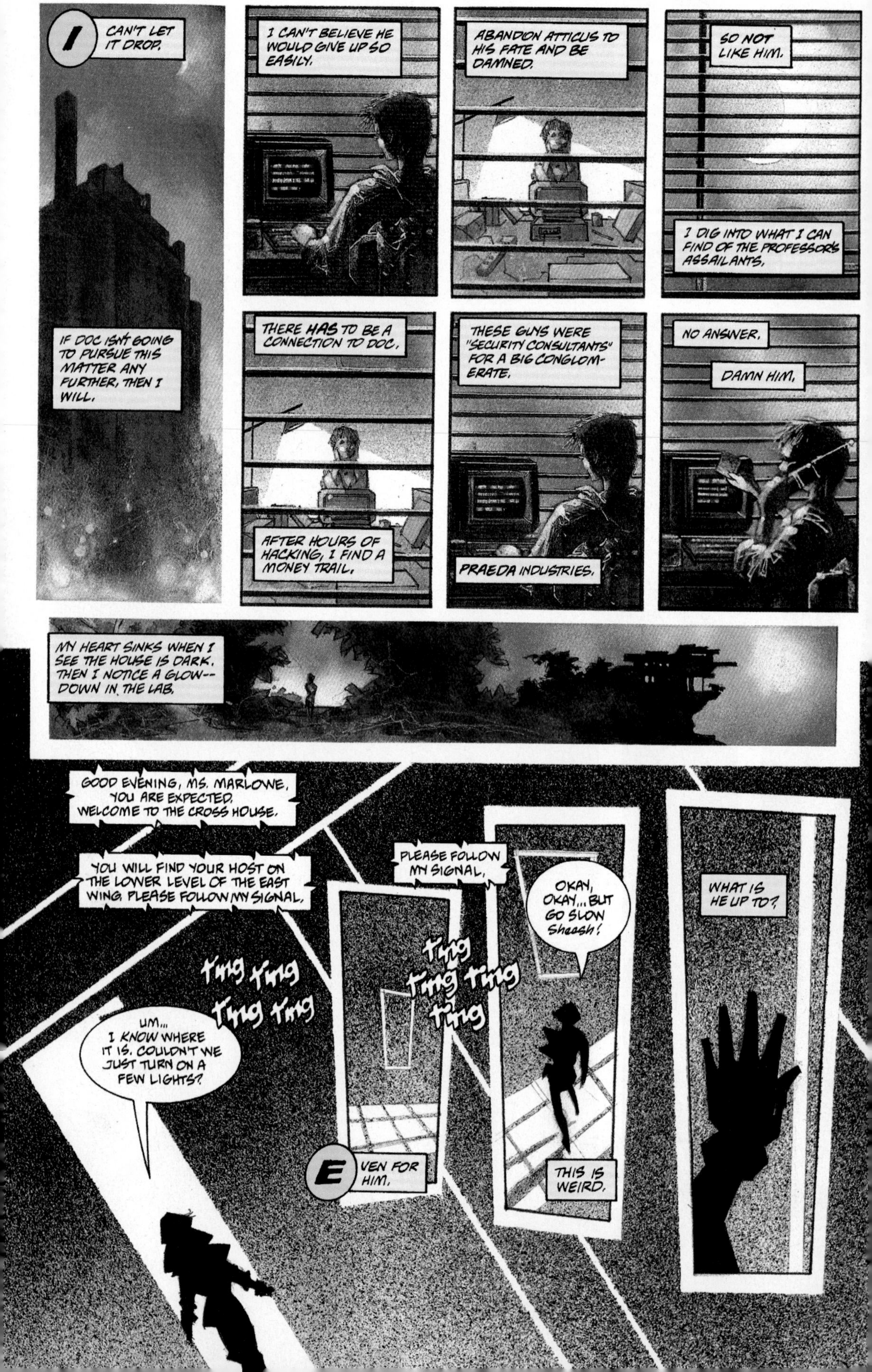
I CAN'T LET IT DROP.
IF DOC ISN'T GOING TO PURSUE THIS MATTER ANY FURTHER, THEN I WILL.
I CAN'T BELIEVE HE WOULD GIVE UP SO EASILY.
ABANDON ATTICUS TO HIS FATE AND BE DAMNED.
SO NOT LIKE HIM.
I DIG INTO WHAT I CAN FIND OF THE PROFESSOR'S ASSAILANTS.
THERE HAS TO BE A CONNECTION TO DOC.
AFTER HOURS OF HACKING, I FIND A MONEY TRAIL.
THESE GUYS WERE "SECURITY CONSULTANTS" FOR A BIG CONGLOMERATE.
PRAEDA INDUSTRIES.
NO ANSWER.
DAMN HIM.
MY HEART SINKS WHEN I SEE THE HOUSE IS DARK. THEN I NOTICE A GLOW-- DOWN IN THE LAB.
GOOD EVENING, MS. MARLOWE. YOU ARE EXPECTED. WELCOME TO THE CROSS HOUSE.
YOU WILL FIND YOUR HOST ON THE LOWER LEVEL OF THE EAST WING. PLEASE FOLLOW MY SIGNAL.
Ting ting ting ting
UM... I KNOW WHERE IT IS. COULDN'T WE JUST TURN ON A FEW LIGHTS?
PLEASE FOLLOW MY SIGNAL.
Ting ting ting ting
EVEN FOR HIM.
OKAY, OKAY... BUT GO SLOW Sheesh!
THIS IS WEIRD.
WHAT IS HE UP TO?

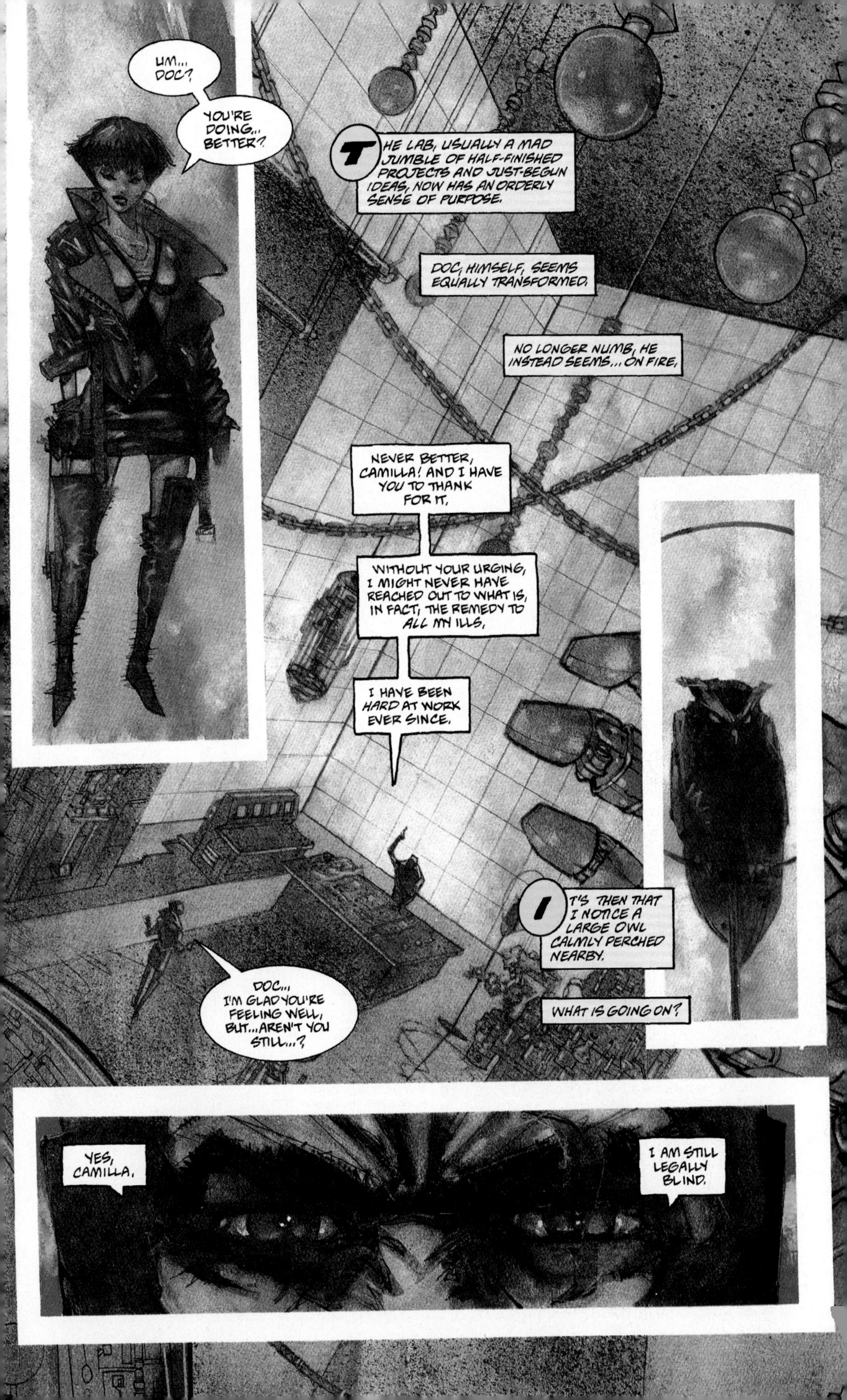

UM... DOC?
YOU'RE DOING... BETTER?
THE LAB, USUALLY A MAD JUMBLE OF HALF-FINISHED PROJECTS AND JUST-BEGUN IDEAS, NOW HAS AN ORDERLY SENSE OF PURPOSE.
DOC, HIMSELF, SEEMS EQUALLY TRANSFORMED.
NO LONGER NUMB, HE INSTEAD SEEMS... ON FIRE.
NEVER BETTER, CAMILLA! AND I HAVE YOU TO THANK FOR IT.
WITHOUT YOUR URGING, I MIGHT NEVER HAVE REACHED OUT TO WHAT IS, IN FACT, THE REMEDY TO ALL MY ILLS.
I HAVE BEEN HARD AT WORK EVER SINCE.
DOC... I'M GLAD YOU'RE FEELING WELL, BUT... AREN'T YOU STILL...?
IT'S THEN THAT I NOTICE A LARGE OWL CALMLY PERCHED NEARBY.
WHAT IS GOING ON?
YES, CAMILLA.
I AM STILL LEGALLY BLIND.

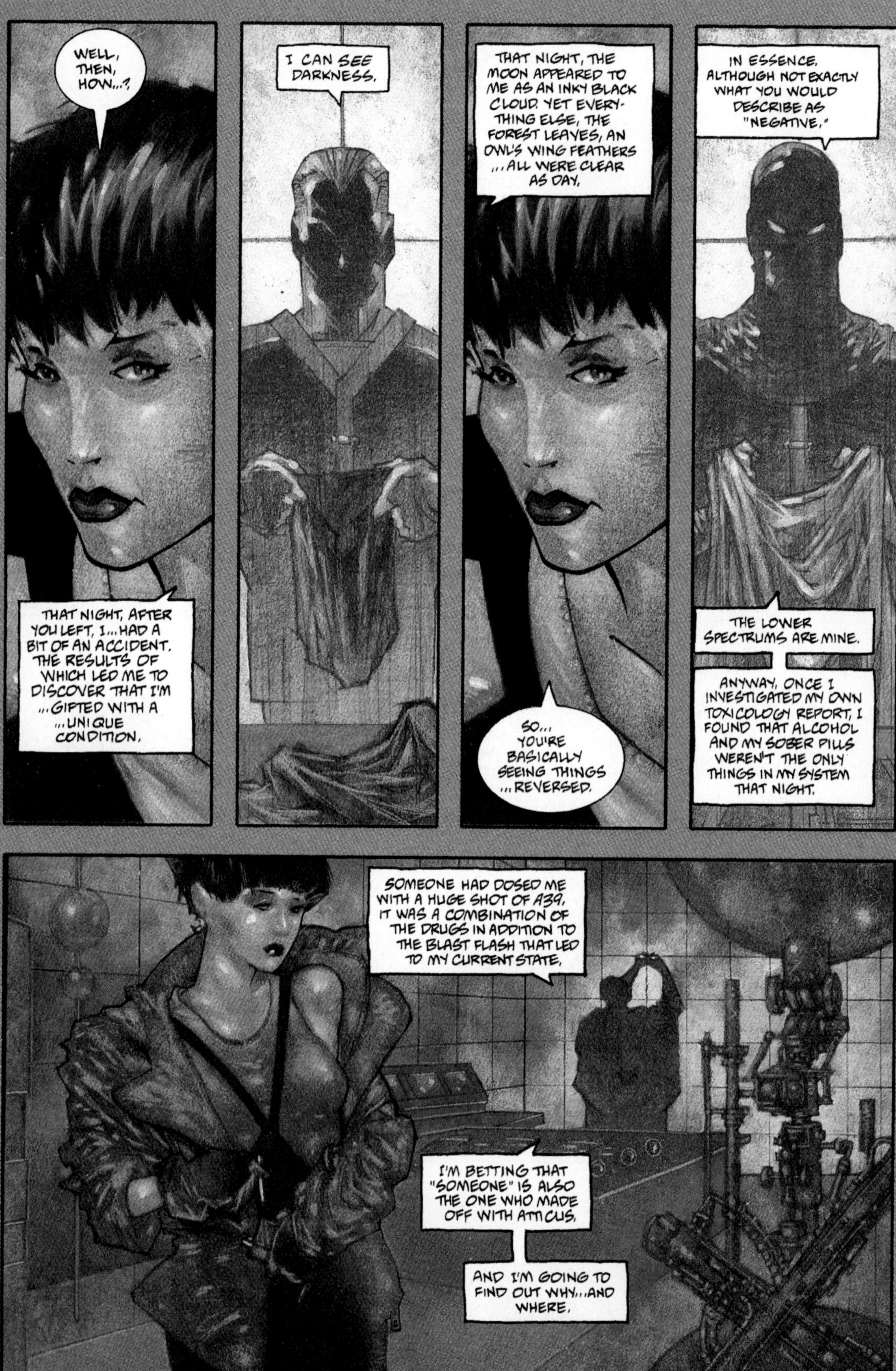
WELL, THEN, HOW...?
THAT NIGHT, AFTER YOU LEFT, I...HAD A BIT OF AN ACCIDENT. THE RESULTS OF WHICH LED ME TO DISCOVER THAT I'M ...GIFTED WITH A ...UNIQUE CONDITION.
I CAN SEE DARKNESS.
THAT NIGHT, THE MOON APPEARED TO ME AS AN INKY BLACK CLOUD. YET EVERY-THING ELSE, THE FOREST LEAVES, AN OWL'S WING FEATHERS ...ALL WERE CLEAR AS DAY.
SO... YOU'RE BASICALLY SEEING THINGS ...REVERSED.
IN ESSENCE. ALTHOUGH NOT EXACTLY WHAT YOU WOULD DESCRIBE AS "NEGATIVE."
THE LOWER SPECTRUMS ARE MINE.
ANYWAY, ONCE I INVESTIGATED MY OWN TOXICOLOGY REPORT, I FOUND THAT ALCOHOL AND MY SOBER PILLS WEREN'T THE ONLY THINGS IN MY SYSTEM THAT NIGHT.
SOMEONE HAD DOSED ME WITH A HUGE SHOT OF A39. IT WAS A COMBINATION OF THE DRUGS IN ADDITION TO THE BLAST FLASH THAT LED TO MY CURRENT STATE.
I'M BETTING THAT "SOMEONE" IS ALSO THE ONE WHO MADE OFF WITH ATTICUS.
AND I'M GOING TO FIND OUT WHY...AND WHERE.

I'VE SUCCEEDED IN FASHIONING LENSES THAT FOCUS BROAD SPECTRUMS INTO MY NEWLY NARROWED RANGE.

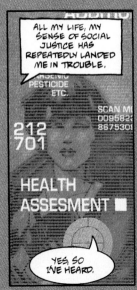

ALL MY LIFE, MY SENSE OF SOCIAL JUSTICE HAS REPEATEDLY LANDED ME IN TROUBLE.

ARSENIC PESTICIDE ETC.

SCAN MO 0095822 8675305

212 701

HEALTH ASSESMENT ■

YES, SO I'VE HEARD.

NEVER AGAIN.

DON'T YOU SEE?

THIS NEW... CONDITION GRANTS ME THE FREEDOM TO FINALLY OPERATE UNDER A TRUE COVER OF DARKNESS.

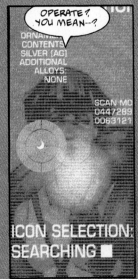

OPERATE? YOU MEAN--?

ORNAMENTAL CONTENTS SILVER [AG] ADDITIONAL ALLOYS: NONE

SCAN MO 0447289 0063121

ICON SELECTION: SEARCHING ■

EXACTLY.

NO ONE WILL CONNECT PIETER CROSS, A BLIND MAN, TO THE ACTIVITIES OF A NEW, NOCTURNAL OPERATIVE.

MAY I...?

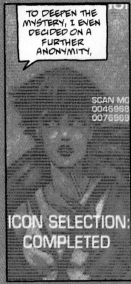

TO DEEPEN THE MYSTERY, I EVEN DECIDED ON A FURTHER ANONYMITY.

SCAN MO 0046968 0076969

ICON SELECTION: COMPLETED

BY ADOPTING AN IDENTITY FROM THE PAST.

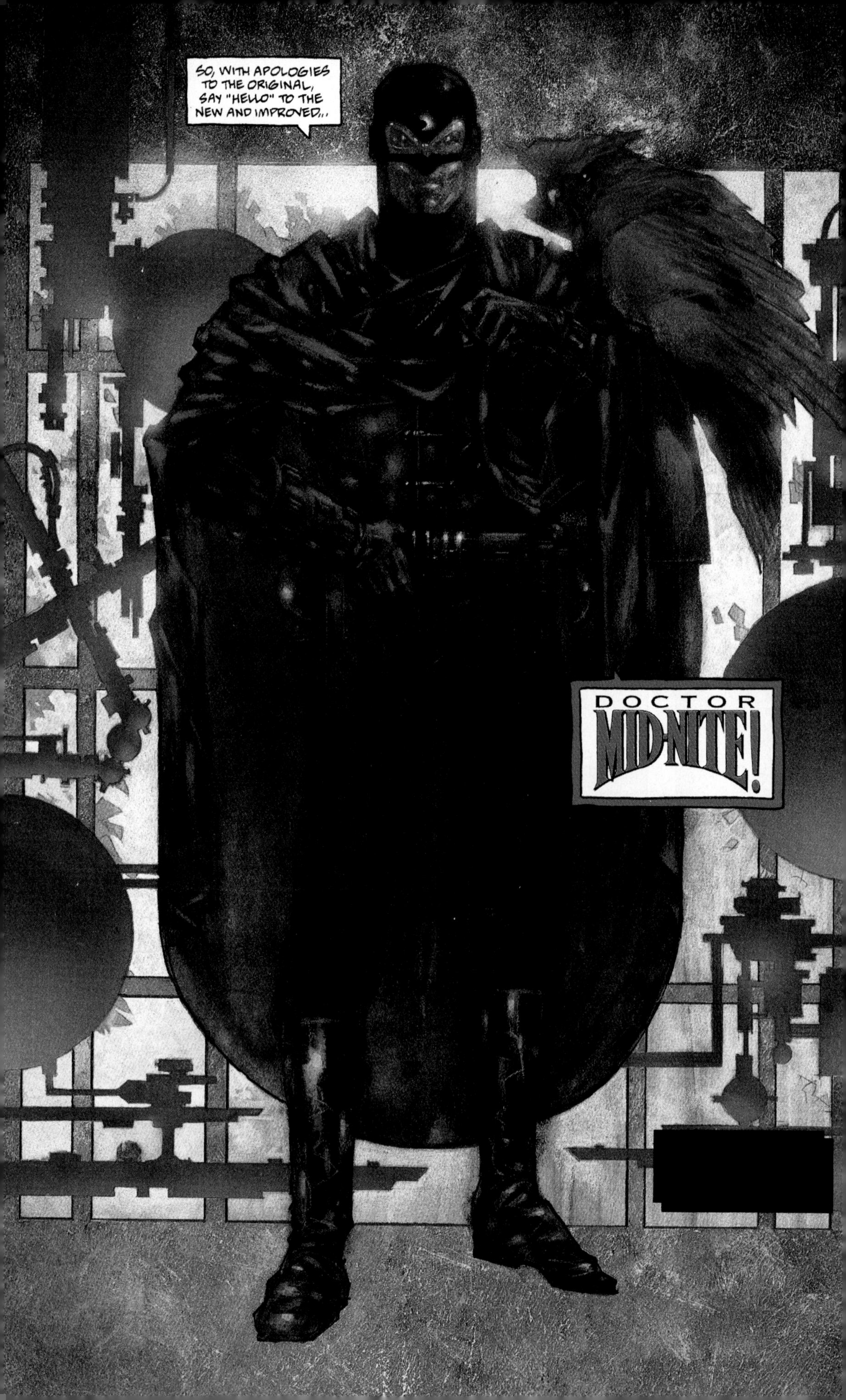
SO, WITH APOLOGIES TO THE ORIGINAL, SAY "HELLO" TO THE NEW AND IMPROVED...
DOCTOR MID-NITE!

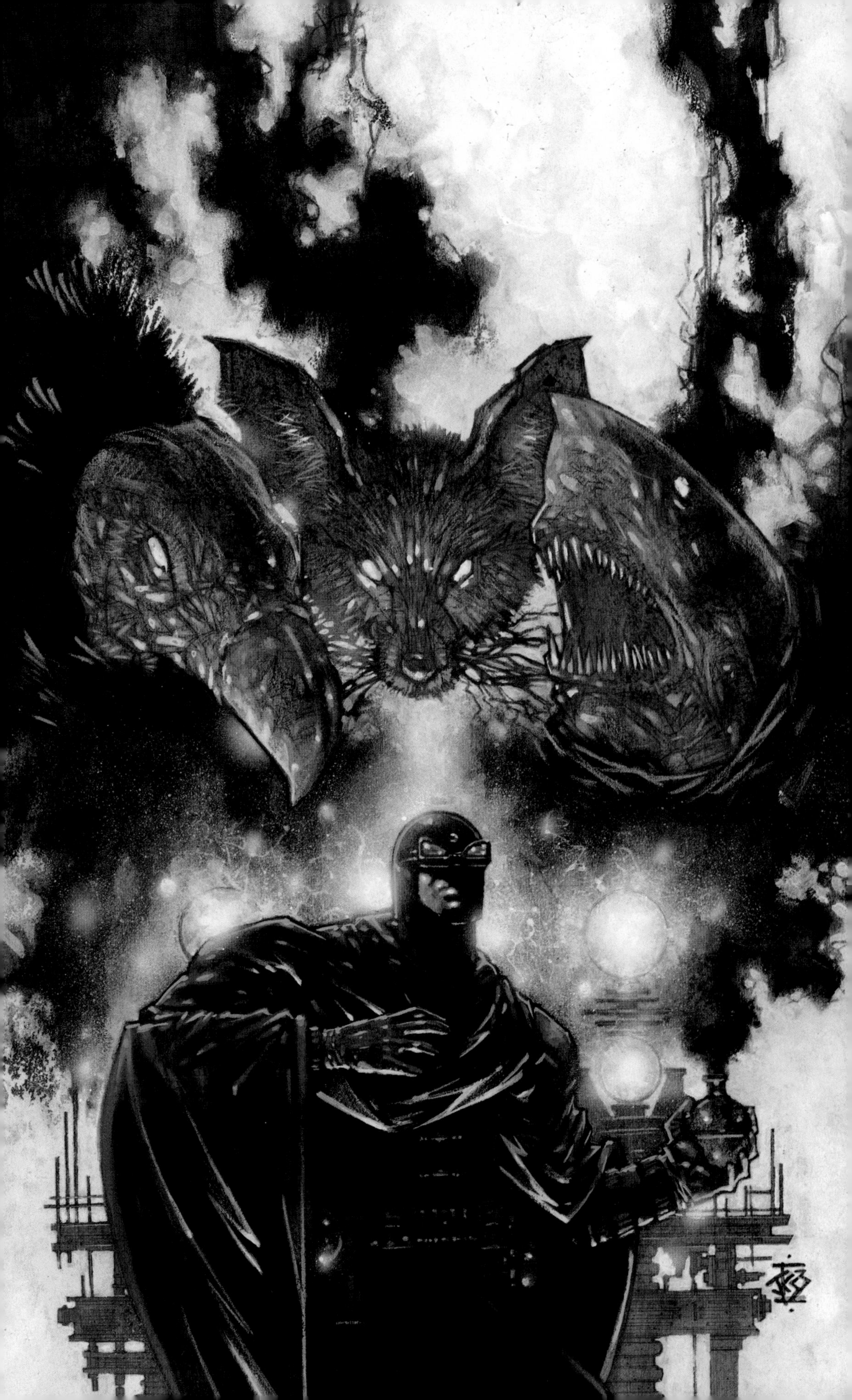

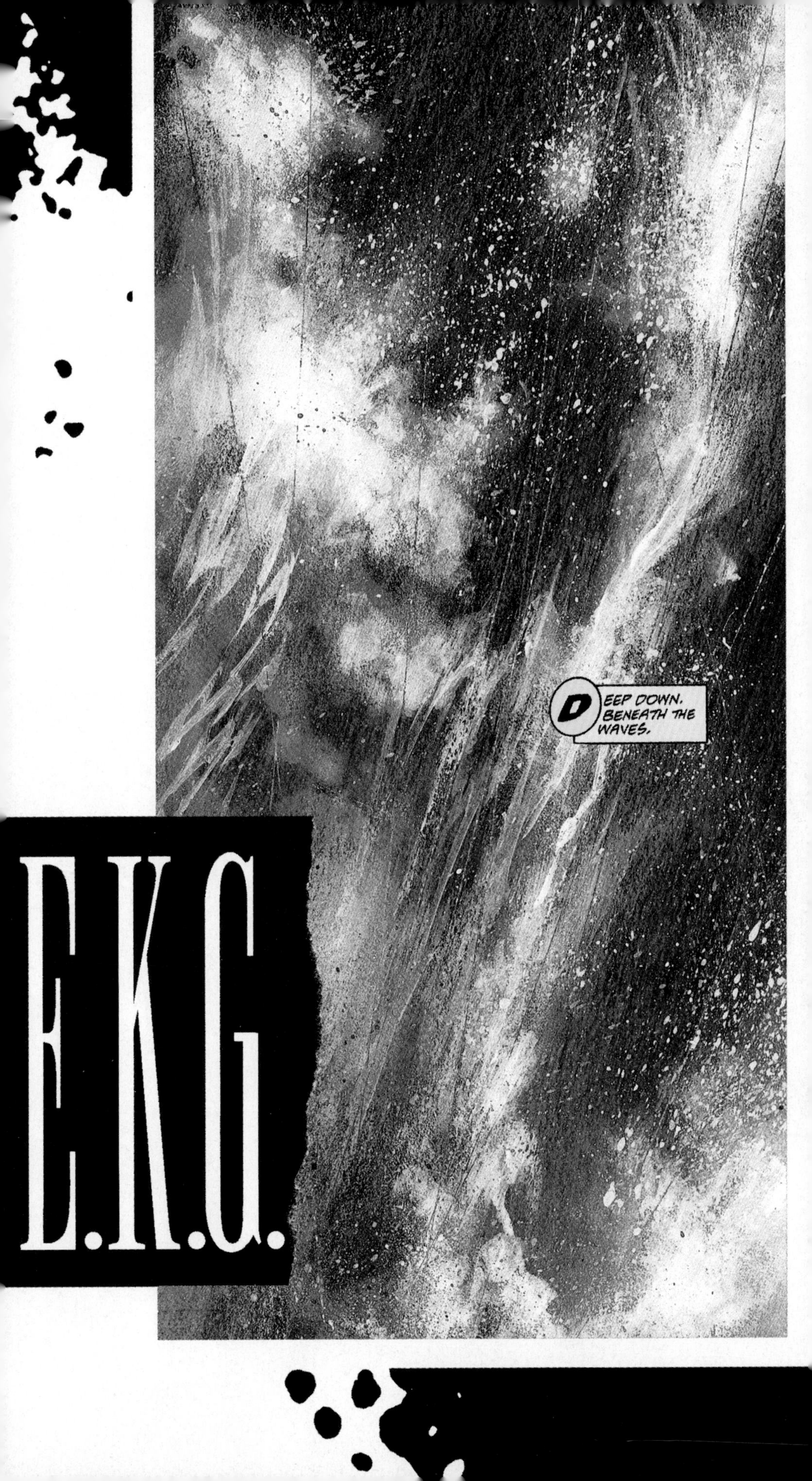
DEEP DOWN, BENEATH THE WAVES.
E.K.G.

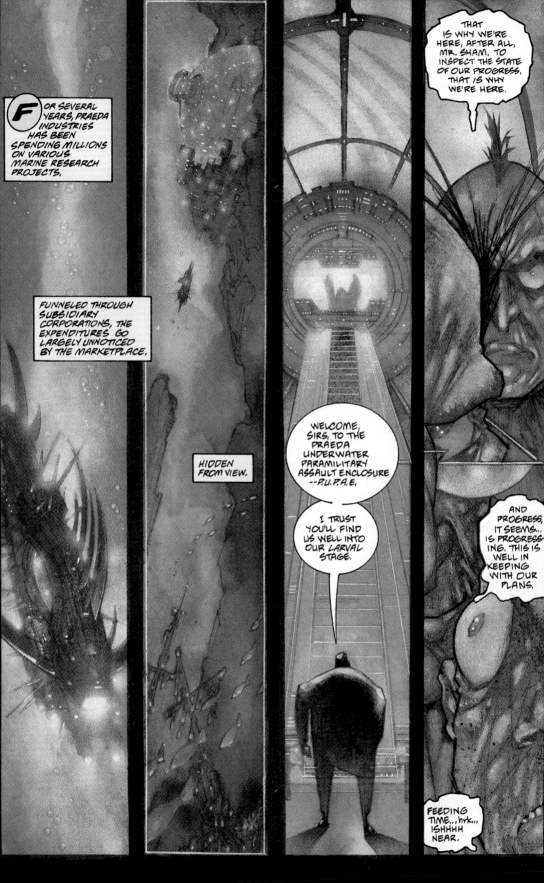

FOR SEVERAL YEARS, PRAEDA INDUSTRIES HAS BEEN SPENDING MILLIONS ON VARIOUS MARINE RESEARCH PROJECTS.

FUNNELED THROUGH SUBSIDIARY CORPORATIONS, THE EXPENDITURES GO LARGELY UNNOTICED BY THE MARKETPLACE.

HIDDEN FROM VIEW.

THAT IS WHY WE'RE HERE, AFTER ALL, MR. SHAM, TO INSPECT THE STATE OF OUR PROGRESS. THAT IS WHY WE'RE HERE.

WELCOME, SIRS, TO THE PRAEDA UNDERWATER PARAMILITARY ASSAULT ENCLOSURE --P.U.P.A.E.

I TRUST YOU'LL FIND US WELL INTO OUR *LARVAL* STAGE.

AND PROGRESS, IT SEEMS... IS PROGRESSING. THIS IS WELL IN KEEPING WITH OUR PLANS.

FEEDING TIME... HYK... ISHHHH NEAR.

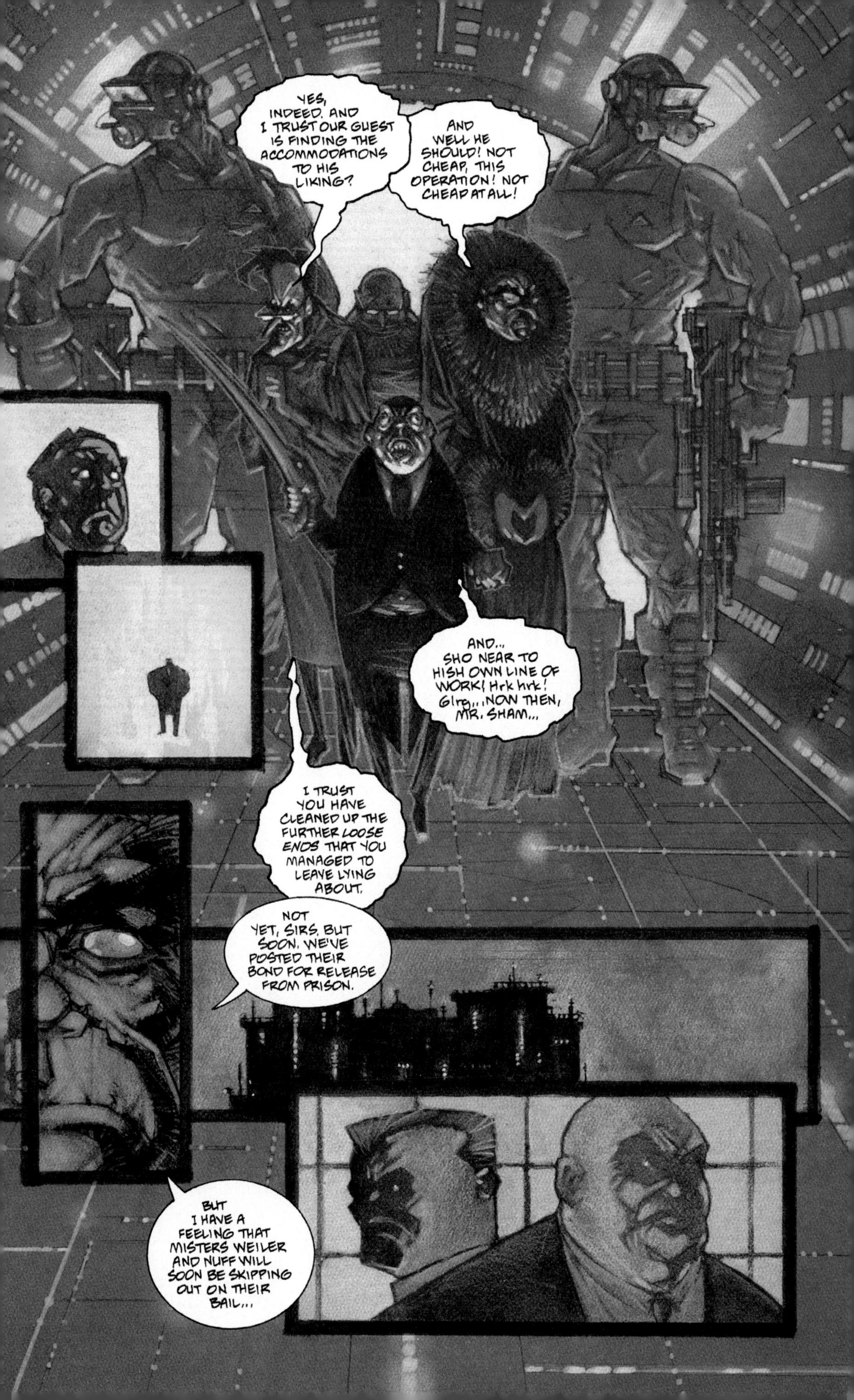
YES, INDEED. AND I TRUST OUR GUEST IS FINDING THE ACCOMMODATIONS TO HIS LIKING?
AND WELL HE SHOULD! NOT CHEAP, THIS OPERATION! NOT CHEAP AT ALL!
AND... SHO NEAR TO HISH OWN LINE OF WORK! Hrk hrk! Glrg... NOW THEN, MR. SHAM...
I TRUST YOU HAVE CLEANED UP THE FURTHER LOOSE ENDS THAT YOU MANAGED TO LEAVE LYING ABOUT.
NOT YET, SIRS, BUT SOON. WE'VE POSTED THEIR BOND FOR RELEASE FROM PRISON.
BUT I HAVE A FEELING THAT MISTERS WEILER AND NUFF WILL SOON BE SKIPPING OUT ON THEIR BAIL...

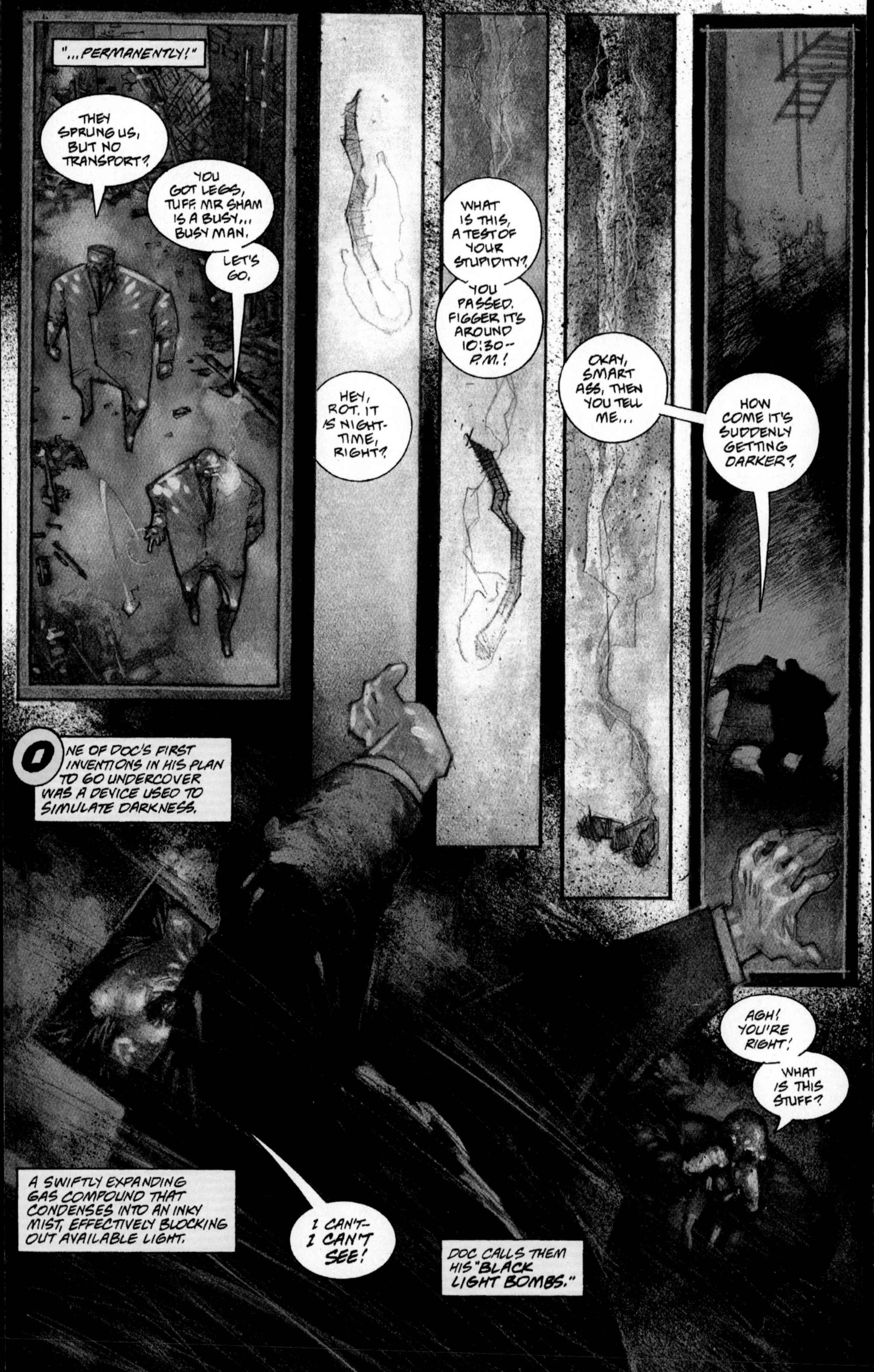
"...PERMANENTLY!"
THEY SPRUNG US, BUT NO TRANSPORT?
YOU GOT LEGS, TUFF. MR SHAM IS A BUSY... BUSY MAN.
LET'S GO.
HEY, ROT. IT IS NIGHT-TIME, RIGHT?
WHAT IS THIS, A TEST OF YOUR STUPIDITY?
YOU PASSED. FIGGER IT'S AROUND 10:30-- P.M.!
OKAY, SMART ASS, THEN YOU TELL ME...
HOW COME IT'S SUDDENLY GETTING DARKER?
ONE OF DOC'S FIRST INVENTIONS IN HIS PLAN TO GO UNDERCOVER WAS A DEVICE USED TO SIMULATE DARKNESS.
AGH! YOU'RE RIGHT!
WHAT IS THIS STUFF?
A SWIFTLY EXPANDING GAS COMPOUND THAT CONDENSES INTO AN INKY MIST, EFFECTIVELY BLOCKING OUT AVAILABLE LIGHT.
I CAN'T-- I CAN'T SEE!
DOC CALLS THEM HIS "BLACK LIGHT BOMBS."

NEXT CAME A VARIETY OF RAPID-INJECTION AMPULES.

TRANQS, TRUTHS AND TRAUMAS.

RELAX, FRIEND. STRESS IS BAD FOR YOUR HEALTH.

¿AKT¿

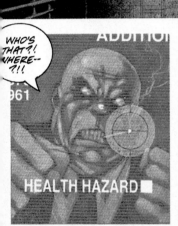

WHO'S THAT?! WHERE--?!!

ADDITIO
961

HEALTH HAZARD ■

AS IS SMOKING.

YOUR PARTNER HAS BEEN SEDATED, MR. WEILER, WHICH LEAVES YOU TO ANSWER MY QUESTIONS.

HOW IS PRAEDA INDUSTRIES CONNECTED TO THE DRUG A39?

I TOLD DOC OF THE PROFESSOR'S ASSAILANTS' LINK TO THE LOCAL MEGA-CORP. HE ALREADY KNEW OF THEIR ADDICTION.

HOW LONG'S IT BEEN SINCE YOU HAD A HIT? FEEL ALL JELLY IN THE LEGS YET?

TUFF-- HUH?

A
520
057
714

HEALTH HAZARD: REQUSITIONED

I DON'T KNOW WHAT YOU'RE—

YOU--?! YOU GOT SOMETHING FOR ME? DID MR. SHAM SEND YOU TO MEET US?

MR. SHAM.

WHERE'D HE GO?

DAMN. LARGO'S NOT GONNA LIKE THIS.

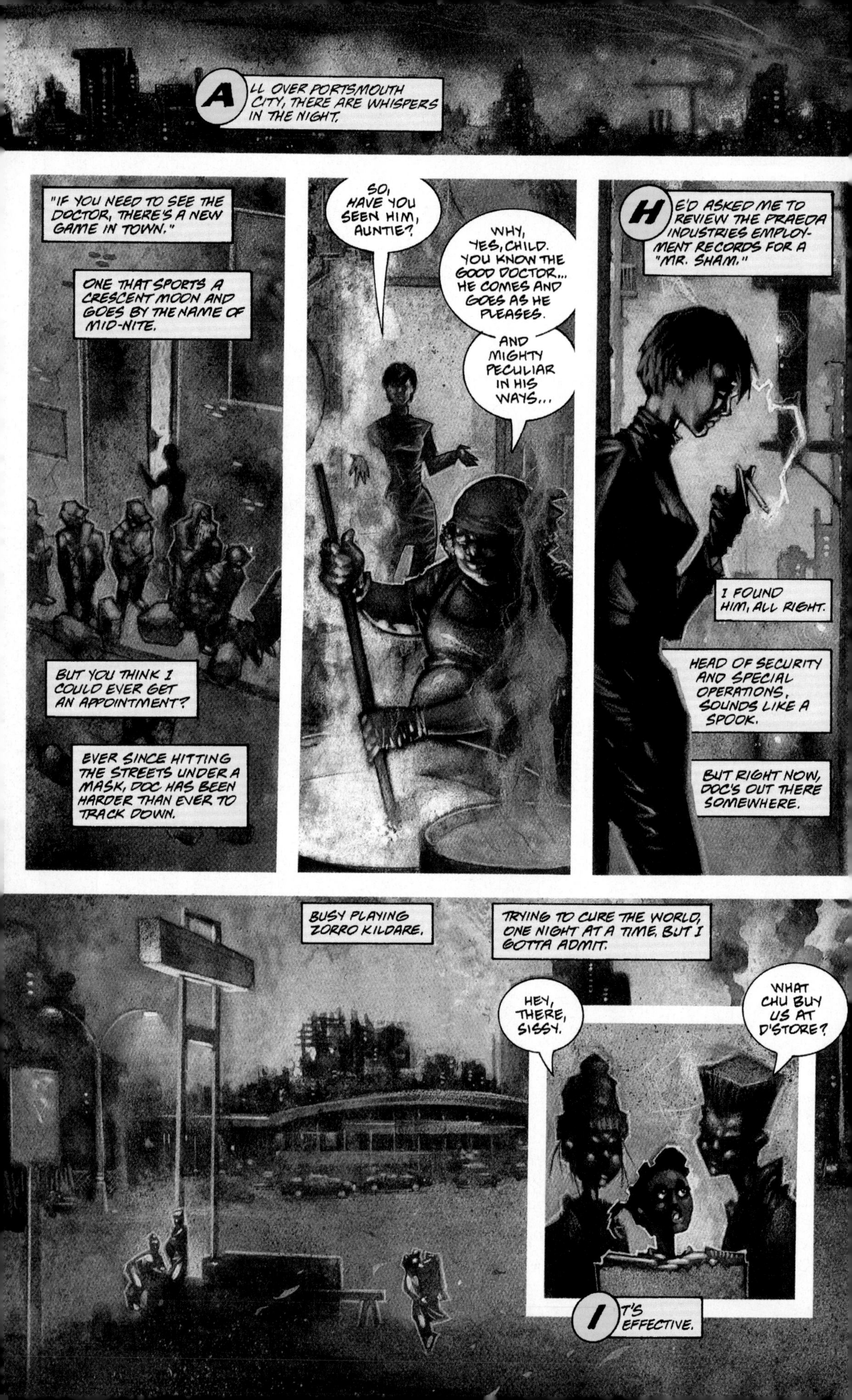
ALL OVER PORTSMOUTH CITY, THERE ARE WHISPERS IN THE NIGHT.
"IF YOU NEED TO SEE THE DOCTOR, THERE'S A NEW GAME IN TOWN."
ONE THAT SPORTS A CRESCENT MOON AND GOES BY THE NAME OF MID-NITE.
BUT YOU THINK I COULD EVER GET AN APPOINTMENT?
EVER SINCE HITTING THE STREETS UNDER A MASK, DOC HAS BEEN HARDER THAN EVER TO TRACK DOWN.
SO, HAVE YOU SEEN HIM, AUNTIE?
WHY, YES, CHILD. YOU KNOW THE GOOD DOCTOR... HE COMES AND GOES AS HE PLEASES.
AND MIGHTY PECULIAR IN HIS WAYS...
HE'D ASKED ME TO REVIEW THE PRAEDA INDUSTRIES EMPLOYMENT RECORDS FOR A "MR. SHAM."
I FOUND HIM, ALL RIGHT.
HEAD OF SECURITY AND SPECIAL OPERATIONS. SOUNDS LIKE A SPOOK.
BUT RIGHT NOW, DOC'S OUT THERE SOMEWHERE.
BUSY PLAYING ZORRO KILDARE.
TRYING TO CURE THE WORLD, ONE NIGHT AT A TIME. BUT I GOTTA ADMIT.
HEY, THERE, SISSY.
WHAT CHU BUY US AT D'STORE?
IT'S EFFECTIVE.

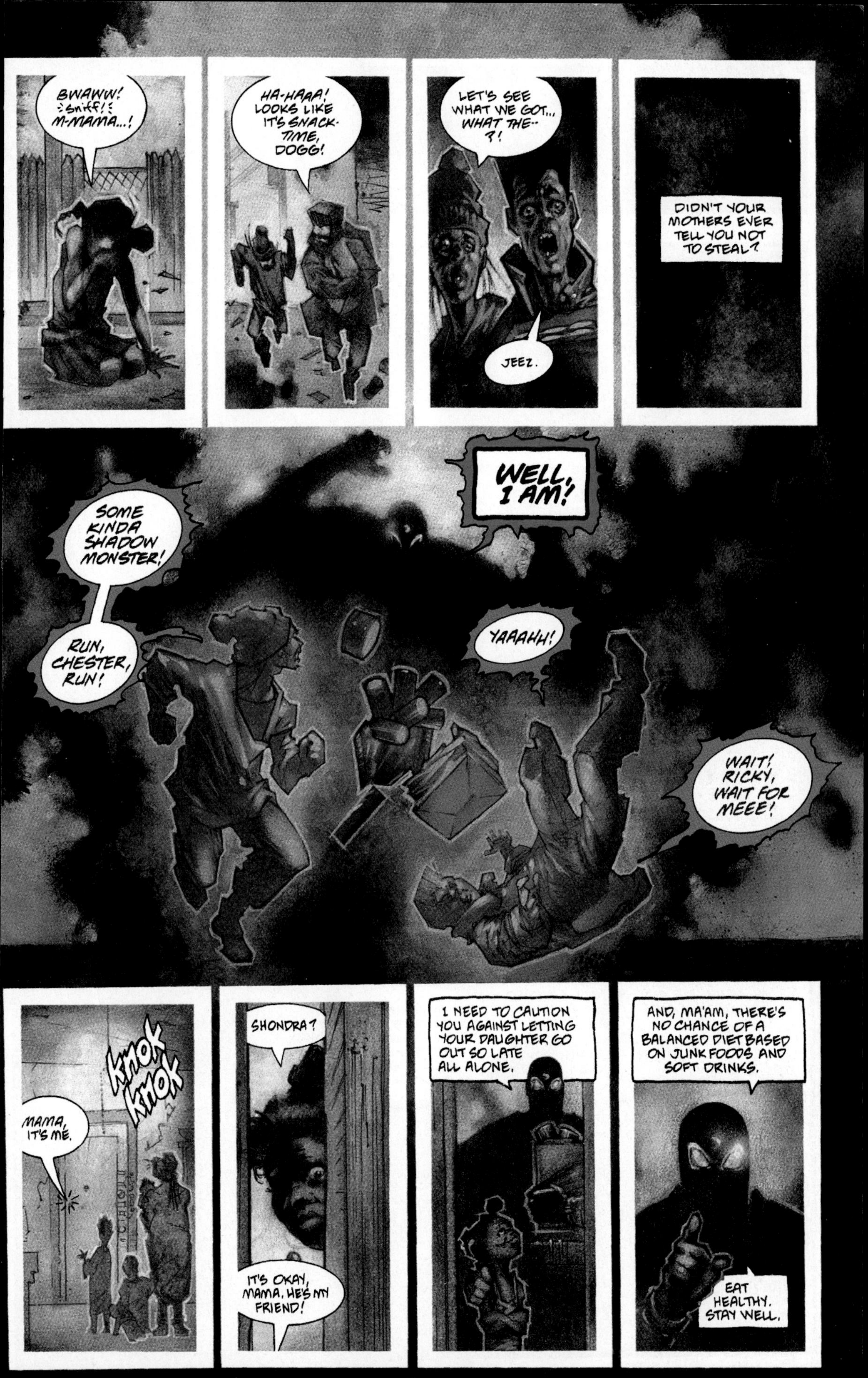
BWAWW! :sniff!: M-MAMA...!
HA-HAAA! LOOKS LIKE IT'S SNACK-TIME, DOGG!
LET'S SEE WHAT WE GOT... WHAT THE-- ?!
JEEZ.
DIDN'T YOUR MOTHERS EVER TELL YOU NOT TO STEAL?
WELL, I AM!
SOME KINDA SHADOW MONSTER!
RUN, CHESTER, RUN!
YAAAHH!
WAIT! RICKY, WAIT FOR MEEE!
KNOK KNOK
MAMA, IT'S ME.
SHONDRA?
IT'S OKAY, MAMA. HE'S MY FRIEND!
I NEED TO CAUTION YOU AGAINST LETTING YOUR DAUGHTER GO OUT SO LATE ALL ALONE.
AND, MA'AM, THERE'S NO CHANCE OF A BALANCED DIET BASED ON JUNK FOODS AND SOFT DRINKS.
EAT HEALTHY. STAY WELL.

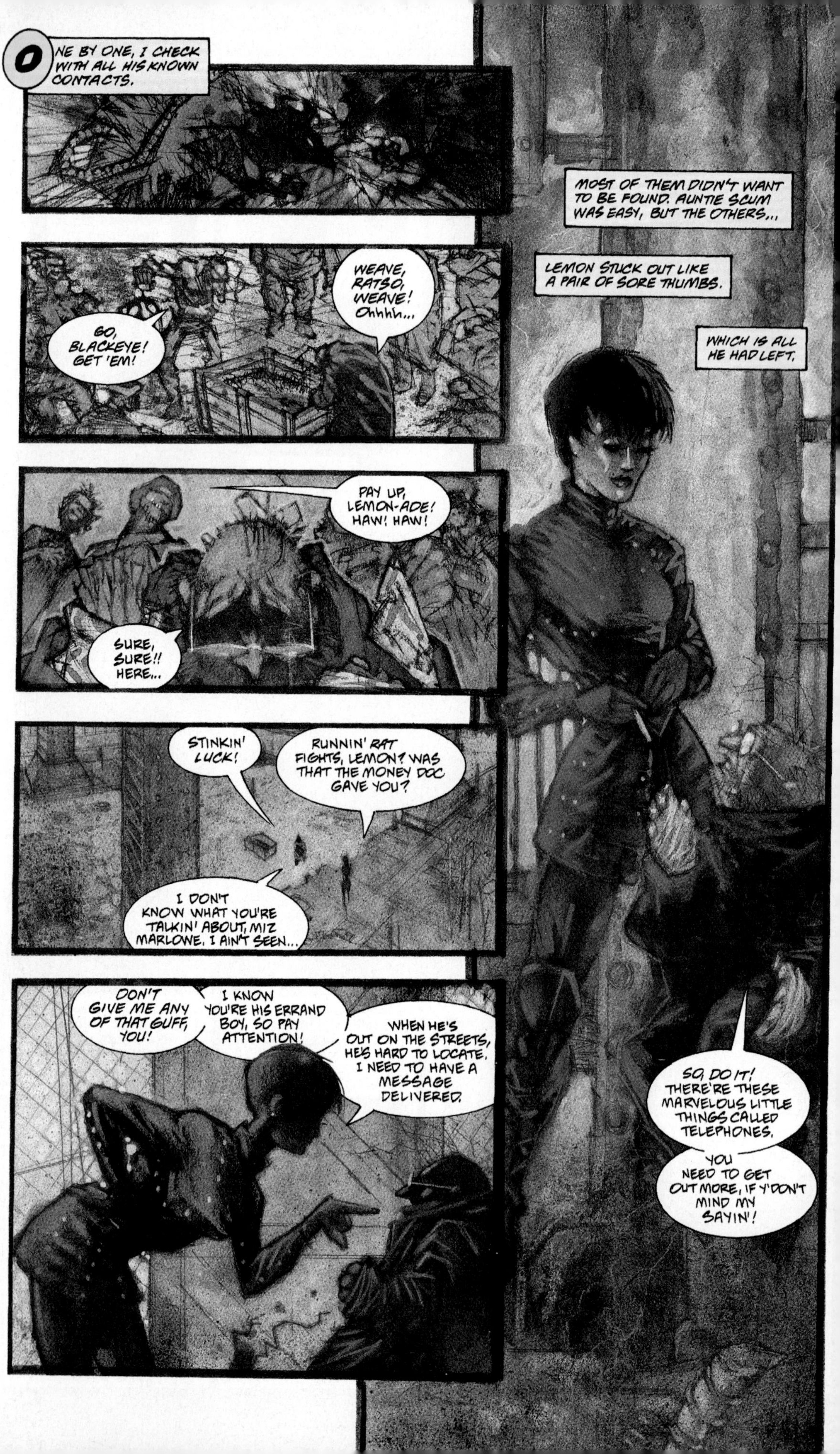
ONE BY ONE, I CHECK WITH ALL HIS KNOWN CONTACTS.
MOST OF THEM DIDN'T WANT TO BE FOUND. AUNTIE SCUM WAS EASY, BUT THE OTHERS...
LEMON STUCK OUT LIKE A PAIR OF SORE THUMBS.
WHICH IS ALL HE HAD LEFT.
GO, BLACKEYE! GET 'EM!
WEAVE, RATSO, WEAVE! Ohhhh...
PAY UP, LEMON-ADE! HAW! HAW!
SURE, SURE!! HERE...
STINKIN' LUCK!
RUNNIN' RAT FIGHTS, LEMON? WAS THAT THE MONEY DOC GAVE YOU?
I DON'T KNOW WHAT YOU'RE TALKIN' ABOUT, MIZ MARLOWE. I AIN'T SEEN...
DON'T GIVE ME ANY OF THAT GUFF, YOU!
I KNOW YOU'RE HIS ERRAND BOY, SO PAY ATTENTION!
WHEN HE'S OUT ON THE STREETS, HE'S HARD TO LOCATE. I NEED TO HAVE A MESSAGE DELIVERED.
SO, DO IT! THERE'RE THESE MARVELOUS LITTLE THINGS CALLED TELEPHONES.
YOU NEED TO GET OUT MORE, IF Y'DON'T MIND MY SAYIN'!

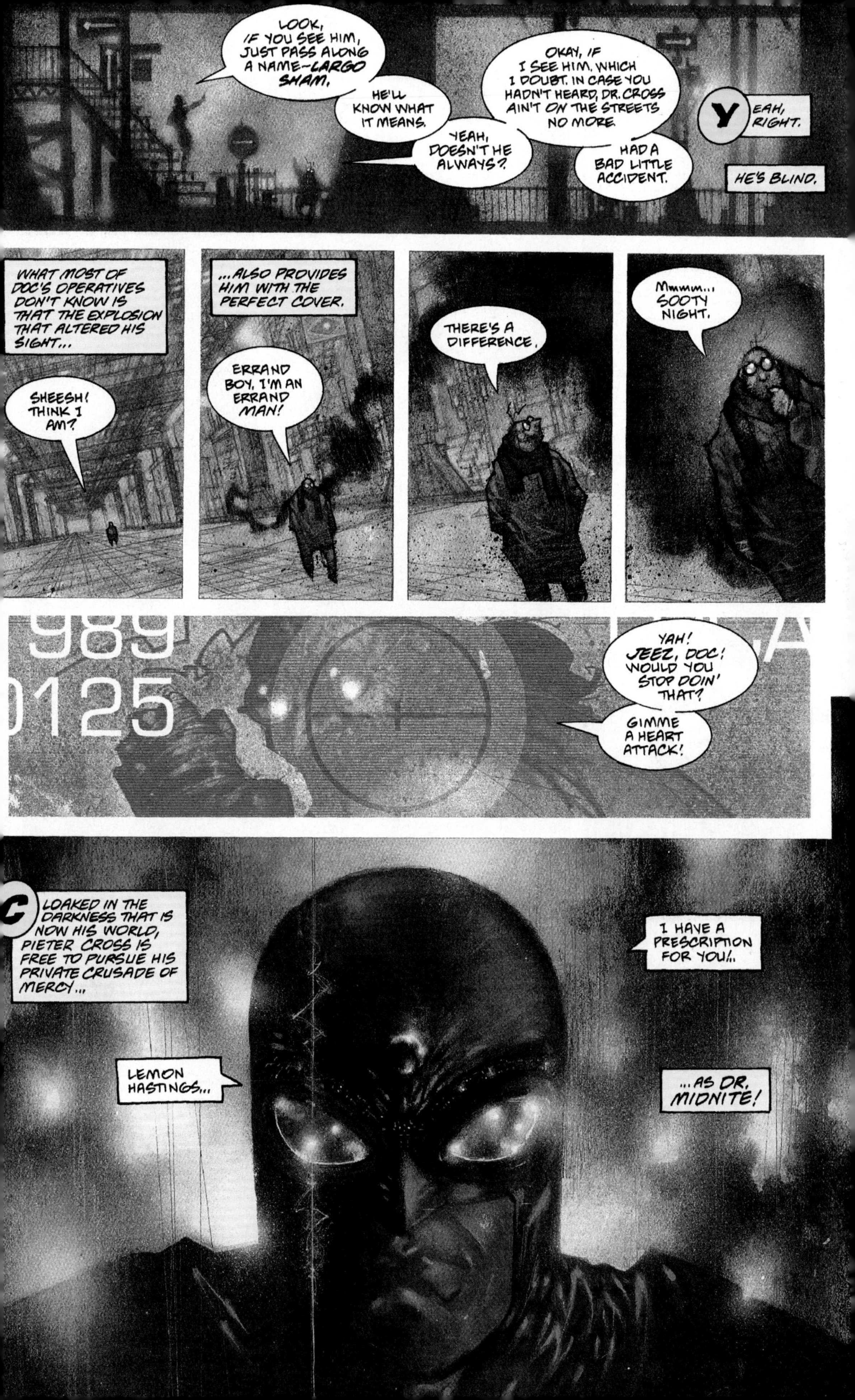
LOOK, IF YOU SEE HIM, JUST PASS ALONG A NAME--LARGO SHAM.
HE'LL KNOW WHAT IT MEANS.
YEAH, DOESN'T HE ALWAYS?
OKAY, IF I SEE HIM, WHICH I DOUBT. IN CASE YOU HADN'T HEARD, DR. CROSS AIN'T ON THE STREETS NO MORE.
HAD A BAD LITTLE ACCIDENT.
YEAH, RIGHT.
HE'S BLIND.
WHAT MOST OF DOC'S OPERATIVES DON'T KNOW IS THAT THE EXPLOSION THAT ALTERED HIS SIGHT...
SHEESH! THINK I AM?
...ALSO PROVIDES HIM WITH THE PERFECT COVER.
ERRAND BOY, I'M AN ERRAND MAN!
THERE'S A DIFFERENCE.
Mmmm... SOOTY NIGHT.
989
0125
YAH! JEEZ, DOC! WOULD YOU STOP DOIN' THAT?
GIMME A HEART ATTACK!
CLOAKED IN THE DARKNESS THAT IS NOW HIS WORLD, PIETER CROSS IS FREE TO PURSUE HIS PRIVATE CRUSADE OF MERCY...
I HAVE A PRESCRIPTION FOR YOU!..
LEMON HASTINGS...
...AS DR. MIDNITE!

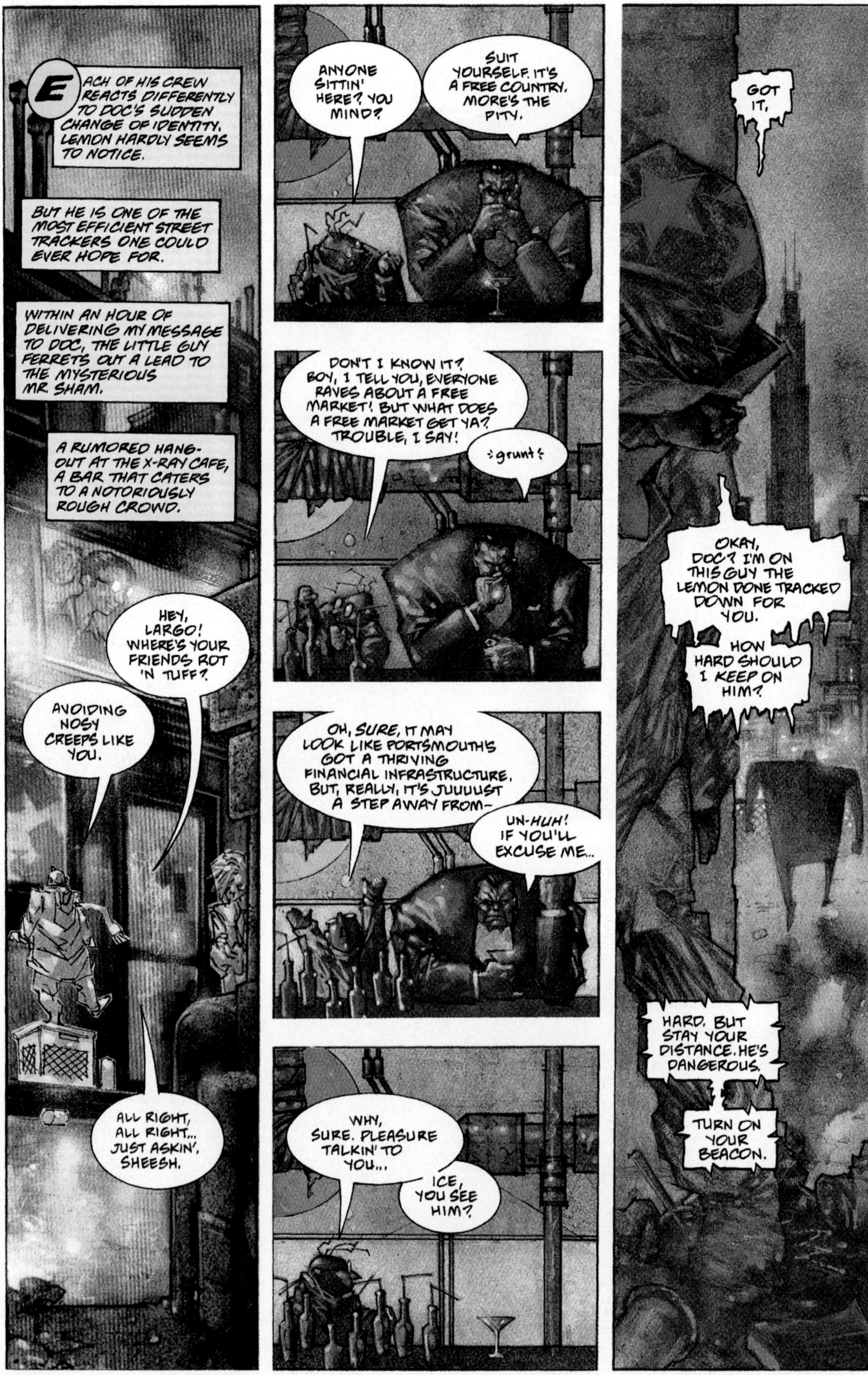
EACH OF HIS CREW REACTS DIFFERENTLY TO DOC'S SUDDEN CHANGE OF IDENTITY. LEMON HARDLY SEEMS TO NOTICE.
BUT HE IS ONE OF THE MOST EFFICIENT STREET TRACKERS ONE COULD EVER HOPE FOR.
WITHIN AN HOUR OF DELIVERING MY MESSAGE TO DOC, THE LITTLE GUY FERRETS OUT A LEAD TO THE MYSTERIOUS MR. SHAM.
A RUMORED HANG-OUT AT THE X-RAY CAFE, A BAR THAT CATERS TO A NOTORIOUSLY ROUGH CROWD.
HEY, LARGO! WHERE'S YOUR FRIENDS ROT 'N TUFF?
AVOIDING NOSY CREEPS LIKE YOU.
ALL RIGHT, ALL RIGHT... JUST ASKIN', SHEESH.
ANYONE SITTIN' HERE? YOU MIND?
SUIT YOURSELF. IT'S A FREE COUNTRY. MORE'S THE PITY.
DON'T I KNOW IT? BOY, I TELL YOU, EVERYONE RAVES ABOUT A FREE MARKET! BUT WHAT DOES A FREE MARKET GET YA? TROUBLE, I SAY!
grunt
OH, SURE, IT MAY LOOK LIKE PORTSMOUTH'S GOT A THRIVING FINANCIAL INFRASTRUCTURE. BUT, REALLY, IT'S JUUUUST A STEP AWAY FROM--
UN-HUH! IF YOU'LL EXCUSE ME...
WHY, SURE. PLEASURE TALKIN' TO YOU...
ICE, YOU SEE HIM?
GOT IT.
OKAY, DOC? I'M ON THIS GUY THE LEMON DONE TRACKED DOWN FOR YOU.
HOW HARD SHOULD I KEEP ON HIM?
HARD. BUT STAY YOUR DISTANCE. HE'S DANGEROUS.
TURN ON YOUR BEACON.

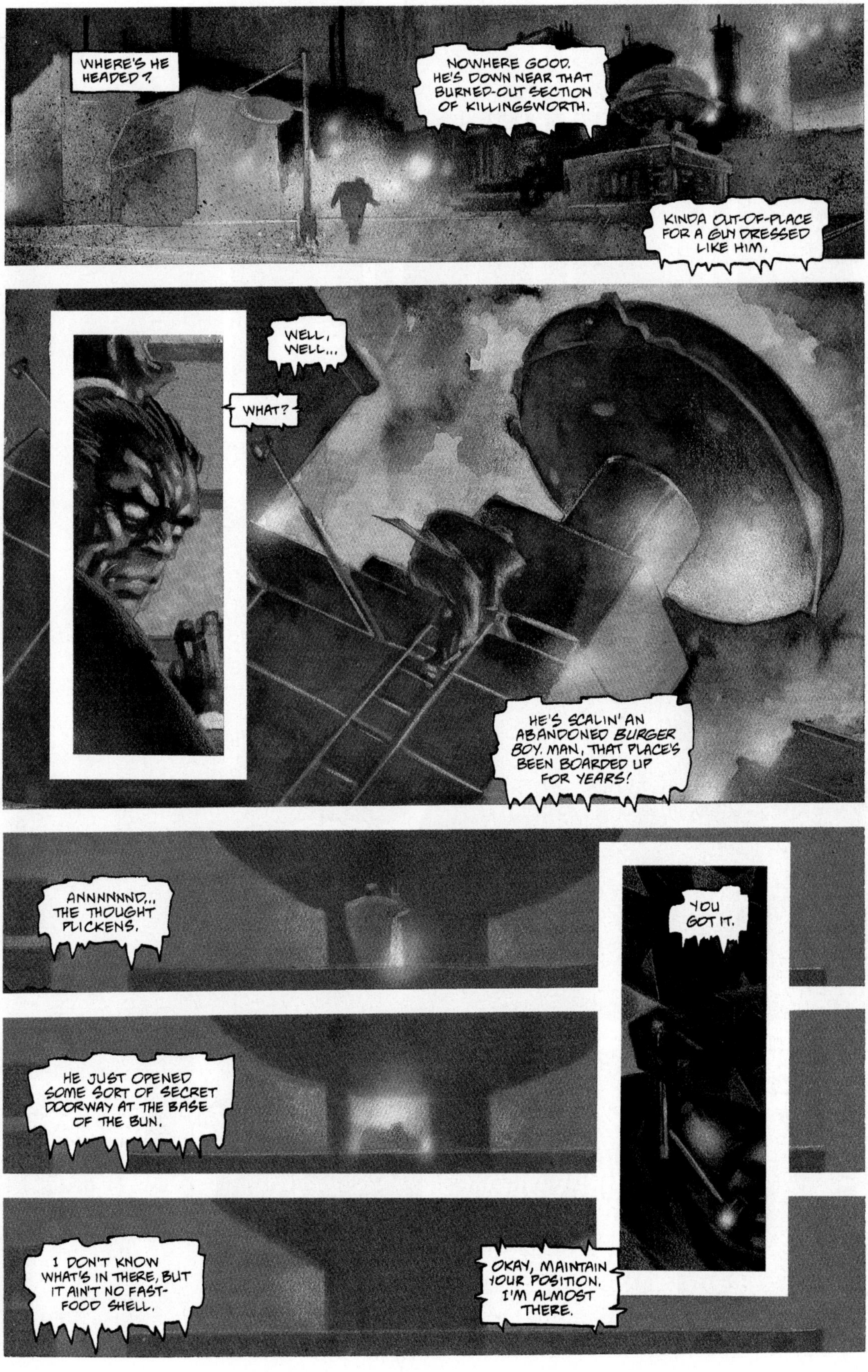
WHERE'S HE HEADED?
NOWHERE GOOD. HE'S DOWN NEAR THAT BURNED-OUT SECTION OF KILLINGSWORTH.
KINDA OUT-OF-PLACE FOR A GUY DRESSED LIKE HIM.
WELL, WELL...
WHAT?
HE'S SCALIN' AN ABANDONED BURGER BOY. MAN, THAT PLACE'S BEEN BOARDED UP FOR YEARS!
ANNNNNND... THE THOUGHT PLICKENS.
YOU GOT IT.
HE JUST OPENED SOME SORT OF SECRET DOORWAY AT THE BASE OF THE BUN.
I DON'T KNOW WHAT'S IN THERE, BUT IT AIN'T NO FAST-FOOD SHELL.
OKAY, MAINTAIN YOUR POSITION. I'M ALMOST THERE.

DOC'S PROTÉGÉ, ICE-SICKLE, STIFLES A SMILE. RICH FOLKS ARE A FUNNY BUNCH.

NICE DUDS.

HERE?

YEAH, YOU CAN JUST SEE THE SEAL OF THE DOOR—HERE AND HERE. BUT I WASN'T CLOSE ENOUGH TO SEE HOW HE OPENED IT.

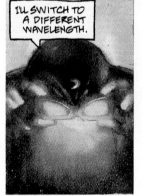

I'LL SWITCH TO A DIFFERENT WAVELENGTH.

HERE.

I'LL BE DAMNED! ON A SESAME SEED BUN!

GOOD WORK. IF I'M NOT BACK IN HALF AN HOUR, CONTACT THE POLICE.

UM... GOOD LUCK.

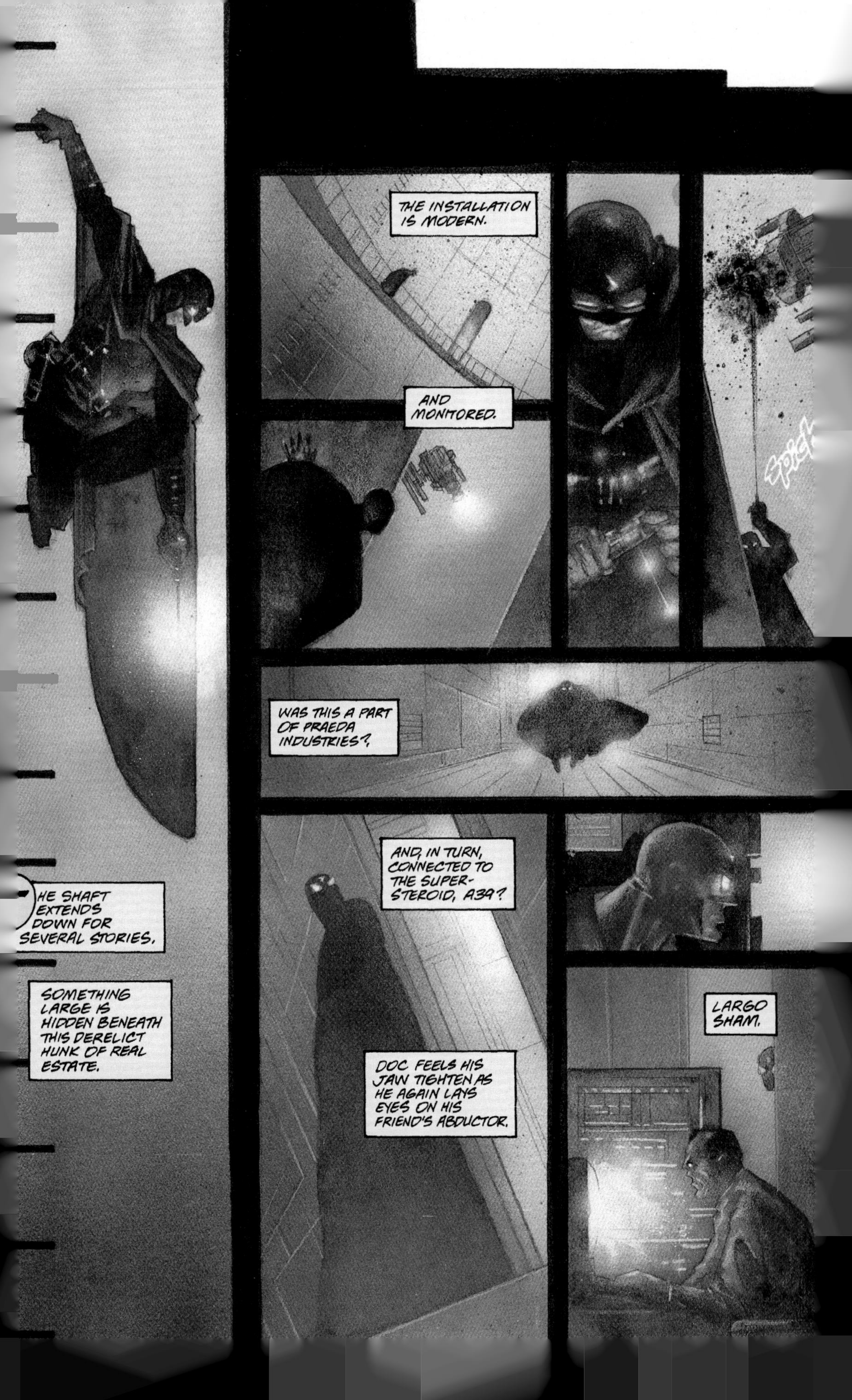
HE SHAFT EXTENDS DOWN FOR SEVERAL STORIES.
SOMETHING LARGE IS HIDDEN BENEATH THIS DERELICT HUNK OF REAL ESTATE.
THE INSTALLATION IS MODERN.
AND MONITORED.
WAS THIS A PART OF PRAEDA INDUSTRIES?
AND, IN TURN, CONNECTED TO THE SUPER-STEROID, A39?
DOC FEELS HIS JAW TIGHTEN AS HE AGAIN LAYS EYES ON HIS FRIEND'S ABDUCTOR.
LARGO SHAM.

S THIS WHERE HE'S KEEPING PROFESSOR SEARLES?

PREADA INDUSTRIES SECURITY CLEARANCE REQUIRED.

PREADA

S O, WHERE'S THE CONNECTION? BETWEEN THE DRUG... THE PROFESSOR... AND THE CORPORATION?

WHY DOES PRAEDA BUILD AND MAINTAIN SUCH A LARGE SUBTERRANEAN COMPLEX?

AND KEEP IT HIDDEN?

SUDDENLY, DOC REALIZES WHAT LARGO IS WAITING FOR...

AN ELEVATOR?

HOW BIG IS THIS PLACE?

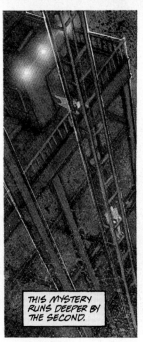

THIS MYSTERY RUNS DEEPER BY THE SECOND.

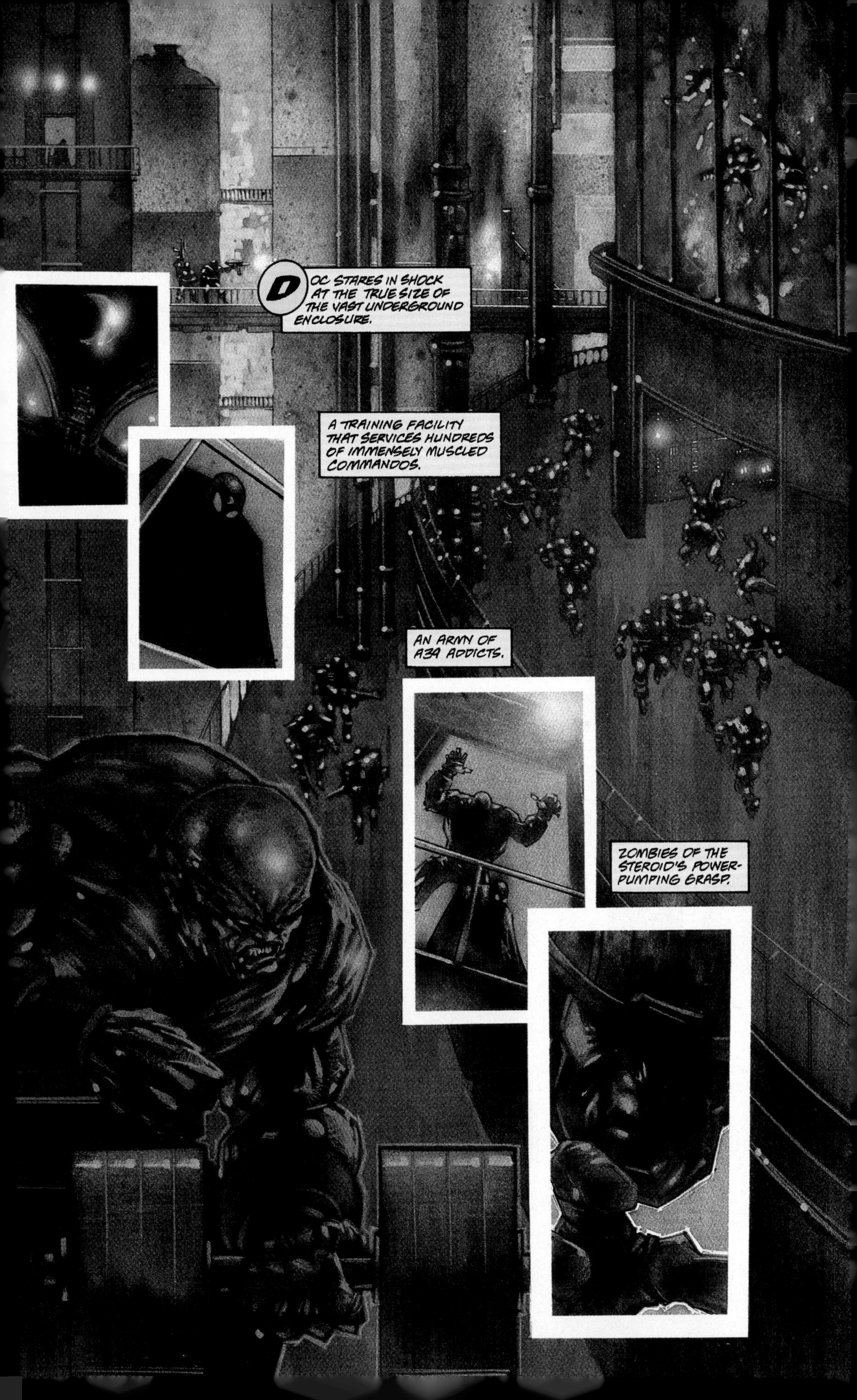
DOC STARES IN SHOCK AT THE TRUE SIZE OF THE VAST UNDERGROUND ENCLOSURE.
A TRAINING FACILITY THAT SERVICES HUNDREDS OF IMMENSELY MUSCLED COMMANDOS.
AN ARMY OF A34 ADDICTS.
ZOMBIES OF THE STEROID'S POWER-PUMPING GRASP.

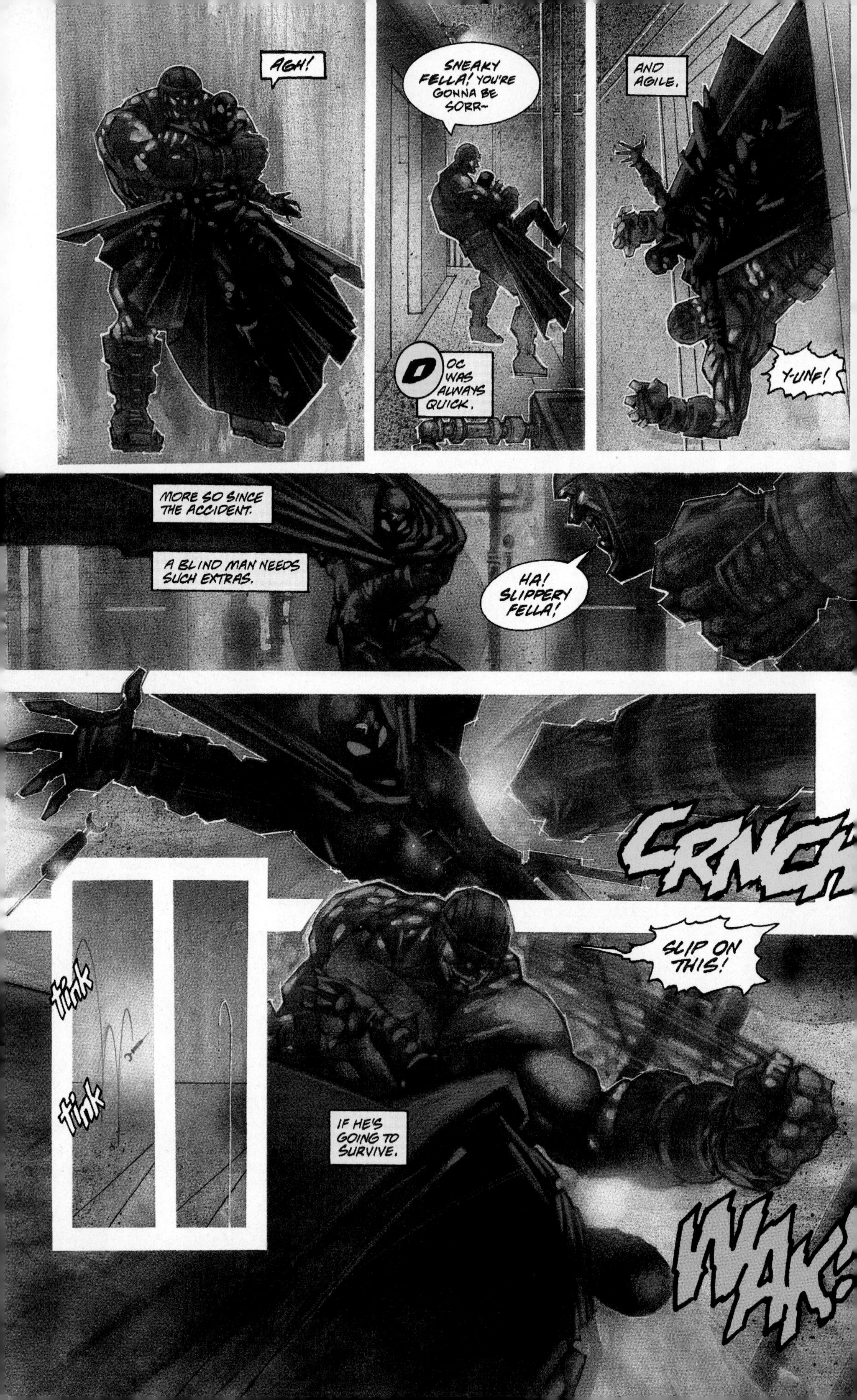
AGH!
SNEAKY FELLA! YOU'RE GONNA BE SORR--
DOC WAS ALWAYS QUICK.
AND AGILE.
Y-UNF!
MORE SO SINCE THE ACCIDENT.
A BLIND MAN NEEDS SUCH EXTRAS.
HA! SLIPPERY FELLA!
CRNCH
tink
tink
SLIP ON THIS!
IF HE'S GOING TO SURVIVE.
WAK

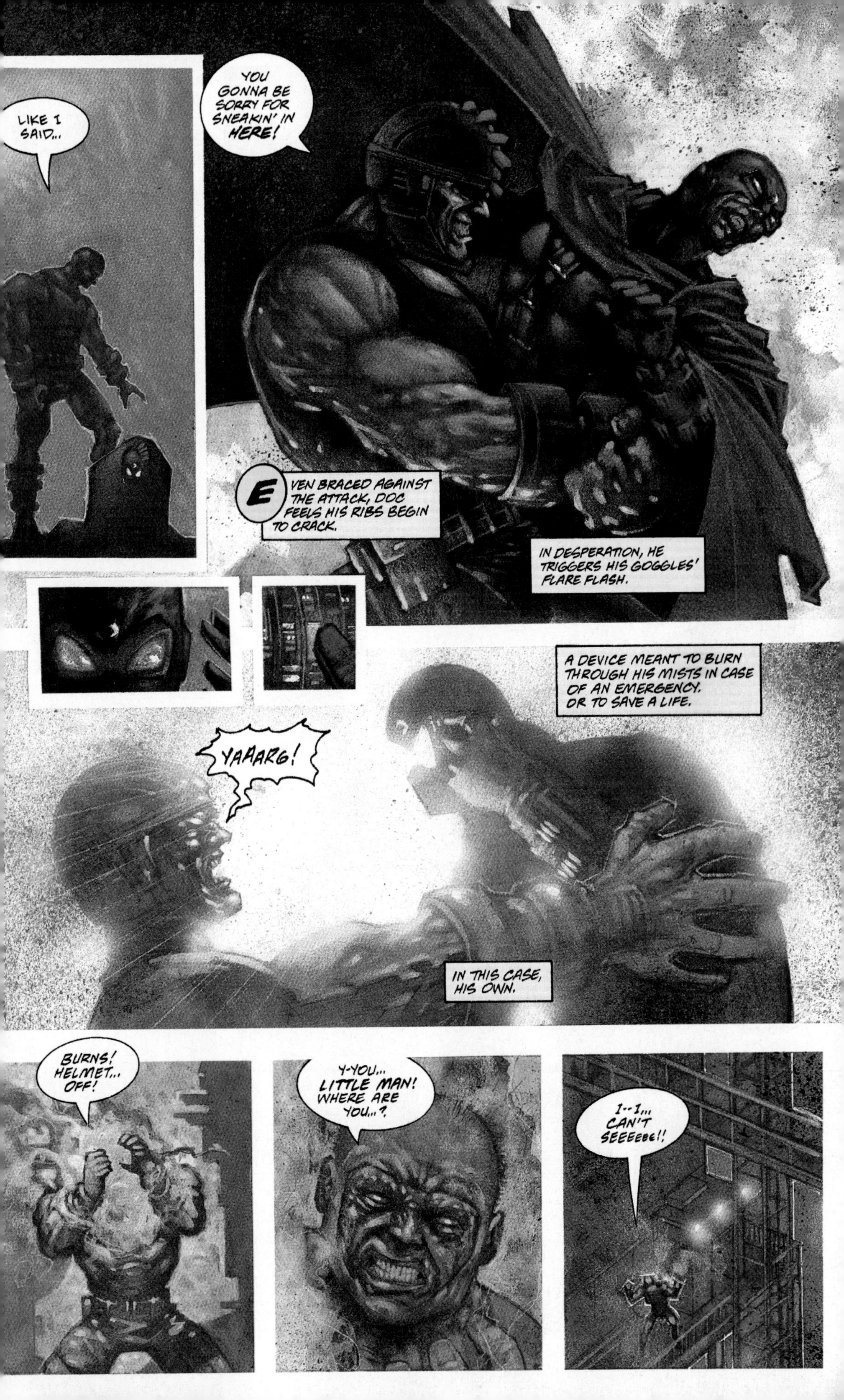
LIKE I SAID...
YOU GONNA BE SORRY FOR SNEAKIN' IN HERE!
EVEN BRACED AGAINST THE ATTACK, DOC FEELS HIS RIBS BEGIN TO CRACK.
IN DESPERATION, HE TRIGGERS HIS GOGGLES' FLARE FLASH.
A DEVICE MEANT TO BURN THROUGH HIS MISTS IN CASE OF AN EMERGENCY. OR TO SAVE A LIFE.
YAAARG!
IN THIS CASE, HIS OWN.
BURNS! HELMET... OFF!
Y-YOU... LITTLE MAN! WHERE ARE YOU...?
I--I... CAN'T SEEEeee!!

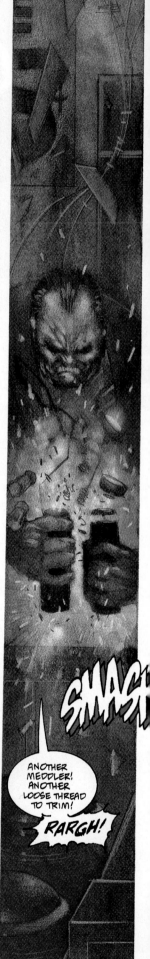

TWENTY-EIGHT MINUTES, THIRTY-SEVEN SECONDS.

CHK.

D-DOC?

DOC!!

QU-QUICKLY, LET'S GET DOWN FROM HERE!

M-MY CAR IS JUST AROUND THE CORNER. UNNG--

ARE YOU ALL RIGHT WHERE DOES IT HURT?

I'LL...BE FINE. I RAN INTO SOME TROUBLE BELOW.

BUT I DON'T THINK ANYONE ELSE SAW ME.

NOW, WHO IS THIS?

SMASH

ANOTHER MEDDLER! ANOTHER LOOSE THREAD TO TRIM!

RARGH!

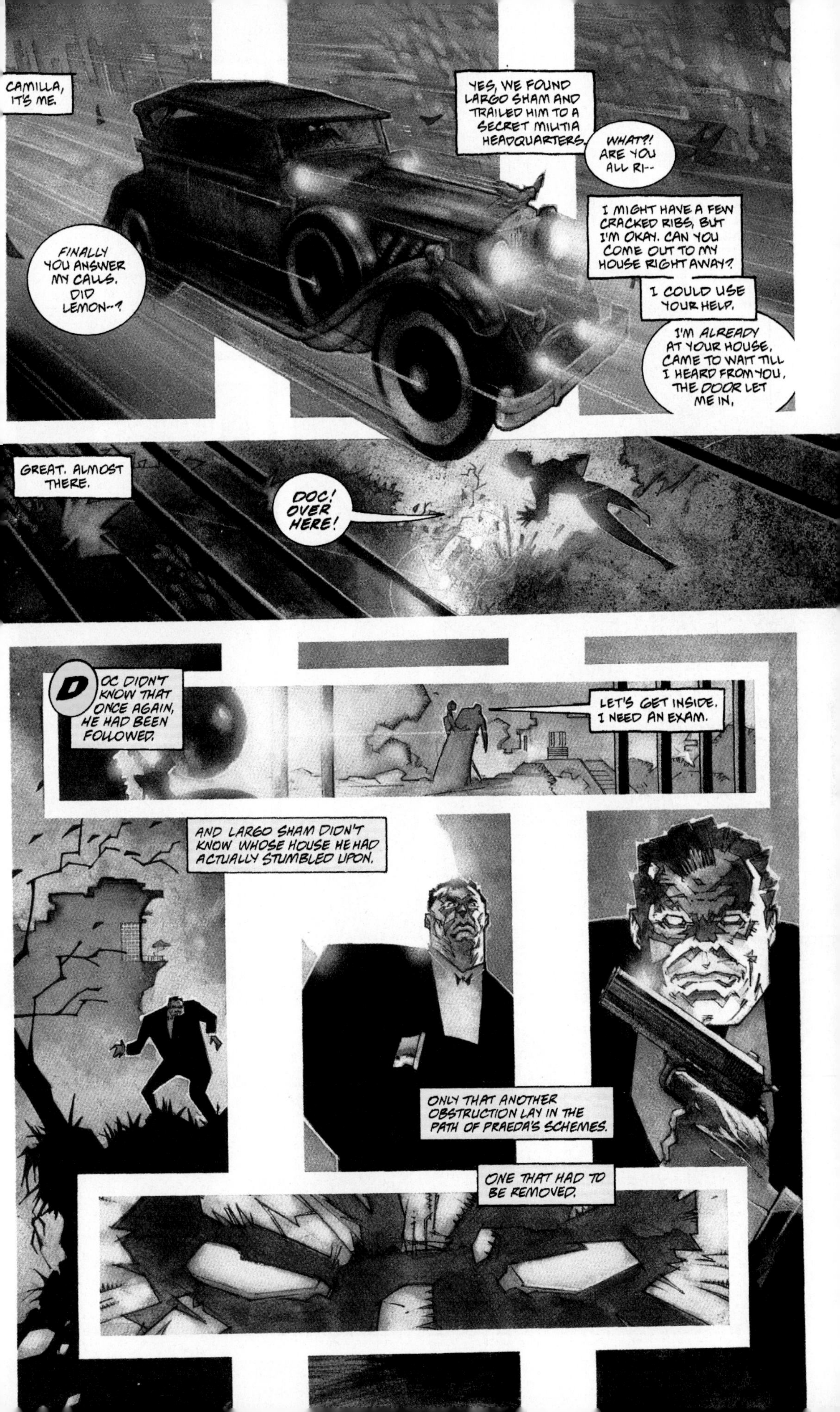
CAMILLA, IT'S ME.
FINALLY YOU ANSWER MY CALLS. DID LEMON--?
YES, WE FOUND LARGO SHAM AND TRAILED HIM TO A SECRET MILITIA HEADQUARTERS.
WHAT?! ARE YOU ALL RI--
I MIGHT HAVE A FEW CRACKED RIBS, BUT I'M OKAY. CAN YOU COME OUT TO MY HOUSE RIGHT AWAY?
I COULD USE YOUR HELP.
I'M ALREADY AT YOUR HOUSE. CAME TO WAIT TILL I HEARD FROM YOU. THE DOOR LET ME IN.
GREAT. ALMOST THERE.
DOC! OVER HERE!
DOC DIDN'T KNOW THAT ONCE AGAIN, HE HAD BEEN FOLLOWED.
LET'S GET INSIDE. I NEED AN EXAM.
AND LARGO SHAM DIDN'T KNOW WHOSE HOUSE HE HAD ACTUALLY STUMBLED UPON.
ONLY THAT ANOTHER OBSTRUCTION LAY IN THE PATH OF PRAEDA'S SCHEMES.
ONE THAT HAD TO BE REMOVED.

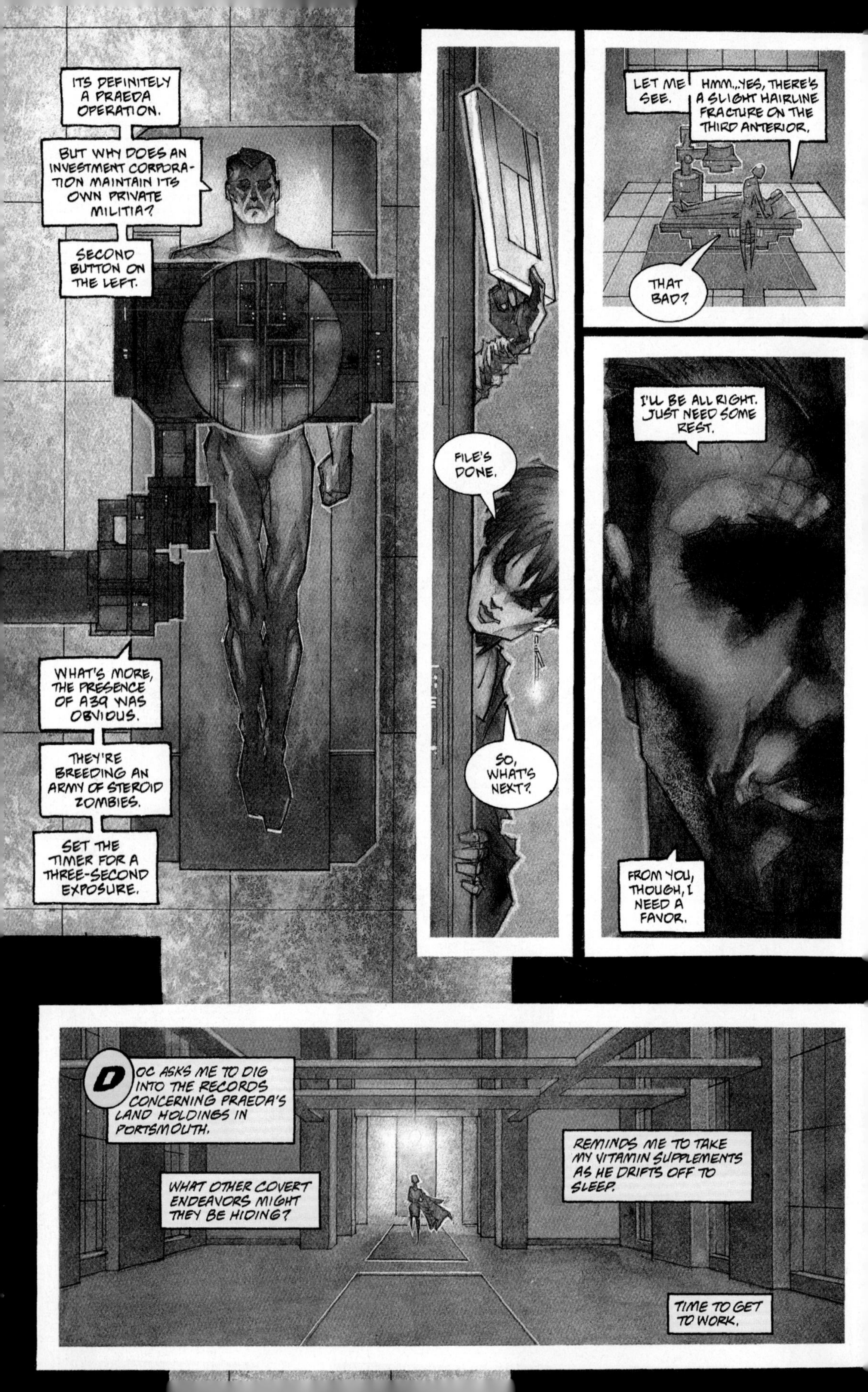
ITS DEFINITELY A PRAEDA OPERATION.
BUT WHY DOES AN INVESTMENT CORPORATION MAINTAIN ITS OWN PRIVATE MILITIA?
SECOND BUTTON ON THE LEFT.
WHAT'S MORE, THE PRESENCE OF A39 WAS OBVIOUS.
THEY'RE BREEDING AN ARMY OF STEROID ZOMBIES.
SET THE TIMER FOR A THREE-SECOND EXPOSURE.
FILE'S DONE.
SO, WHAT'S NEXT?
LET ME SEE.
HMM...YES, THERE'S A SLIGHT HAIRLINE FRACTURE ON THE THIRD ANTERIOR.
THAT BAD?
I'LL BE ALL RIGHT. JUST NEED SOME REST.
FROM YOU, THOUGH, I NEED A FAVOR.
DOC ASKS ME TO DIG INTO THE RECORDS CONCERNING PRAEDA'S LAND HOLDINGS IN PORTSMOUTH.
WHAT OTHER COVERT ENDEAVORS MIGHT THEY BE HIDING?
REMINDS ME TO TAKE MY VITAMIN SUPPLEMENTS AS HE DRIFTS OFF TO SLEEP.
TIME TO GET TO WORK.

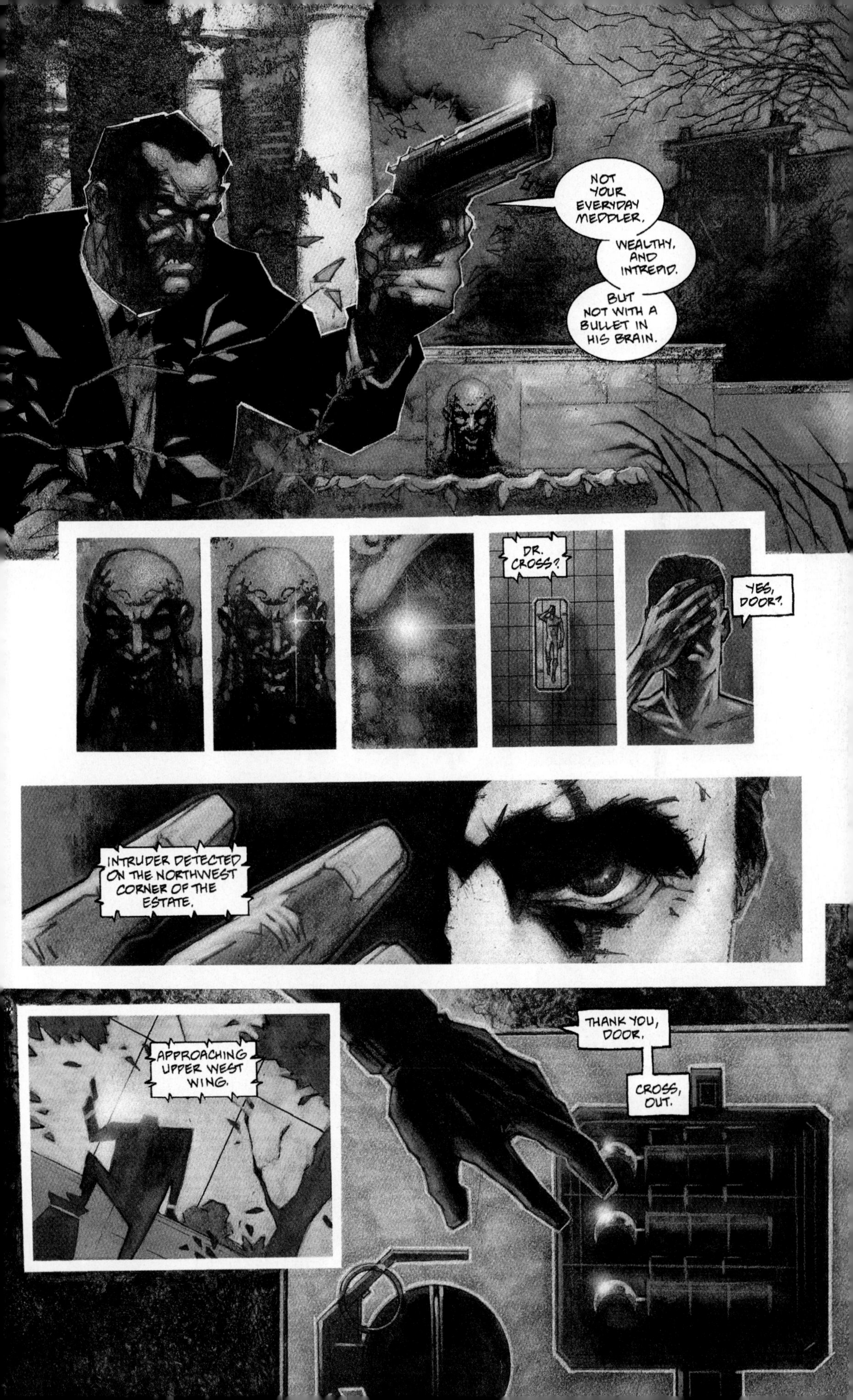
NOT YOUR EVERYDAY MEDDLER.
WEALTHY. AND INTREPID.
BUT NOT WITH A BULLET IN HIS BRAIN.
DR. CROSS?
YES, DOOR?
INTRUDER DETECTED ON THE NORTHWEST CORNER OF THE ESTATE.
APPROACHING UPPER WEST WING.
THANK YOU, DOOR.
CROSS, OUT.

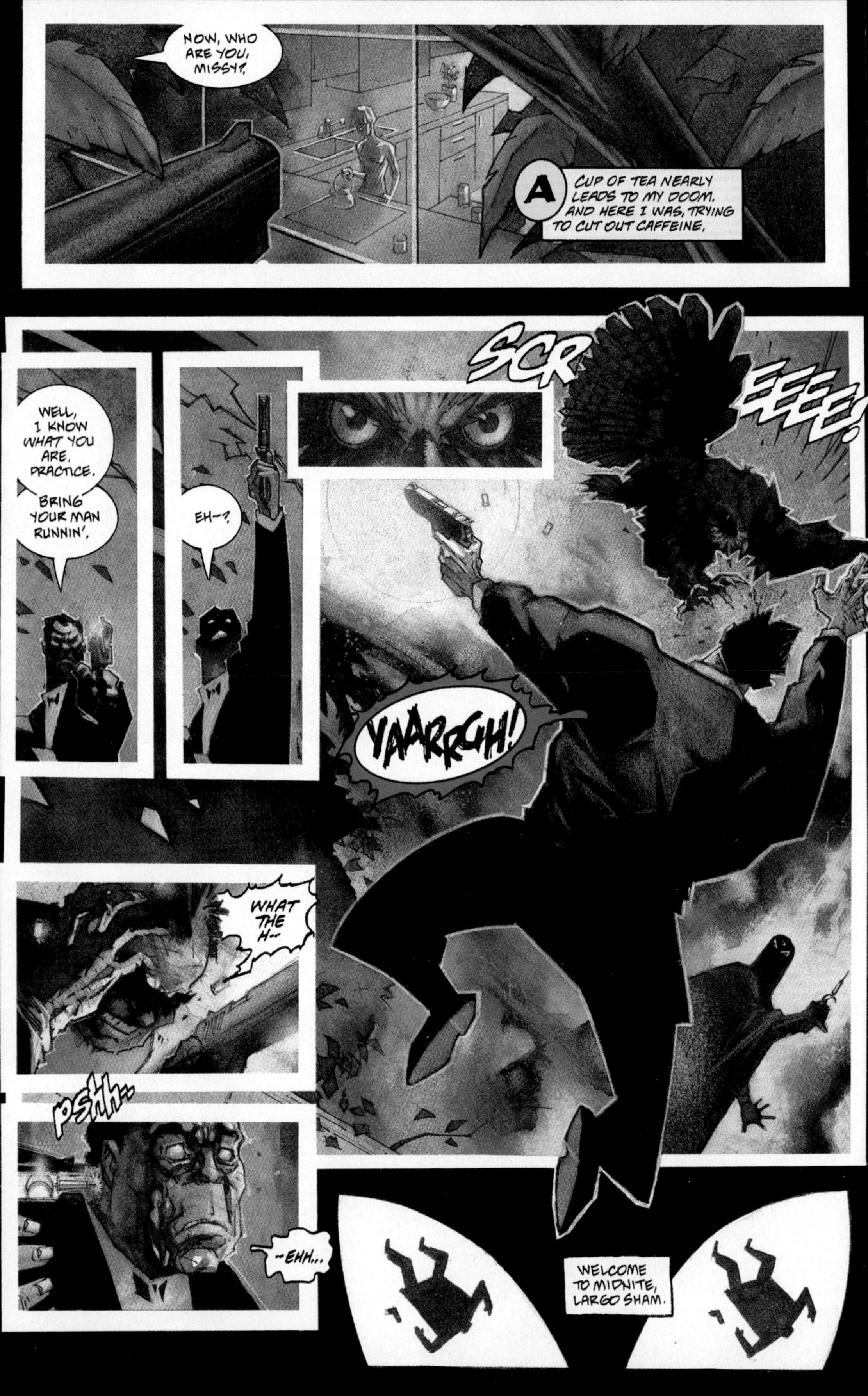
NOW, WHO ARE YOU, MISSY?
A CUP OF TEA NEARLY LEADS TO MY DOOM. AND HERE I WAS, TRYING TO CUT OUT CAFFEINE.
WELL, I KNOW WHAT YOU ARE, PRACTICE.
BRING YOUR MAN RUNNIN'.
EH--?
SCR
EEEE!
YAARRGH!
WHAT THE H--
pshh--
--EHH...
WELCOME TO MIDNITE, LARGO SHAM.

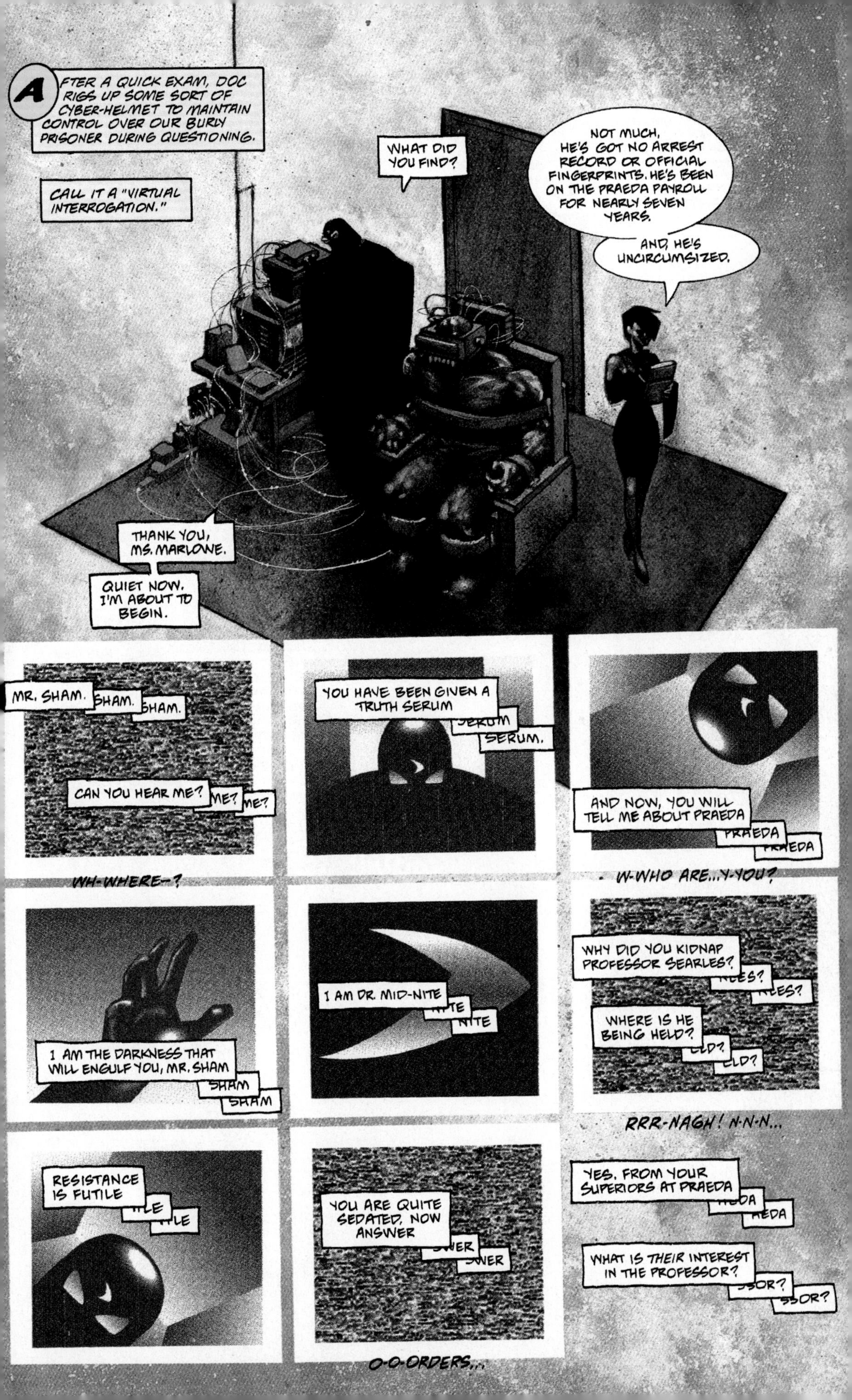
AFTER A QUICK EXAM, DOC RIGS UP SOME SORT OF CYBER-HELMET TO MAINTAIN CONTROL OVER OUR BURLY PRISONER DURING QUESTIONING.
CALL IT A "VIRTUAL INTERROGATION."
WHAT DID YOU FIND?
NOT MUCH. HE'S GOT NO ARREST RECORD OR OFFICIAL FINGERPRINTS. HE'S BEEN ON THE PRAEDA PAYROLL FOR NEARLY SEVEN YEARS.
AND, HE'S UNCIRCUMSIZED.
THANK YOU, MS. MARLOWE.
QUIET NOW. I'M ABOUT TO BEGIN.
MR. SHAM. SHAM. SHAM.
CAN YOU HEAR ME? ME? ME?
WH-WHERE--?
YOU HAVE BEEN GIVEN A TRUTH SERUM SERUM SERUM.
AND NOW, YOU WILL TELL ME ABOUT PRAEDA PRAEDA PRAEDA
W-WHO ARE...Y-YOU?
I AM THE DARKNESS THAT WILL ENGULF YOU, MR. SHAM SHAM SHAM
I AM DR. MID-NITE NITE NITE
WHY DID YOU KIDNAP PROFESSOR SEARLES? LES? LES?
WHERE IS HE BEING HELD? ELD? ELD?
RRR-NAGH! N-N-N...
RESISTANCE IS FUTILE ILE ILE
YOU ARE QUITE SEDATED. NOW ANSWER SWER SWER
O-O-ORDERS...
YES. FROM YOUR SUPERIORS AT PRAEDA EDA EDA
WHAT IS THEIR INTEREST IN THE PROFESSOR? SSOR? SSOR?

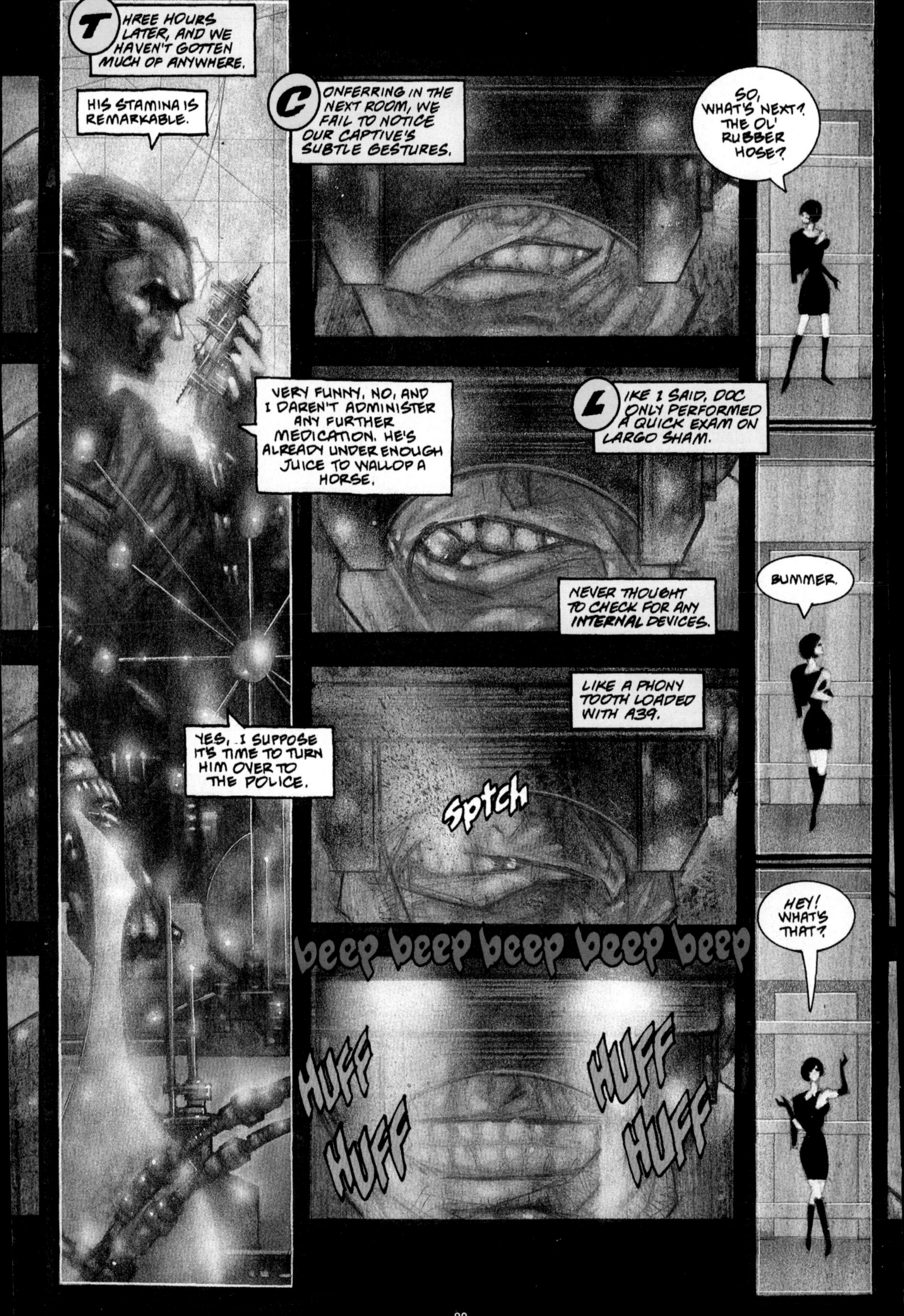
THREE HOURS LATER, AND WE HAVEN'T GOTTEN MUCH OF ANYWHERE.
HIS STAMINA IS REMARKABLE.
CONFERRING IN THE NEXT ROOM, WE FAIL TO NOTICE OUR CAPTIVE'S SUBTLE GESTURES.
SO, WHAT'S NEXT? THE OL' RUBBER HOSE?
VERY FUNNY. NO, AND I DAREN'T ADMINISTER ANY FURTHER MEDICATION. HE'S ALREADY UNDER ENOUGH JUICE TO WALLOP A HORSE.
LIKE I SAID, DOC ONLY PERFORMED A QUICK EXAM ON LARGO SHAM.
BUMMER.
NEVER THOUGHT TO CHECK FOR ANY INTERNAL DEVICES.
LIKE A PHONY TOOTH LOADED WITH A39.
YES, I SUPPOSE IT'S TIME TO TURN HIM OVER TO THE POLICE.
sptch
HEY! WHAT'S THAT?
beep beep beep beep beep
HUFF HUFF
HUFF HUFF

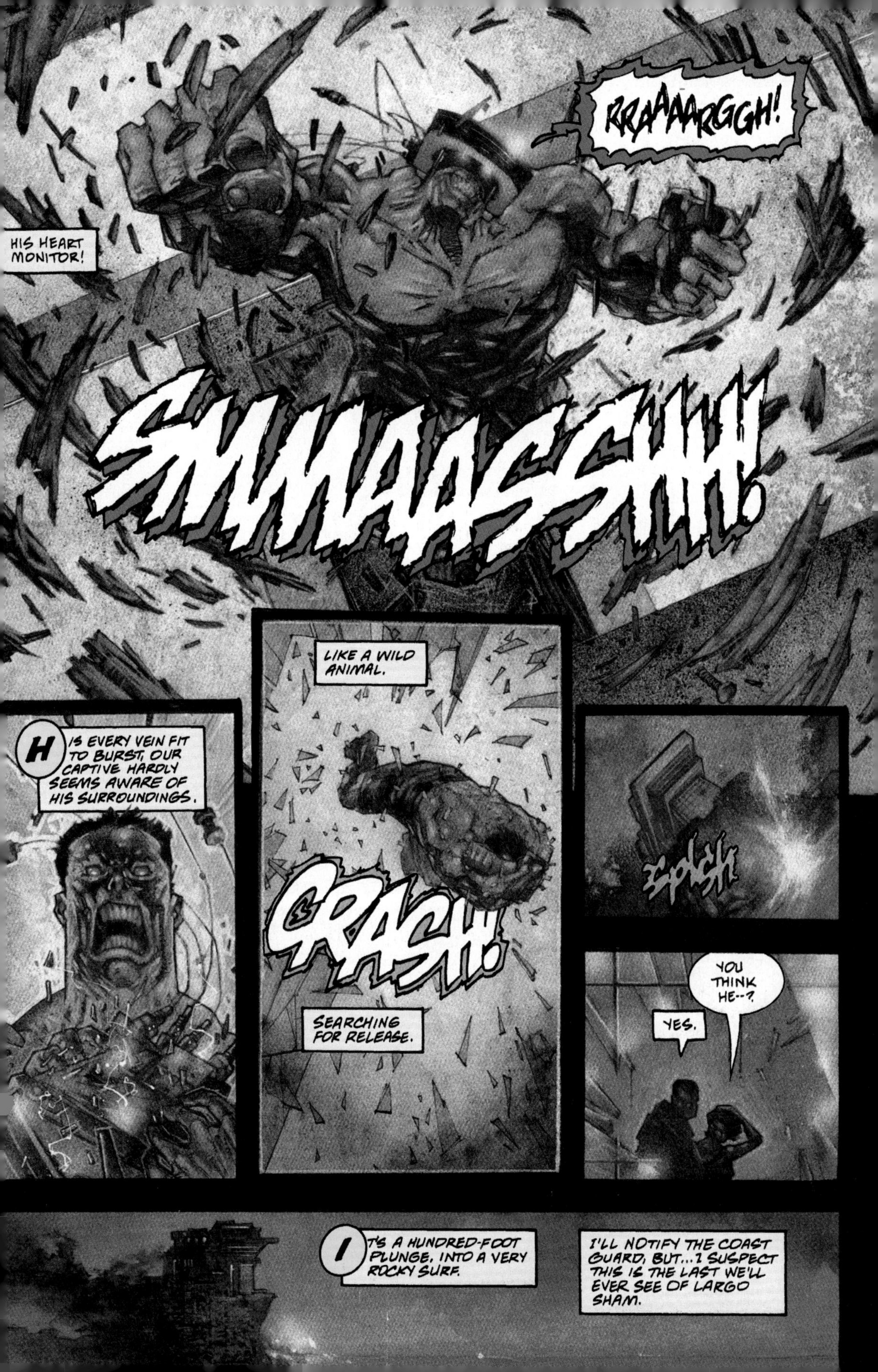
RRAAAARGGH!
HIS HEART MONITOR!
SMMAASSHH!
HIS EVERY VEIN FIT TO BURST, OUR CAPTIVE HARDLY SEEMS AWARE OF HIS SURROUNDINGS.
LIKE A WILD ANIMAL.
CRASH!
SEARCHING FOR RELEASE.
SPLSH
YOU THINK HE--?
YES.
IT'S A HUNDRED-FOOT PLUNGE, INTO A VERY ROCKY SURF.
I'LL NOTIFY THE COAST GUARD, BUT...I SUSPECT THIS IS THE LAST WE'LL EVER SEE OF LARGO SHAM.

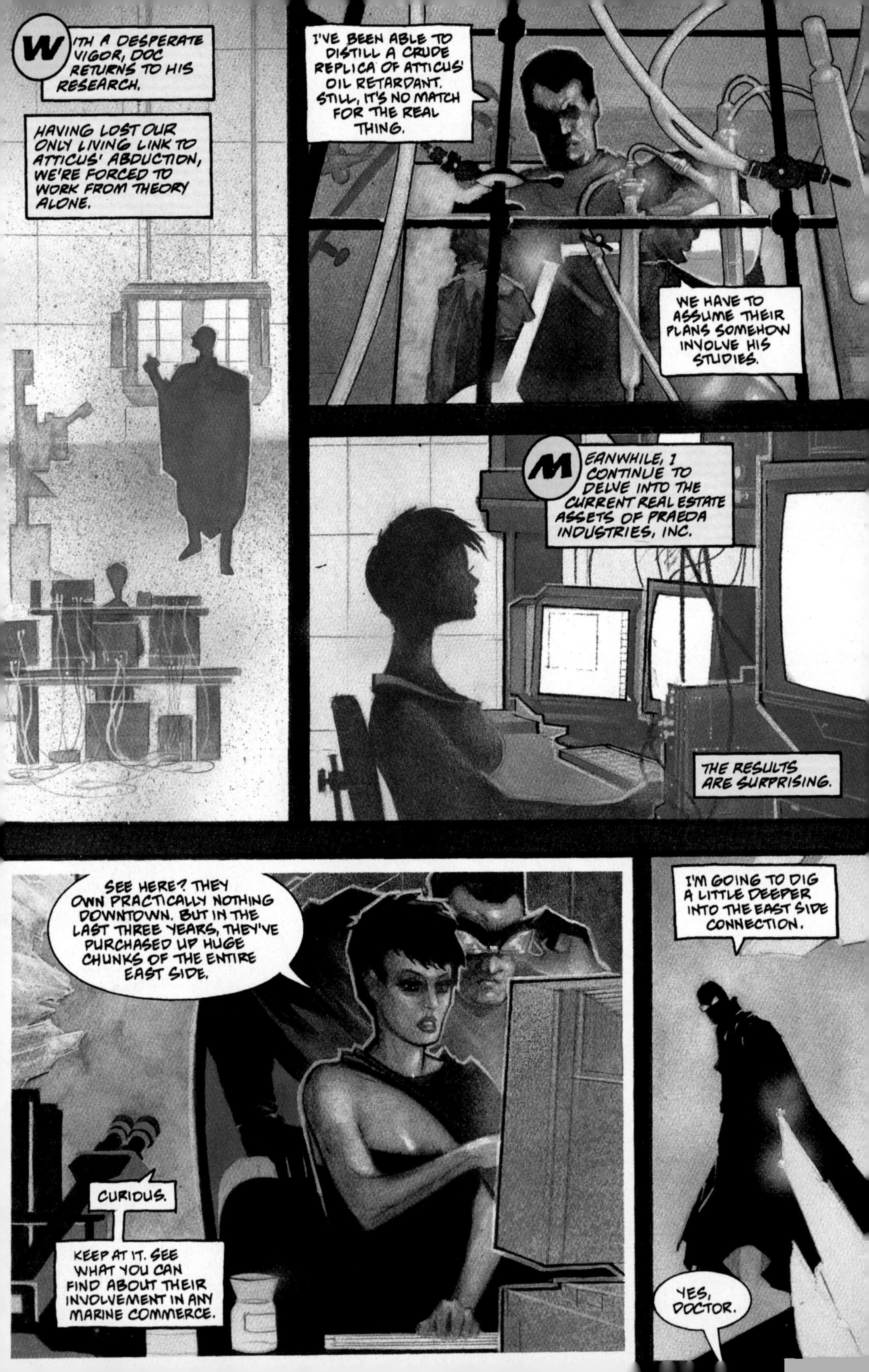
WITH A DESPERATE VIGOR, DOC RETURNS TO HIS RESEARCH.
HAVING LOST OUR ONLY LIVING LINK TO ATTICUS' ABDUCTION, WE'RE FORCED TO WORK FROM THEORY ALONE.
I'VE BEEN ABLE TO DISTILL A CRUDE REPLICA OF ATTICUS' OIL RETARDANT. STILL, IT'S NO MATCH FOR THE REAL THING.
WE HAVE TO ASSUME THEIR PLANS SOMEHOW INVOLVE HIS STUDIES.
MEANWHILE, I CONTINUE TO DELVE INTO THE CURRENT REAL ESTATE ASSETS OF PRAEDA INDUSTRIES, INC.
THE RESULTS ARE SURPRISING.
SEE HERE? THEY OWN PRACTICALLY NOTHING DOWNTOWN. BUT IN THE LAST THREE YEARS, THEY'VE PURCHASED UP HUGE CHUNKS OF THE ENTIRE EAST SIDE.
CURIOUS.
KEEP AT IT. SEE WHAT YOU CAN FIND ABOUT THEIR INVOLVEMENT IN ANY MARINE COMMERCE.
I'M GOING TO DIG A LITTLE DEEPER INTO THE EAST SIDE CONNECTION.
YES, DOCTOR.

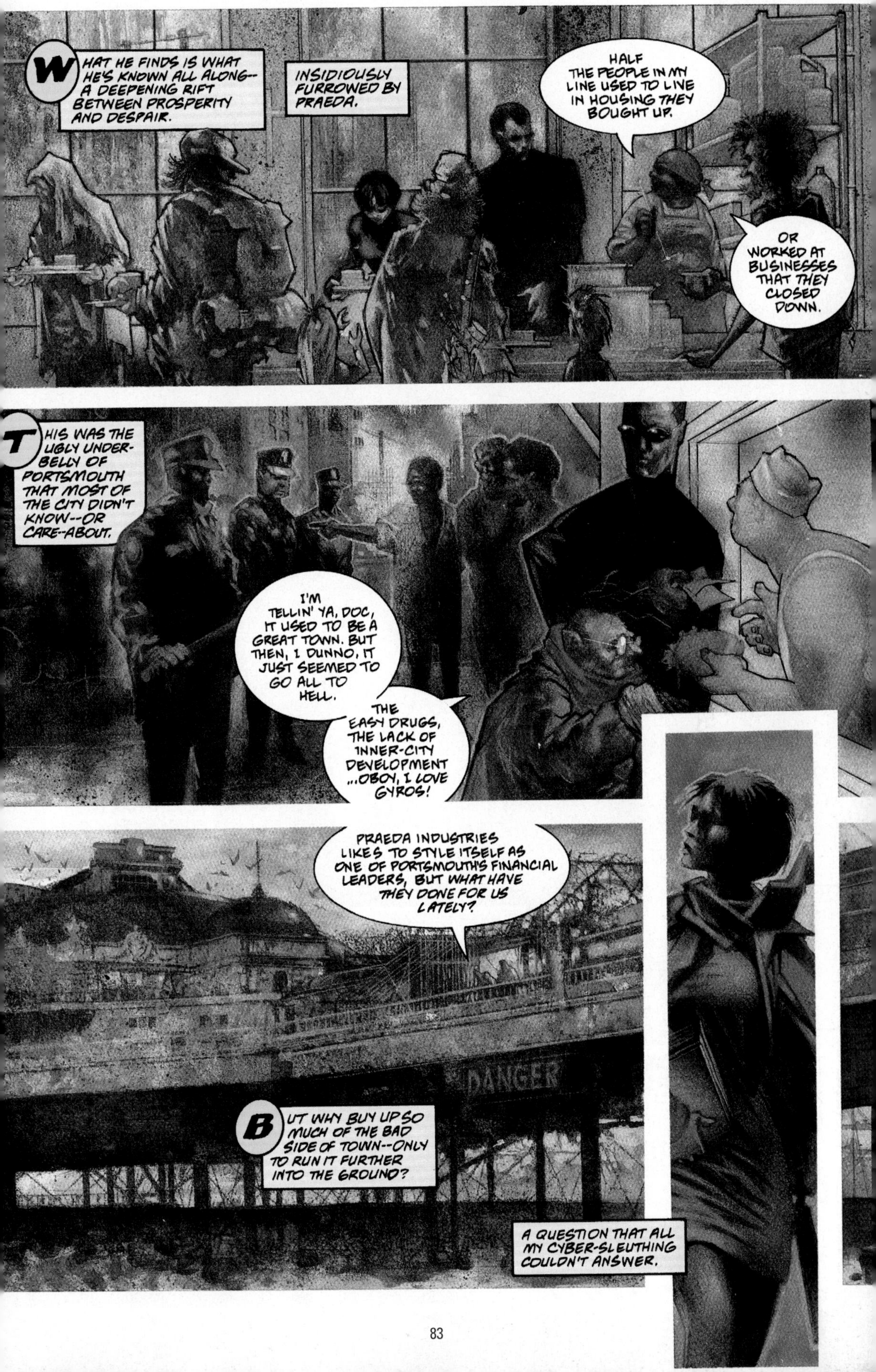
WHAT HE FINDS IS WHAT HE'S KNOWN ALL ALONG-- A DEEPENING RIFT BETWEEN PROSPERITY AND DESPAIR.
INSIDIOUSLY FURROWED BY PRAEDA.
HALF THE PEOPLE IN MY LINE USED TO LIVE IN HOUSING THEY BOUGHT UP.
OR WORKED AT BUSINESSES THAT THEY CLOSED DOWN.
THIS WAS THE UGLY UNDER-BELLY OF PORTSMOUTH THAT MOST OF THE CITY DIDN'T KNOW--OR CARE--ABOUT.
I'M TELLIN' YA, DOC, IT USED TO BE A GREAT TOWN. BUT THEN, I DUNNO, IT JUST SEEMED TO GO ALL TO HELL.
THE EASY DRUGS, THE LACK OF INNER-CITY DEVELOPMENT ...OBOY, I LOVE GYROS!
PRAEDA INDUSTRIES LIKES TO STYLE ITSELF AS ONE OF PORTSMOUTH'S FINANCIAL LEADERS, BUT WHAT HAVE THEY DONE FOR US LATELY?
DANGER
BUT WHY BUY UP SO MUCH OF THE BAD SIDE OF TOWN--ONLY TO RUN IT FURTHER INTO THE GROUND?
A QUESTION THAT ALL MY CYBER-SLEUTHING COULDN'T ANSWER.

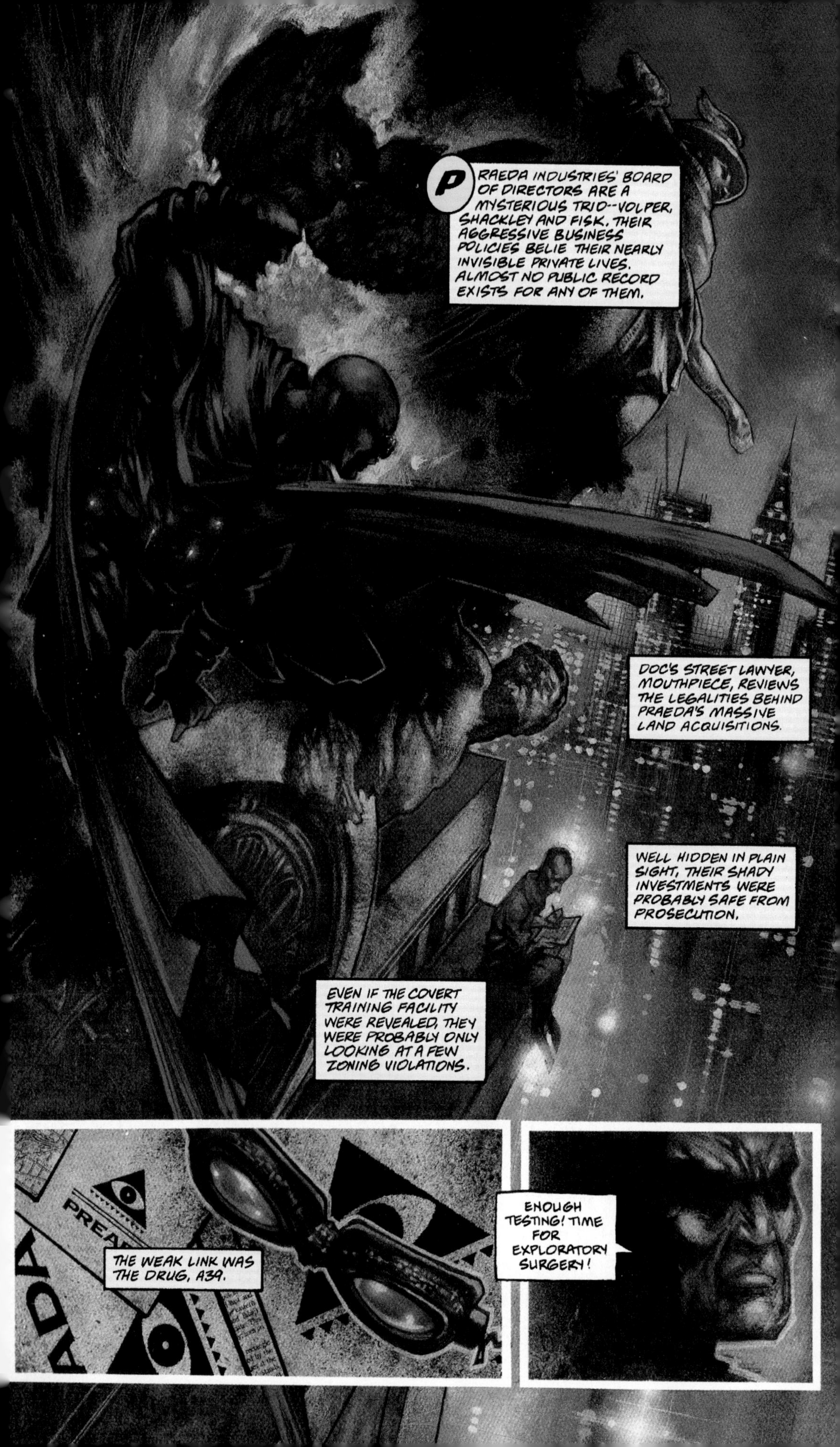
PRAEDA INDUSTRIES' BOARD OF DIRECTORS ARE A MYSTERIOUS TRIO--VOLPER, SHACKLEY AND FISK. THEIR AGGRESSIVE BUSINESS POLICIES BELIE THEIR NEARLY INVISIBLE PRIVATE LIVES. ALMOST NO PUBLIC RECORD EXISTS FOR ANY OF THEM.
DOC'S STREET LAWYER, MOUTHPIECE, REVIEWS THE LEGALITIES BEHIND PRAEDA'S MASSIVE LAND ACQUISITIONS.
WELL HIDDEN IN PLAIN SIGHT, THEIR SHADY INVESTMENTS WERE PROBABLY SAFE FROM PROSECUTION.
EVEN IF THE COVERT TRAINING FACILITY WERE REVEALED, THEY WERE PROBABLY ONLY LOOKING AT A FEW ZONING VIOLATIONS.
THE WEAK LINK WAS THE DRUG, A39.
ENOUGH TESTING! TIME FOR EXPLORATORY SURGERY!

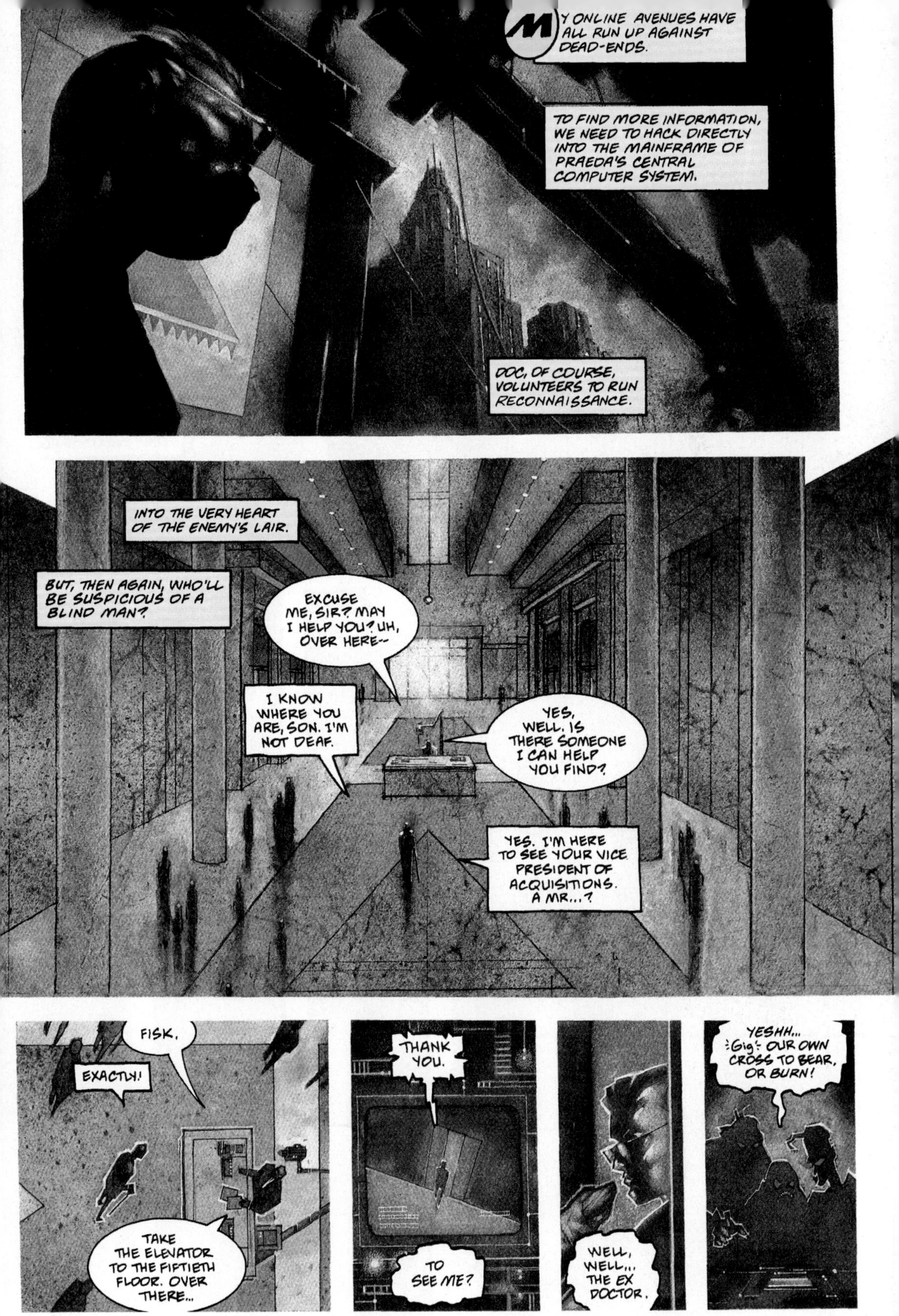
MY ONLINE AVENUES HAVE ALL RUN UP AGAINST DEAD-ENDS.
TO FIND MORE INFORMATION, WE NEED TO HACK DIRECTLY INTO THE MAINFRAME OF PRAEDA'S CENTRAL COMPUTER SYSTEM.
DOC, OF COURSE, VOLUNTEERS TO RUN RECONNAISSANCE.
INTO THE VERY HEART OF THE ENEMY'S LAIR.
BUT, THEN AGAIN, WHO'LL BE SUSPICIOUS OF A BLIND MAN?
EXCUSE ME, SIR? MAY I HELP YOU? UH, OVER HERE--
I KNOW WHERE YOU ARE, SON. I'M NOT DEAF.
YES, WELL. IS THERE SOMEONE I CAN HELP YOU FIND?
YES. I'M HERE TO SEE YOUR VICE PRESIDENT OF ACQUISITIONS. A MR...?
FISK.
EXACTLY!
TAKE THE ELEVATOR TO THE FIFTIETH FLOOR. OVER THERE...
THANK YOU.
TO SEE ME?
WELL, WELL... THE EX DOCTOR.
YESHH... Gig OUR OWN CROSS TO BEAR, OR BURN!

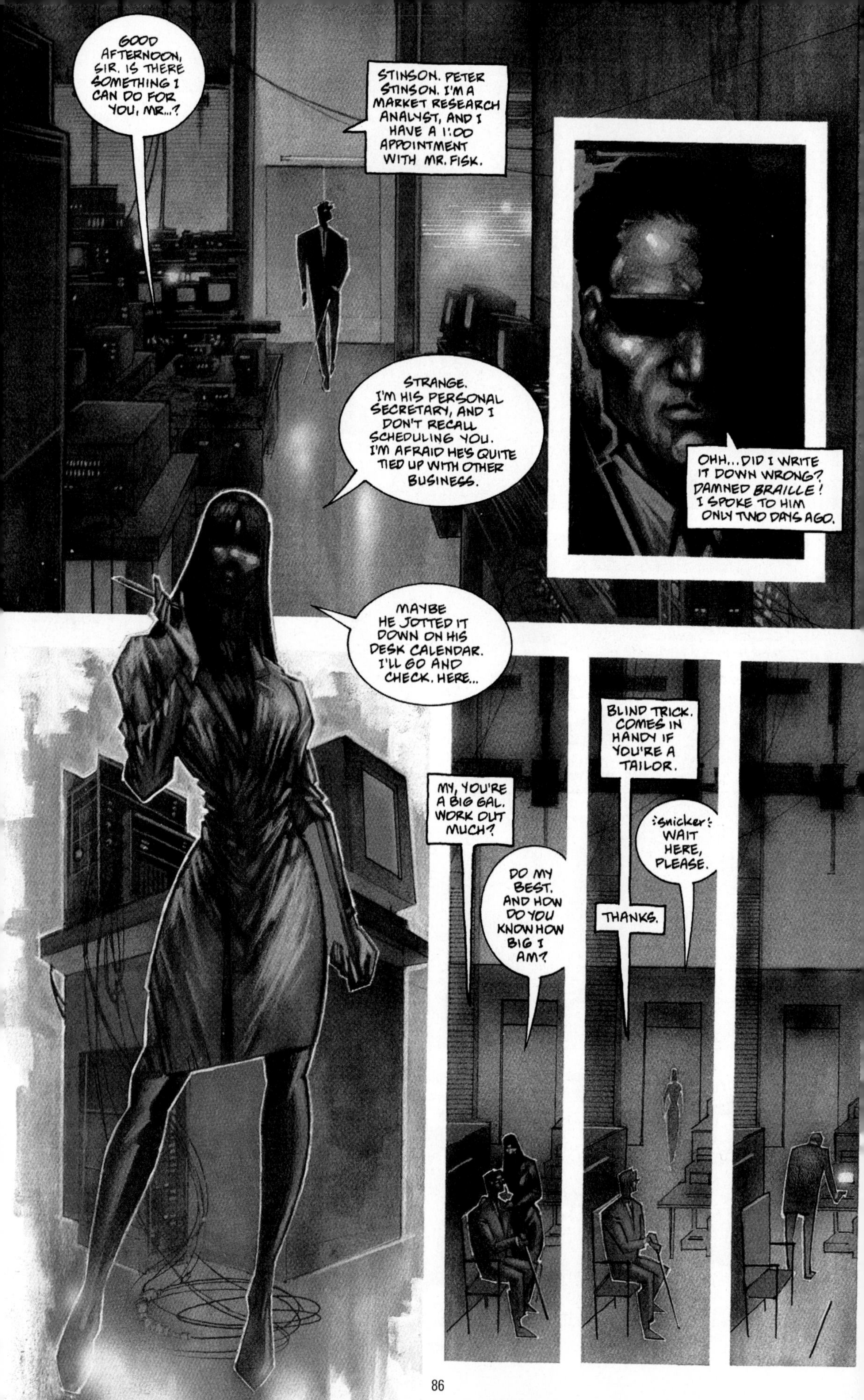
GOOD AFTERNOON, SIR. IS THERE SOMETHING I CAN DO FOR YOU, MR...?
STINSON. PETER STINSON. I'M A MARKET RESEARCH ANALYST, AND I HAVE A 1:00 APPOINTMENT WITH MR. FISK.
STRANGE. I'M HIS PERSONAL SECRETARY, AND I DON'T RECALL SCHEDULING YOU. I'M AFRAID HE'S QUITE TIED UP WITH OTHER BUSINESS.
OHH... DID I WRITE IT DOWN WRONG? DAMNED BRAILLE! I SPOKE TO HIM ONLY TWO DAYS AGO.
MAYBE HE JOTTED IT DOWN ON HIS DESK CALENDAR. I'LL GO AND CHECK. HERE...
MY, YOU'RE A BIG GAL. WORK OUT MUCH?
DO MY BEST. AND HOW DO YOU KNOW HOW BIG I AM?
BLIND TRICK. COMES IN HANDY IF YOU'RE A TAILOR.
THANKS.
:snicker: WAIT HERE, PLEASE.

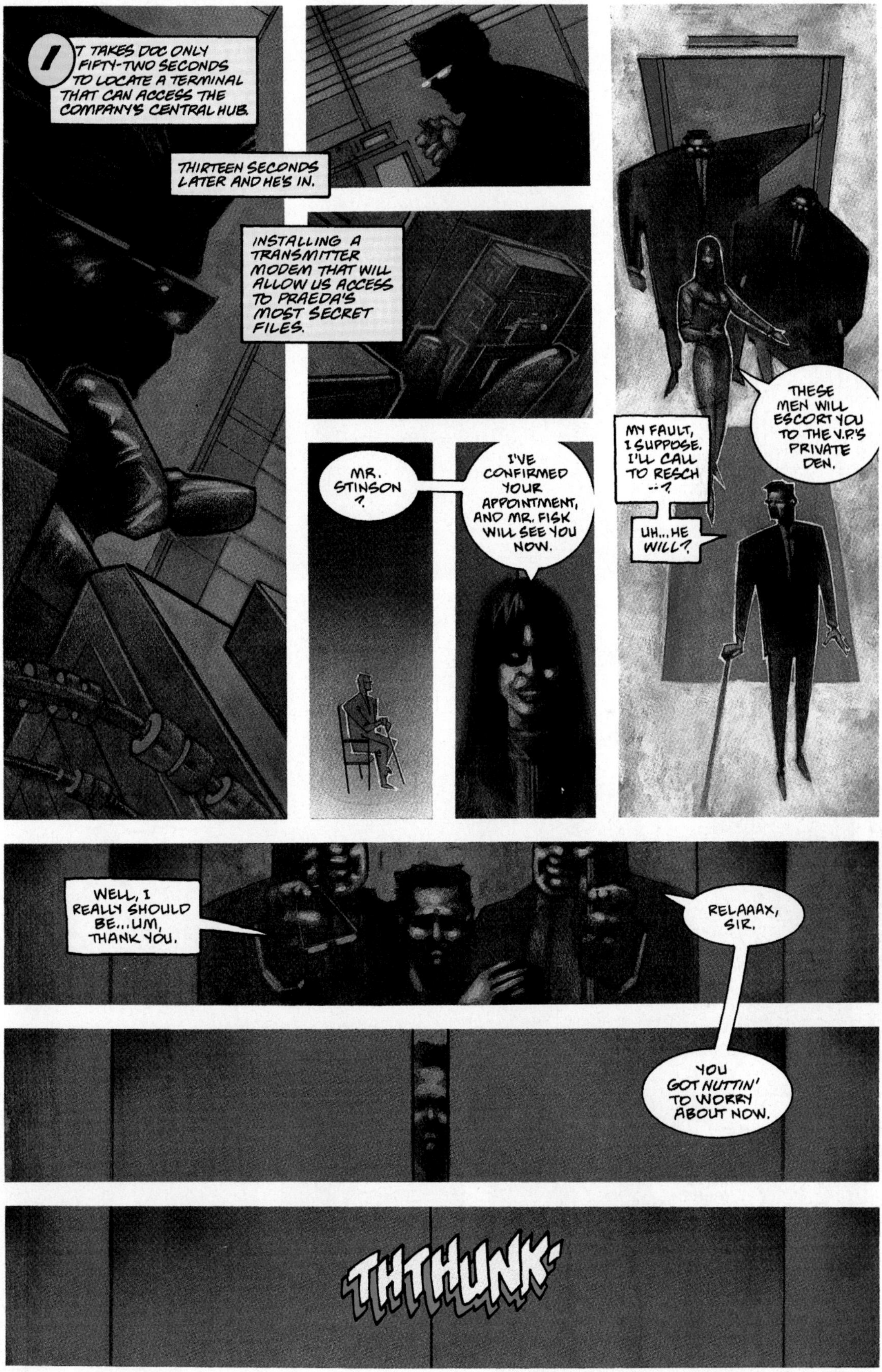
IT TAKES DOC ONLY FIFTY-TWO SECONDS TO LOCATE A TERMINAL THAT CAN ACCESS THE COMPANY'S CENTRAL HUB.
THIRTEEN SECONDS LATER AND HE'S IN.
INSTALLING A TRANSMITTER MODEM THAT WILL ALLOW US ACCESS TO PRAEDA'S MOST SECRET FILES.
MR. STINSON?
I'VE CONFIRMED YOUR APPOINTMENT, AND MR. FISK WILL SEE YOU NOW.
THESE MEN WILL ESCORT YOU TO THE V.P.'S PRIVATE DEN.
MY FAULT, I SUPPOSE. I'LL CALL TO RESCH--?
UH... HE WILL?
WELL, I REALLY SHOULD BE... UM, THANK YOU.
RELAAAX, SIR.
YOU GOT NUTTIN' TO WORRY ABOUT NOW.
THTHUNK

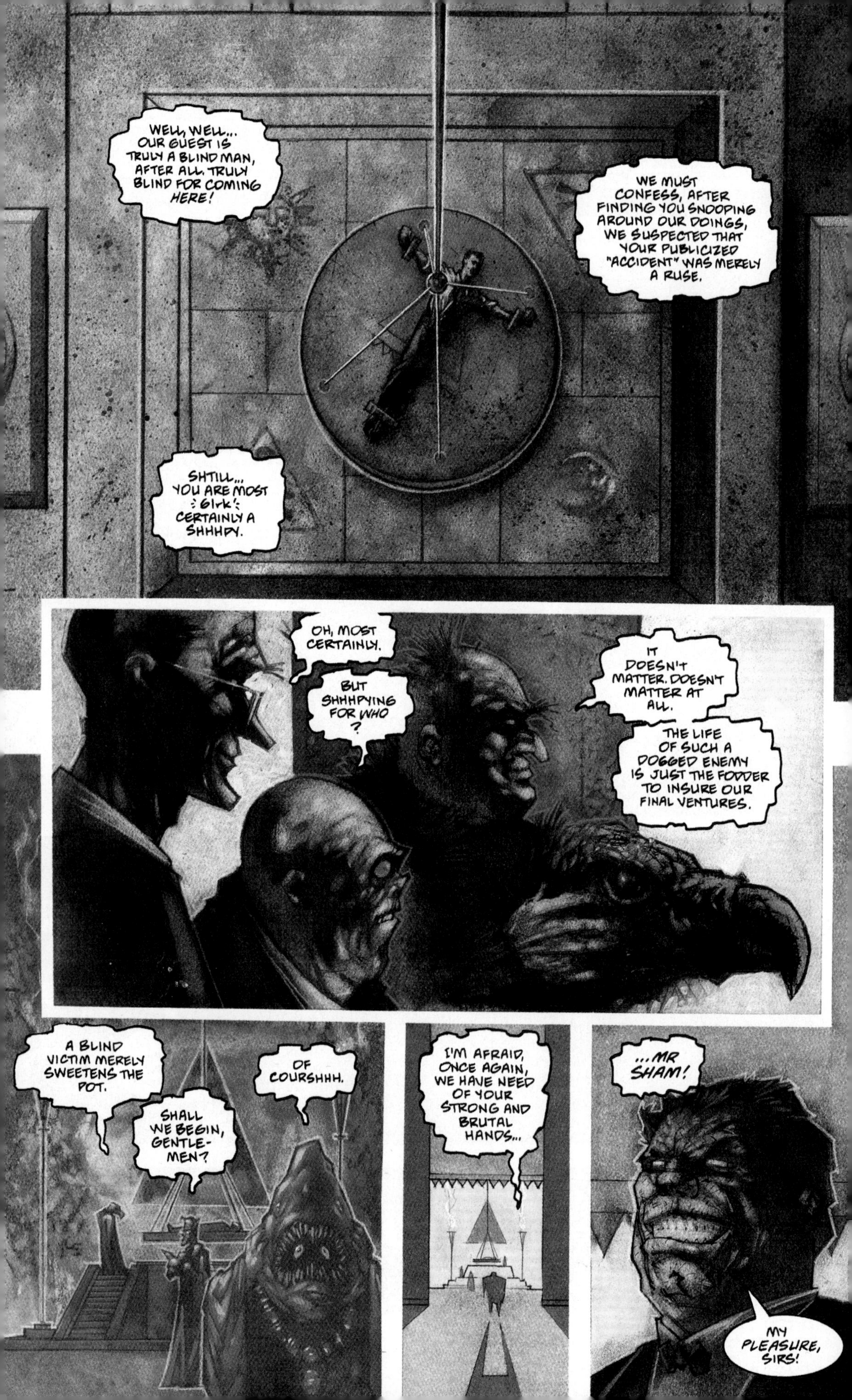
WELL, WELL... OUR GUEST IS TRULY A BLIND MAN, AFTER ALL. TRULY BLIND FOR COMING HERE!
WE MUST CONFESS, AFTER FINDING YOU SNOOPING AROUND OUR DOINGS, WE SUSPECTED THAT YOUR PUBLICIZED "ACCIDENT" WAS MERELY A RUSE.
SHTILL... YOU ARE MOST :GLRK: CERTAINLY A SHHHPY.
OH, MOST CERTAINLY.
BUT SHHHPYING FOR WHO?
IT DOESN'T MATTER. DOESN'T MATTER AT ALL.
THE LIFE OF SUCH A DOGGED ENEMY IS JUST THE FODDER TO INSURE OUR FINAL VENTURES.
A BLIND VICTIM MERELY SWEETENS THE POT.
OF COURSHHH.
SHALL WE BEGIN, GENTLE-MEN?
I'M AFRAID, ONCE AGAIN, WE HAVE NEED OF YOUR STRONG AND BRUTAL HANDS...
...MR SHAM!
MY PLEASURE, SIRS!

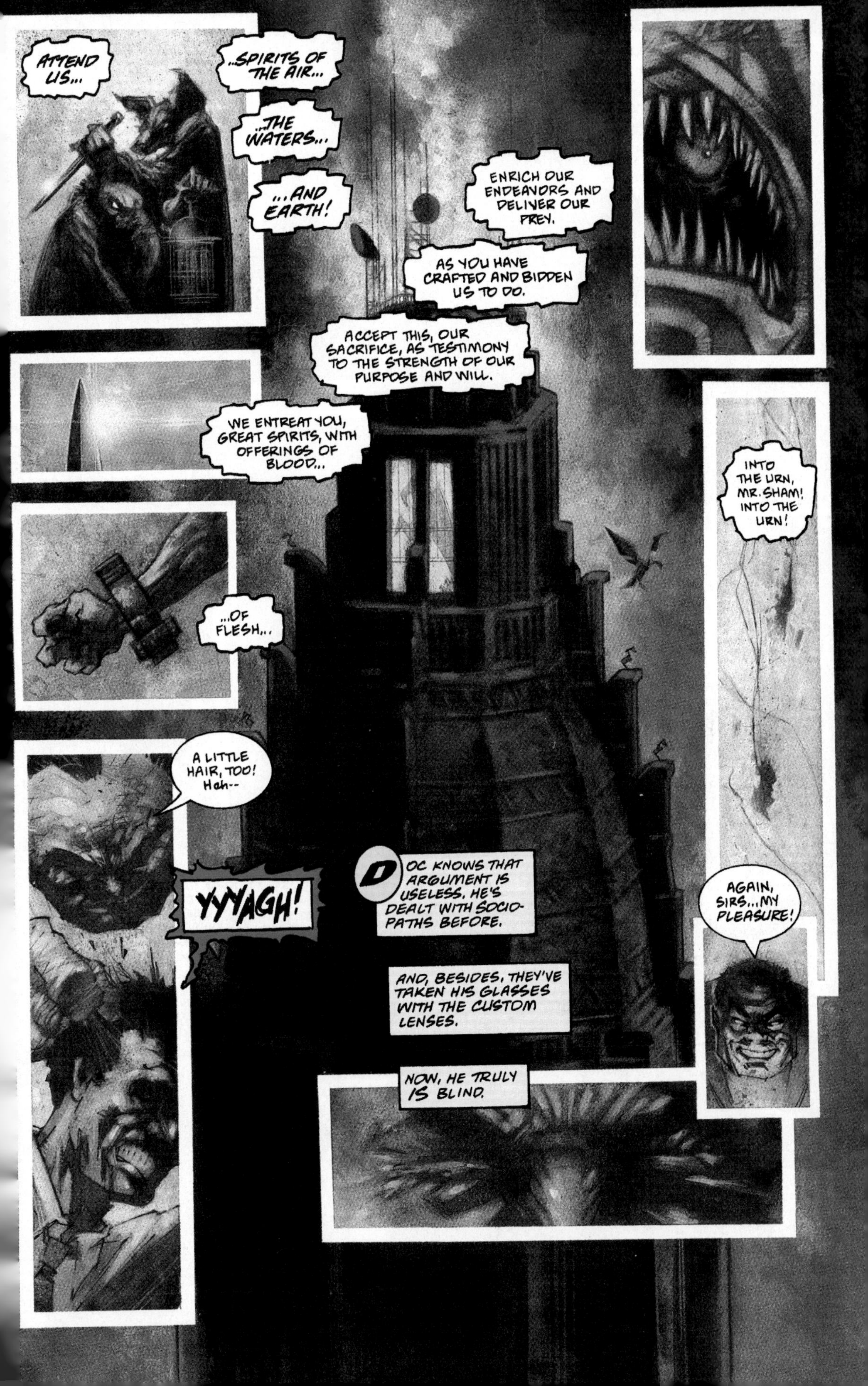
ATTEND US...
..SPIRITS OF THE AIR...
...THE WATERS...
...AND EARTH!
ENRICH OUR ENDEAVORS AND DELIVER OUR PREY.
AS YOU HAVE CRAFTED AND BIDDEN US TO DO.
ACCEPT THIS, OUR SACRIFICE, AS TESTIMONY TO THE STRENGTH OF OUR PURPOSE AND WILL.
WE ENTREAT YOU, GREAT SPIRITS, WITH OFFERINGS OF BLOOD...
...OF FLESH...
INTO THE URN, MR. SHAM! INTO THE URN!
A LITTLE HAIR, TOO! Hah--
YYYAGH!
DOC KNOWS THAT ARGUMENT IS USELESS. HE'S DEALT WITH SOCIO-PATHS BEFORE.
AND, BESIDES, THEY'VE TAKEN HIS GLASSES WITH THE CUSTOM LENSES.
AGAIN, SIRS...MY PLEASURE!
NOW, HE TRULY IS BLIND.

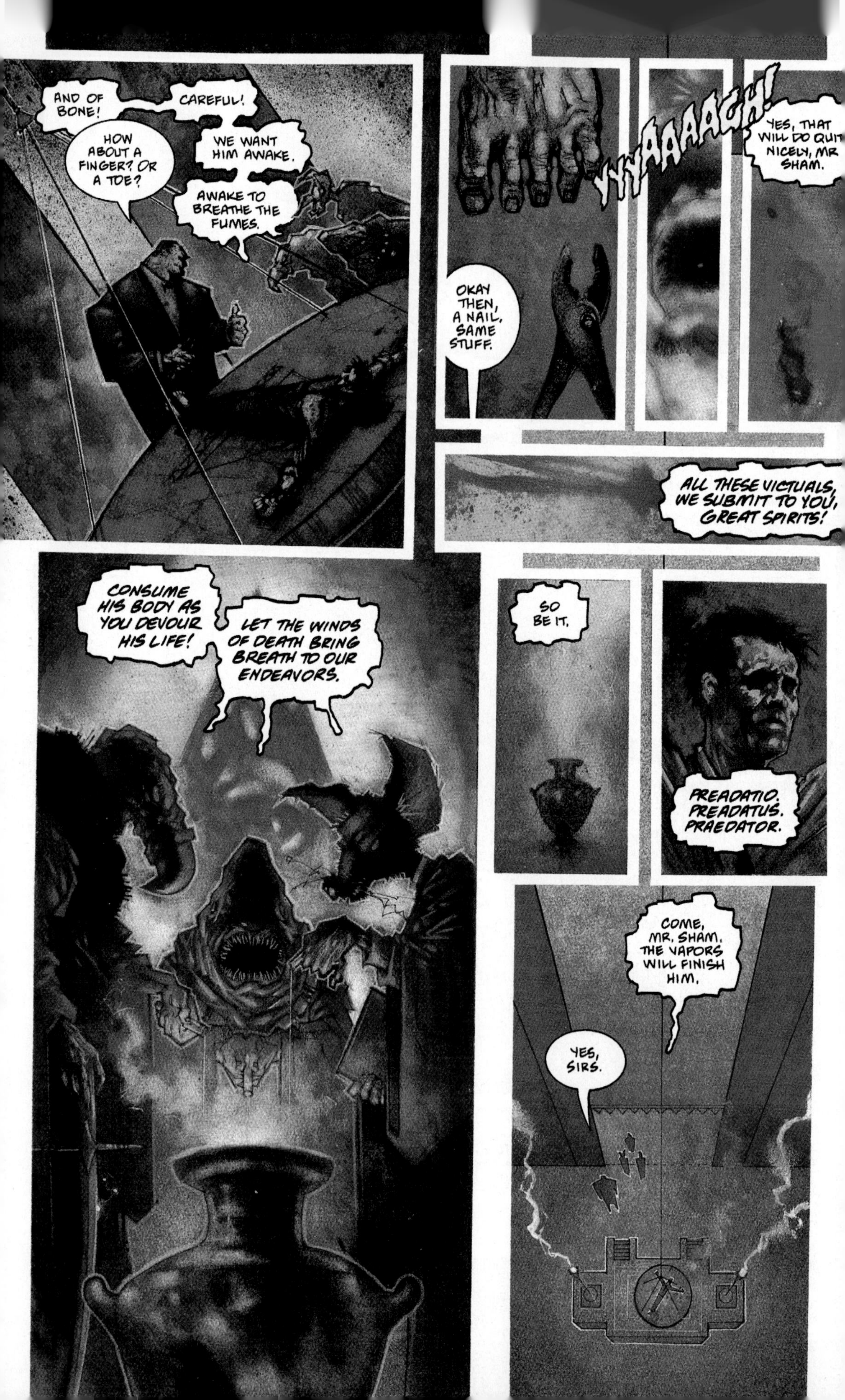
AND OF BONE!
CAREFUL!
HOW ABOUT A FINGER? OR A TOE?
WE WANT HIM AWAKE.
AWAKE TO BREATHE THE FUMES.
OKAY THEN, A NAIL, SAME STUFF.
YYYAAAAACH!
YES, THAT WILL DO QUIT NICELY, MR SHAM.
ALL THESE VICTUALS, WE SUBMIT TO YOU, GREAT SPIRITS!
CONSUME HIS BODY AS YOU DEVOUR HIS LIFE!
LET THE WINDS OF DEATH BRING BREATH TO OUR ENDEAVORS.
SO BE IT.
PREADATIO. PREADATUS. PRAEDATOR.
COME, MR. SHAM. THE VAPORS WILL FINISH HIM.
YES, SIRS.

"I HAVE SOME SOME FURTHER LOOSE ENDS TO TIDY UP, ANYWAY."

AW, C'MON...HOW 'BOUT IT? ANY LOOSE CHANGE?

NOT TODAY, BROTHER.

SHEESH. THIS TOWN'S DRYIN'...

...UP--

H-HEY, PAL! LONG TIME NO SEE! WH--

IT FINALLY OCCURRED TO ME, WHERE THE STEM OF THIS TRAIL MIGHT LEAD.

THAT DO-GOODER IN BLACK. YOU LED HIM TO ME.

N-NO! I, UM...DON'T KNOW WHAT--

ONE TOE.

YEEOOW!

POW

NINE TO GO. HE HAS A GIRL. PALE, BLACK HAIR.

WHO IS SHE?

I DON'... I SWEAR-- I DON' KNOW!!

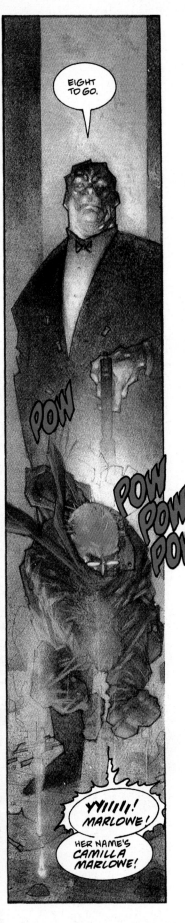

EIGHT TO GO.

POW

POW POW POW

YYIIIII! MARLOWE!

HER NAME'S CAMILLA MARLOWE!

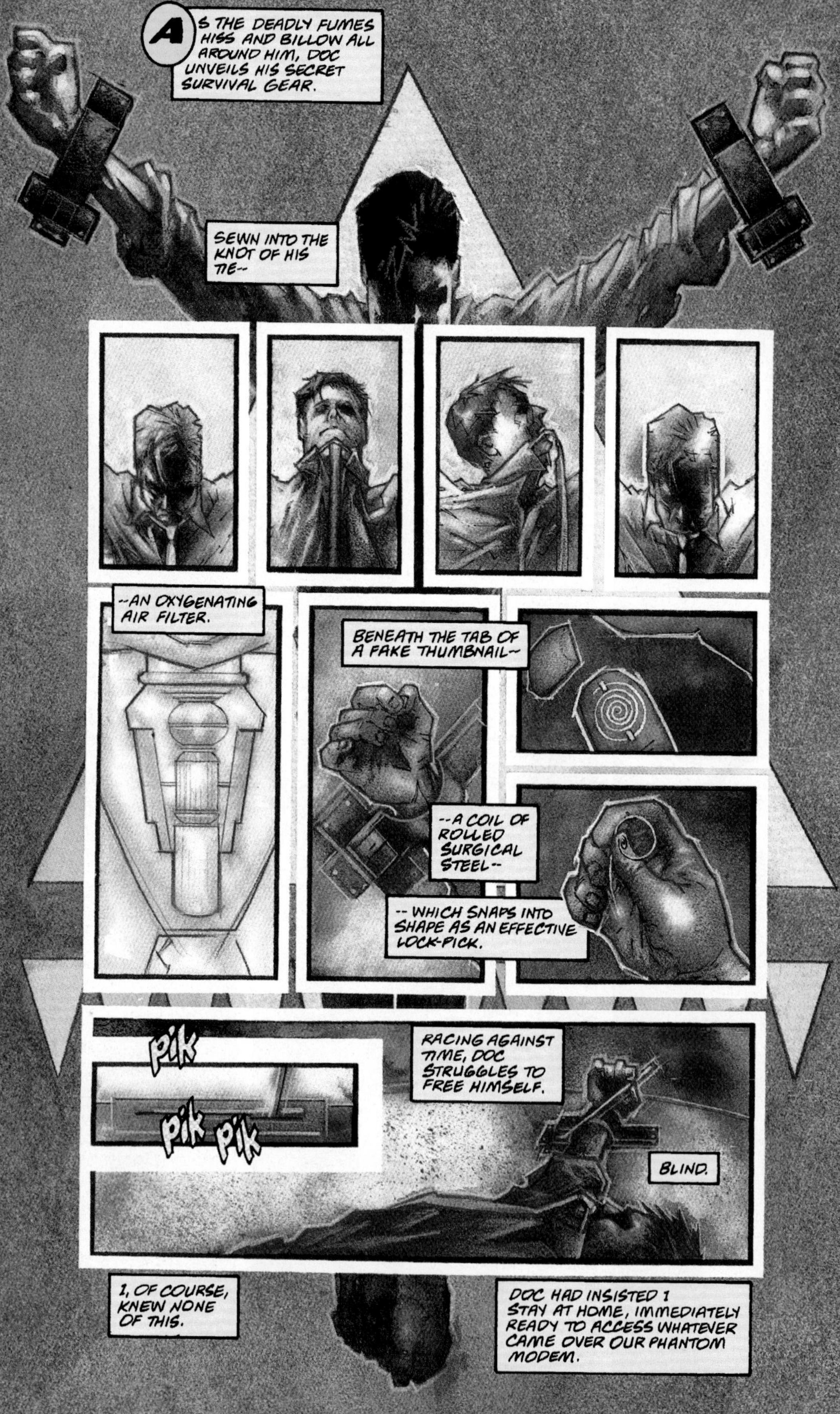
AS THE DEADLY FUMES HISS AND BILLOW ALL AROUND HIM, DOC UNVEILS HIS SECRET SURVIVAL GEAR.
SEWN INTO THE KNOT OF HIS TIE--
--AN OXYGENATING AIR FILTER.
BENEATH THE TAB OF A FAKE THUMBNAIL--
--A COIL OF ROLLED SURGICAL STEEL--
-- WHICH SNAPS INTO SHAPE AS AN EFFECTIVE LOCK-PICK.
pik
pik pik
RACING AGAINST TIME, DOC STRUGGLES TO FREE HIMSELF.
BLIND.
I, OF COURSE, KNEW NONE OF THIS.
DOC HAD INSISTED I STAY AT HOME, IMMEDIATELY READY TO ACCESS WHATEVER CAME OVER OUR PHANTOM MODEM.

**D**URING THE LENGTHY DOWNLOAD, I GO OUT FOR CIGARETTES AND STUFF.

I STARTED SMOKING WHEN I WAS TWELVE.

ONE OF MY ONLY FRIENDS, A FELLOW XENODERM, SHOWED ME HOW.

FOR YEARS, I'D BEEN FORCED TO STAY AWAY FROM BRIGHT LIGHTS, HOT THINGS.

NOW I WAS IN CONTROL.

PACK OF MENTHOLS, PLEASE?

NICOTINE HELPED EASE THE STRESS OF THE OCCASIONS I DID GET BURNED.

FOR YEARS, IT WAS BEST FOR WHAT AILED ME.

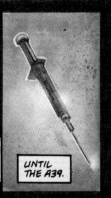UNTIL THE A39.

NO, THEY'VE GONE UP TO A BUCK-FORTY.

IN FACT, SINCE I'VE MET DOC... SINCE HE TOOK UP THIS NEW CRUSADE...

...I'VE BEEN AMAZED AT HOW CALM AND FOCUSED I'VE BECOME.

HIS TREATMENTS HAVE HELPED STRENGTHEN MY RESISTANCE. AND MY RESOLVE.

FOR THE FIRST TIME IN YEARS...

I'M DEEPLY CONCERNED ABOUT SOMETHING.

OTHER THAN MYSELF.

LET'S SEE THAT PROFILE!

WHAT TH-A-A-A-H-H!

YOU?! LARGO SHAM?! YOU'RE ALIVE?!

YESSS... YOU'RE THE ONE, ALL RIGHT.

AND THAT'S MORE THAN THEY'LL SOON SAY ABOUT YOU!

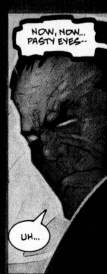NOW, NOW... PASTY EYES--

UH...

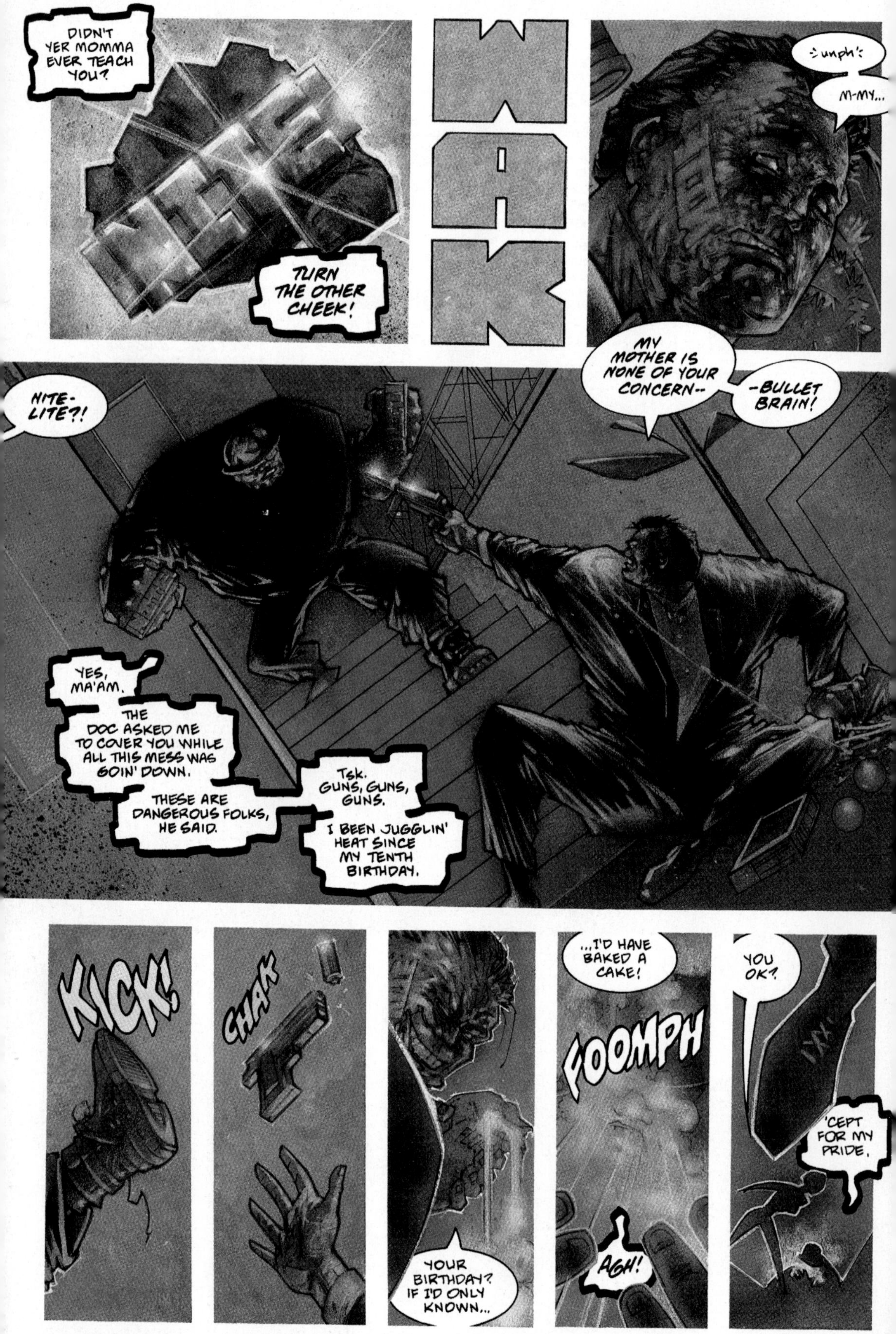
DIDN'T YER MOMMA EVER TEACH YOU?
TURN THE OTHER CHEEK!
WAK
unph
M-MY...
NITE-LITE?!
MY MOTHER IS NONE OF YOUR CONCERN--
-BULLET BRAIN!
YES, MA'AM.
THE DOC ASKED ME TO COVER YOU WHILE ALL THIS MESS WAS GOIN' DOWN.
THESE ARE DANGEROUS FOLKS, HE SAID.
Tsk. GUNS, GUNS, GUNS.
I BEEN JUGGLIN' HEAT SINCE MY TENTH BIRTHDAY.
KICK!
CHAK
YOUR BIRTHDAY? IF I'D ONLY KNOWN...
...I'D HAVE BAKED A CAKE!
FOOMPH
AGH!
YOU OK?
'CEPT FOR MY PRIDE.

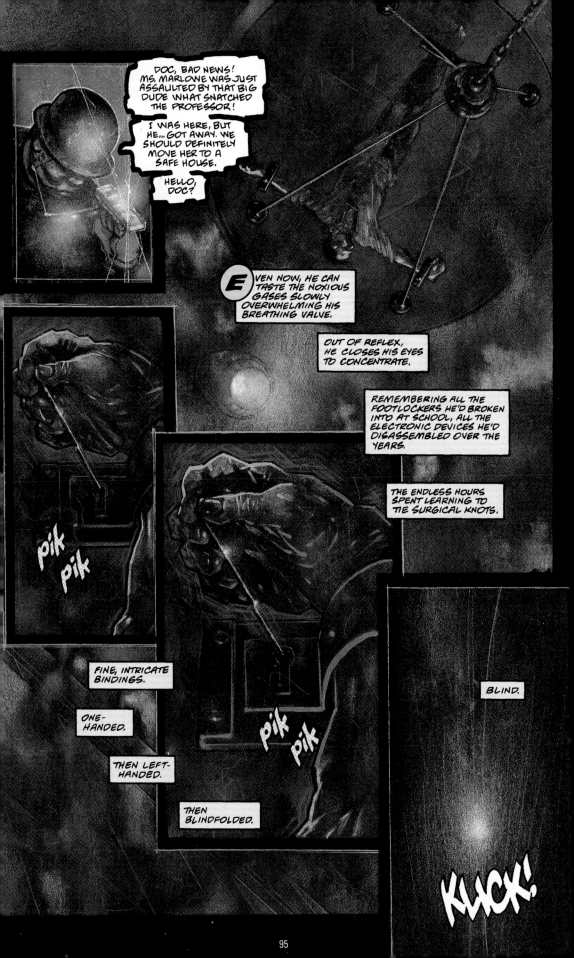

DOC, BAD NEWS! MS. MARLOWE WAS JUST ASSAULTED BY THAT BIG DUDE WHAT SNATCHED THE PROFESSOR!

I WAS HERE, BUT HE... GOT AWAY. WE SHOULD DEFINITELY MOVE HER TO A SAFE HOUSE.

HELLO, DOC?

EVEN NOW, HE CAN TASTE THE NOXIOUS GASES SLOWLY OVERWHELMING HIS BREATHING VALVE.

OUT OF REFLEX, HE CLOSES HIS EYES TO CONCENTRATE.

REMEMBERING ALL THE FOOTLOCKERS HE'D BROKEN INTO AT SCHOOL, ALL THE ELECTRONIC DEVICES HE'D DISASSEMBLED OVER THE YEARS.

THE ENDLESS HOURS SPENT LEARNING TO TIE SURGICAL KNOTS.

pik pik

FINE, INTRICATE BINDINGS.

ONE-HANDED.

THEN LEFT-HANDED.

THEN BLINDFOLDED.

pik pik

BLIND.

KLICK!

95

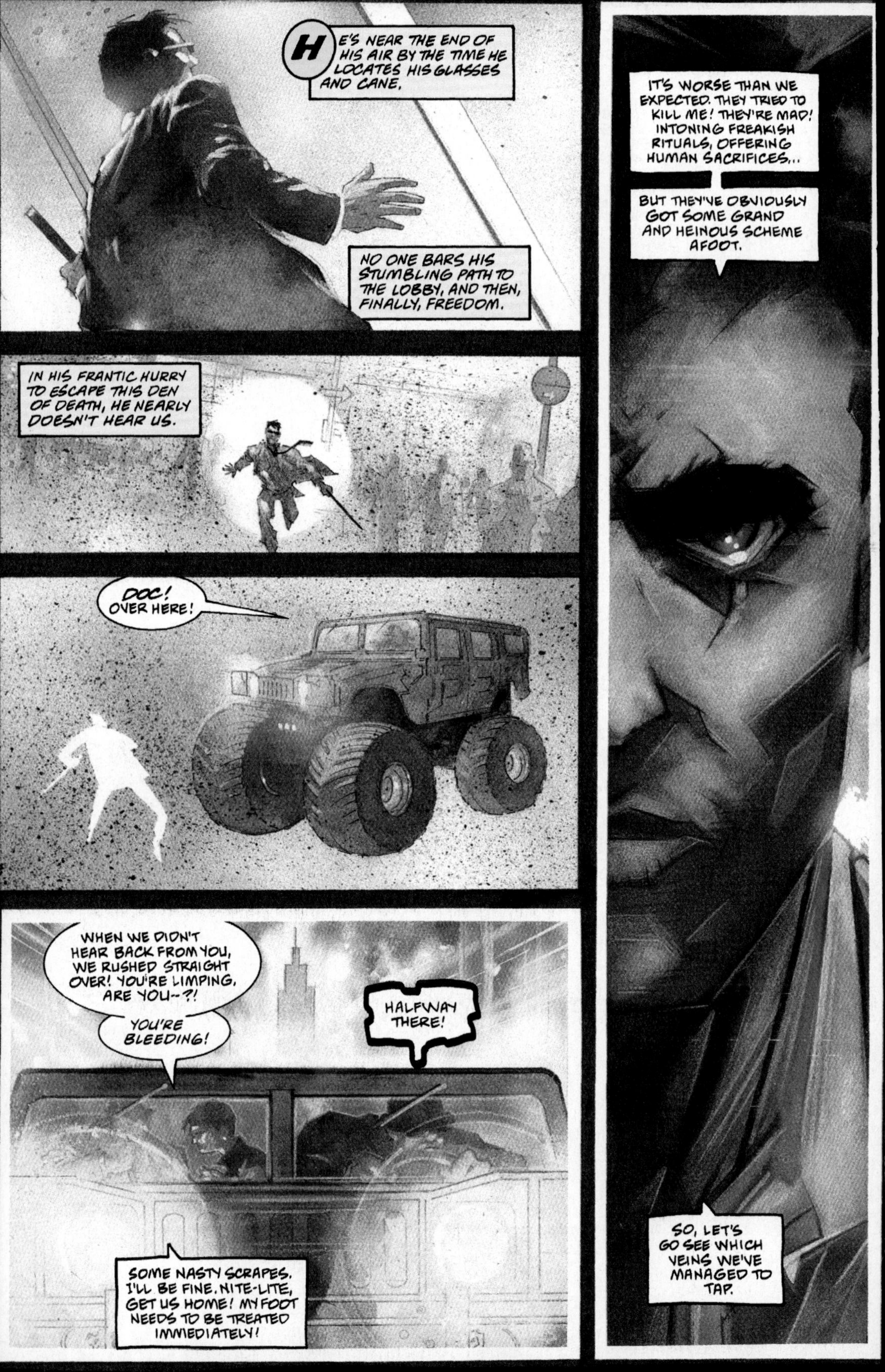

HE'S NEAR THE END OF HIS AIR BY THE TIME HE LOCATES HIS GLASSES AND CANE.
NO ONE BARS HIS STUMBLING PATH TO THE LOBBY, AND THEN, FINALLY, FREEDOM.
IN HIS FRANTIC HURRY TO ESCAPE THIS DEN OF DEATH, HE NEARLY DOESN'T HEAR US.
DOC! OVER HERE!
WHEN WE DIDN'T HEAR BACK FROM YOU, WE RUSHED STRAIGHT OVER! YOU'RE LIMPING, ARE YOU--?!
YOU'RE BLEEDING!
HALFWAY THERE!
SOME NASTY SCRAPES. I'LL BE FINE. NITE-LITE, GET US HOME! MY FOOT NEEDS TO BE TREATED IMMEDIATELY!
IT'S WORSE THAN WE EXPECTED. THEY TRIED TO KILL ME! THEY'RE MAD! INTONING FREAKISH RITUALS, OFFERING HUMAN SACRIFICES...
BUT THEY'VE OBVIOUSLY GOT SOME GRAND AND HEINOUS SCHEME AFOOT.
SO, LET'S GO SEE WHICH VEINS WE'VE MANAGED TO TAP.

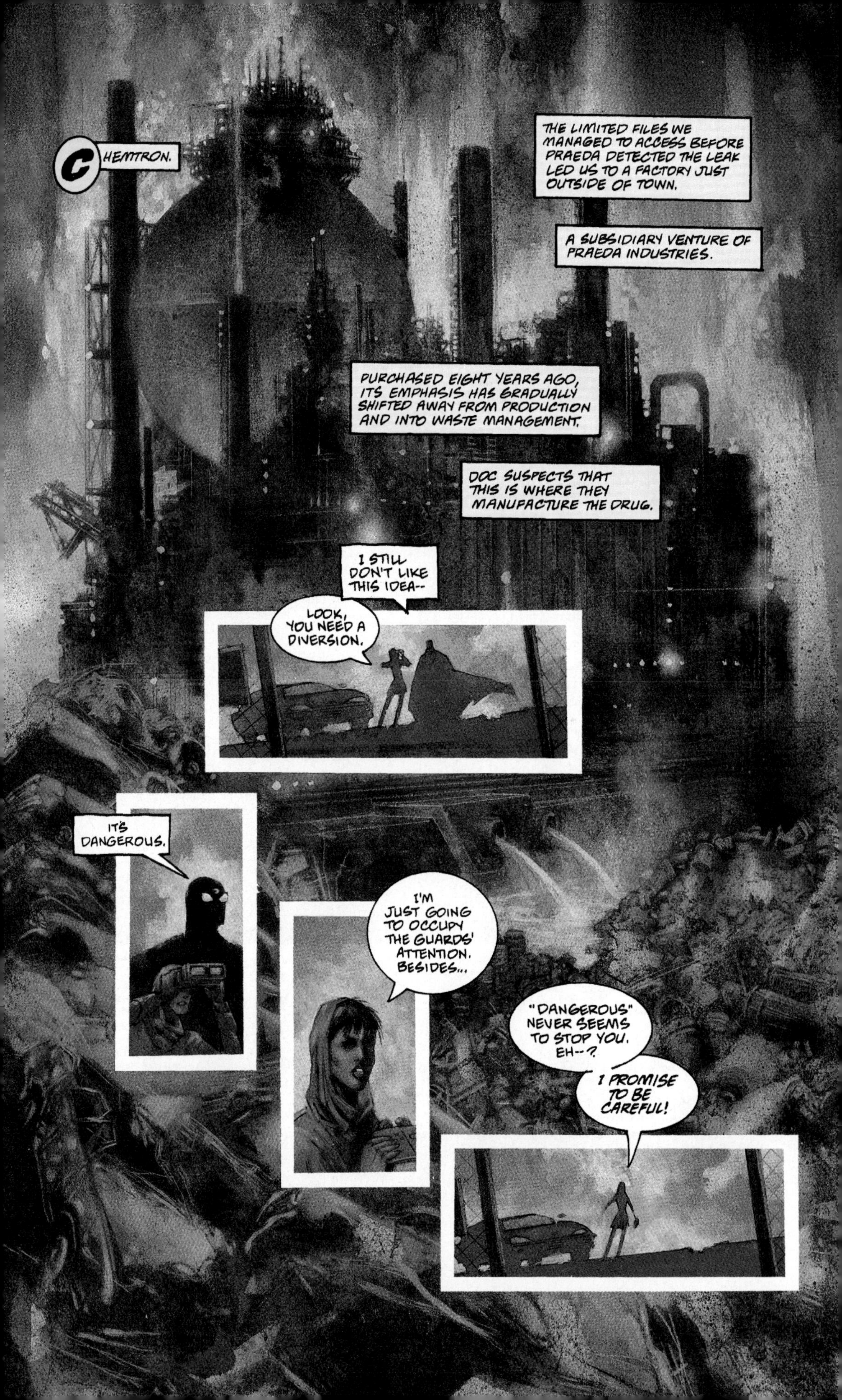
CHEMTRON.
THE LIMITED FILES WE MANAGED TO ACCESS BEFORE PRAEDA DETECTED THE LEAK LED US TO A FACTORY JUST OUTSIDE OF TOWN.
A SUBSIDIARY VENTURE OF PRAEDA INDUSTRIES.
PURCHASED EIGHT YEARS AGO, ITS EMPHASIS HAS GRADUALLY SHIFTED AWAY FROM PRODUCTION AND INTO WASTE MANAGEMENT.
DOC SUSPECTS THAT THIS IS WHERE THEY MANUFACTURE THE DRUG.
I STILL DON'T LIKE THIS IDEA--
LOOK, YOU NEED A DIVERSION.
IT'S DANGEROUS.
I'M JUST GOING TO OCCUPY THE GUARDS' ATTENTION. BESIDES...
"DANGEROUS" NEVER SEEMS TO STOP YOU. EH--?
I PROMISE TO BE CAREFUL!

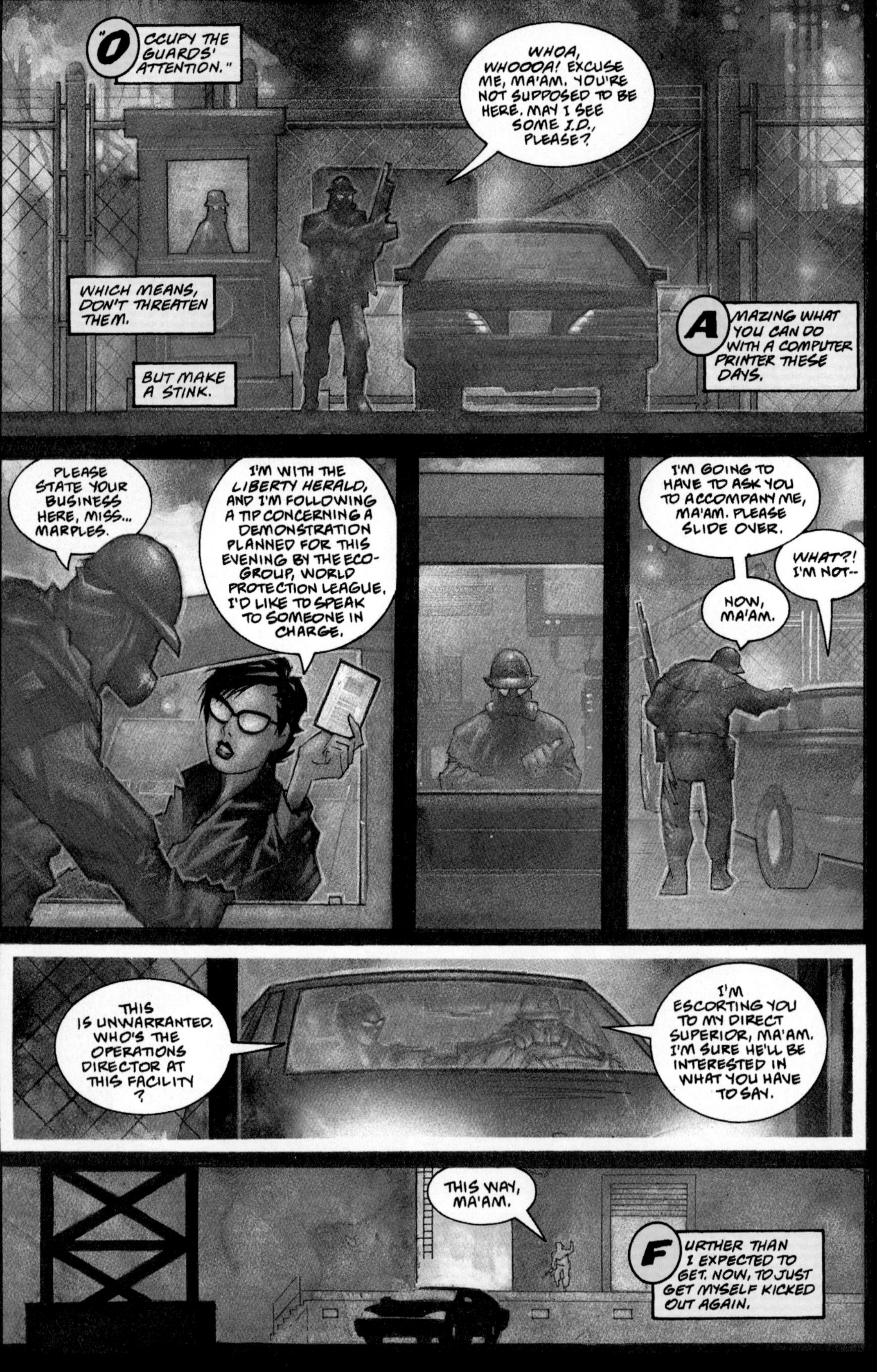
"OCCUPY THE GUARDS' ATTENTION."
WHOA, WHOOOA! EXCUSE ME, MA'AM. YOU'RE NOT SUPPOSED TO BE HERE. MAY I SEE SOME I.D., PLEASE?
WHICH MEANS, DON'T THREATEN THEM.
BUT MAKE A STINK.
AMAZING WHAT YOU CAN DO WITH A COMPUTER PRINTER THESE DAYS.
PLEASE STATE YOUR BUSINESS HERE, MISS... MARPLES.
I'M WITH THE LIBERTY HERALD, AND I'M FOLLOWING A TIP CONCERNING A DEMONSTRATION PLANNED FOR THIS EVENING BY THE ECO-GROUP, WORLD PROTECTION LEAGUE. I'D LIKE TO SPEAK TO SOMEONE IN CHARGE.
I'M GOING TO HAVE TO ASK YOU TO ACCOMPANY ME, MA'AM. PLEASE SLIDE OVER.
WHAT?! I'M NOT--
NOW, MA'AM.
THIS IS UNWARRANTED. WHO'S THE OPERATIONS DIRECTOR AT THIS FACILITY?
I'M ESCORTING YOU TO MY DIRECT SUPERIOR, MA'AM. I'M SURE HE'LL BE INTERESTED IN WHAT YOU HAVE TO SAY.
THIS WAY, MA'AM.
FURTHER THAN I EXPECTED TO GET. NOW, TO JUST GET MYSELF KICKED OUT AGAIN.

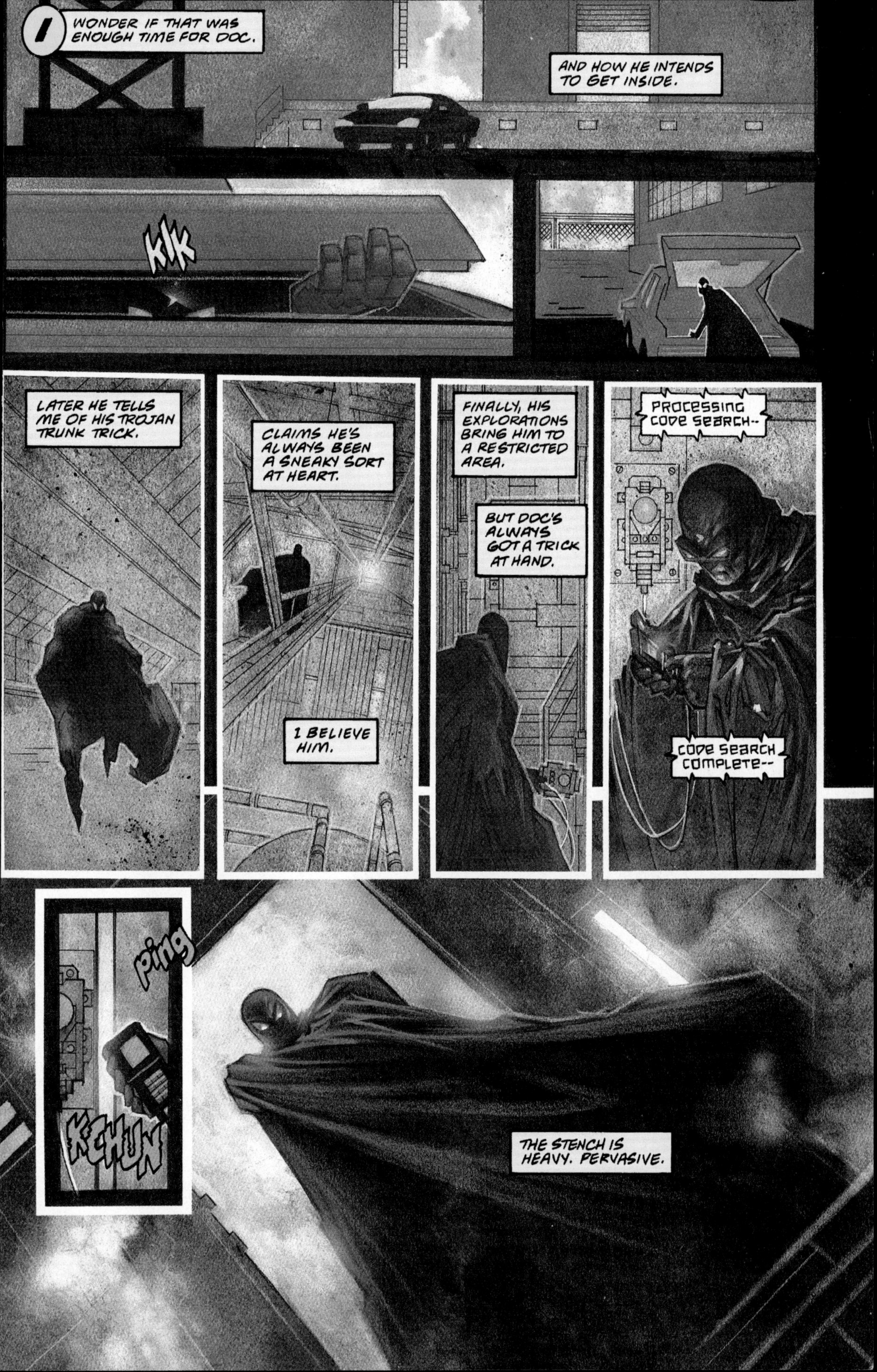
I WONDER IF THAT WAS ENOUGH TIME FOR DOC.
AND HOW HE INTENDS TO GET INSIDE.
KLK
LATER HE TELLS ME OF HIS TROJAN TRUNK TRICK.
CLAIMS HE'S ALWAYS BEEN A SNEAKY SORT AT HEART.
I BELIEVE HIM.
FINALLY, HIS EXPLORATIONS BRING HIM TO A RESTRICTED AREA.
BUT DOC'S ALWAYS GOT A TRICK AT HAND.
PROCESSING CODE SEARCH--
CODE SEARCH COMPLETE--
PING
K-CHUN
THE STENCH IS HEAVY. PERVASIVE.

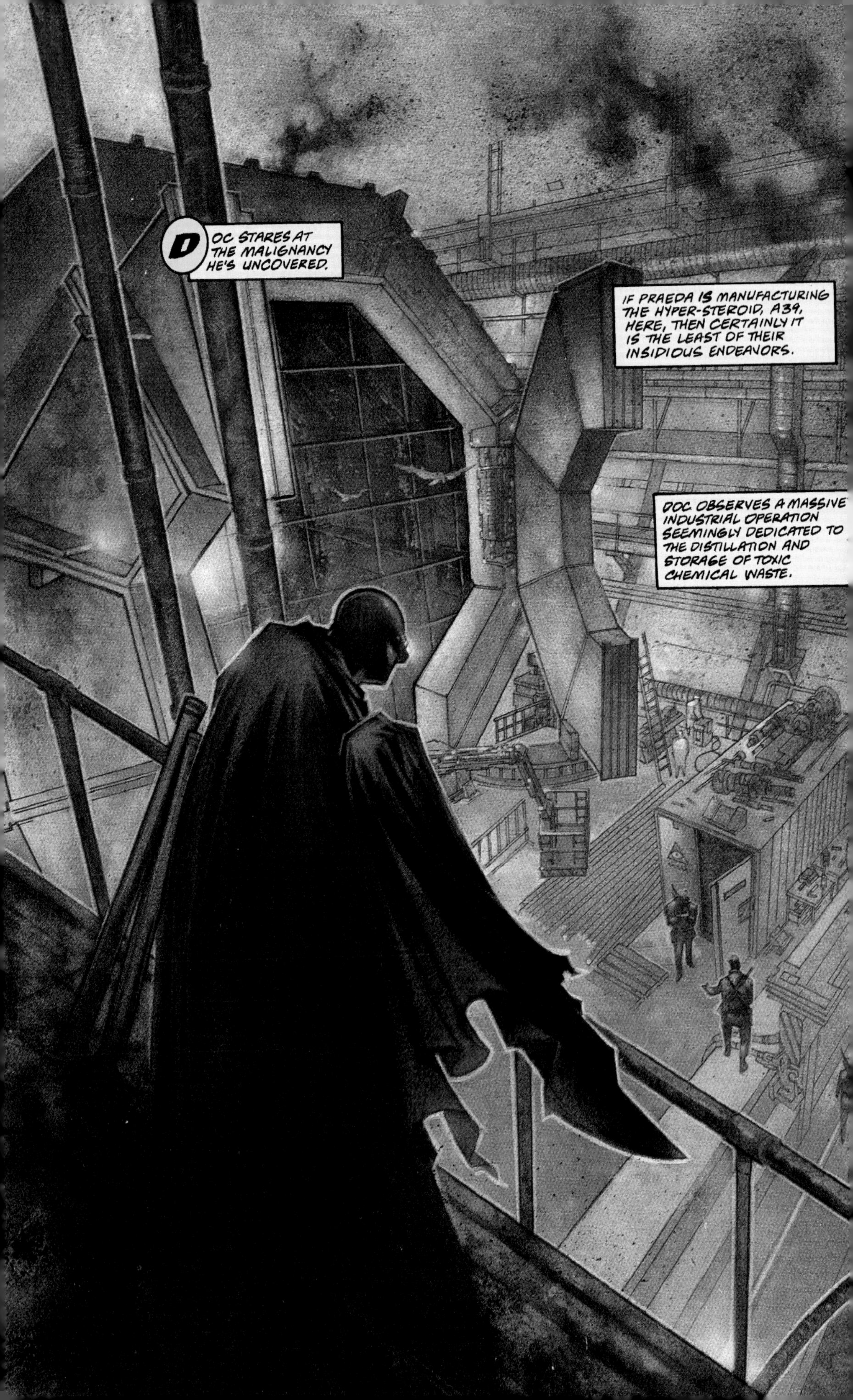
DOC STARES AT THE MALIGNANCY HE'S UNCOVERED.
IF PRAEDA IS MANUFACTURING THE HYPER-STEROID, A39, HERE, THEN CERTAINLY IT IS THE LEAST OF THEIR INSIDIOUS ENDEAVORS.
DOC OBSERVES A MASSIVE INDUSTRIAL OPERATION SEEMINGLY DEDICATED TO THE DISTILLATION AND STORAGE OF TOXIC CHEMICAL WASTE.

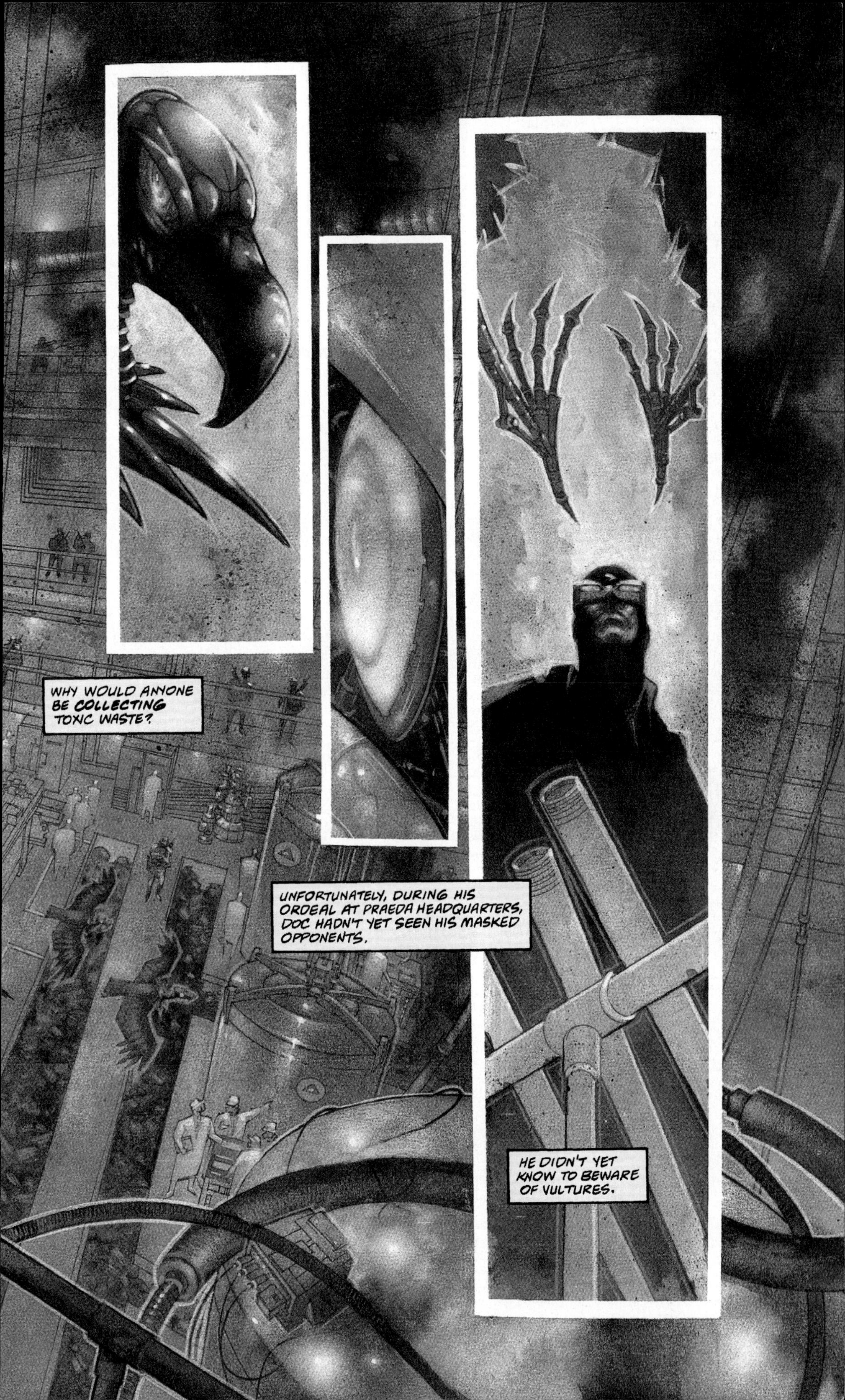
WHY WOULD ANYONE BE COLLECTING TOXIC WASTE?
UNFORTUNATELY, DURING HIS ORDEAL AT PRAEDA HEADQUARTERS, DOC HADN'T YET SEEN HIS MASKED OPPONENTS.
HE DIDN'T YET KNOW TO BEWARE OF VULTURES.

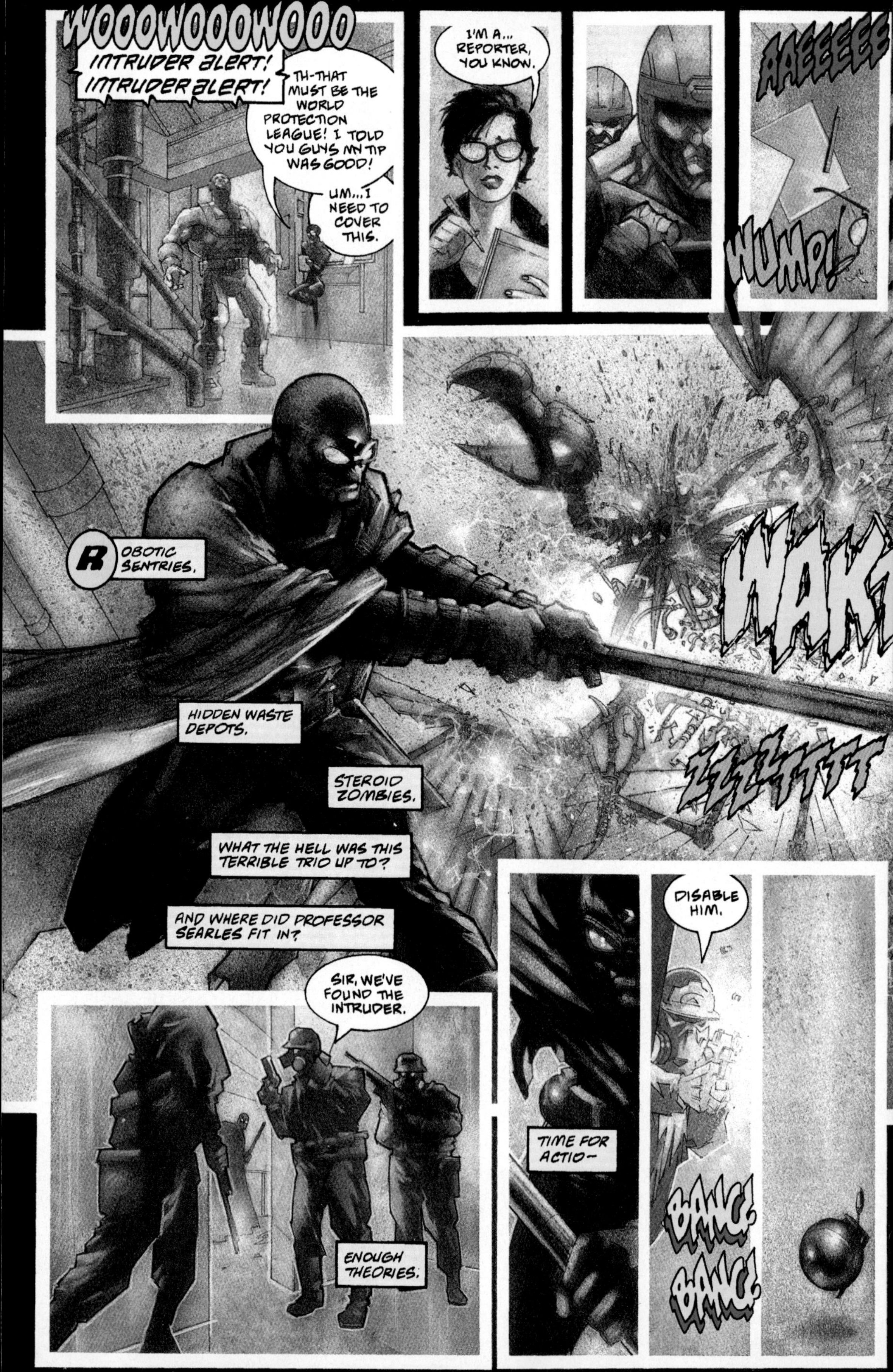
WOOOWOOOWOOO
INTRUDER ALERT! INTRUDER ALERT!
TH-THAT MUST BE THE WORLD PROTECTION LEAGUE! I TOLD YOU GUYS MY TIP WAS GOOD!
UM... I NEED TO COVER THIS.
I'M A... REPORTER, YOU KNOW.
AAEEEEE
WUMP!
ROBOTIC SENTRIES.
WAK
HIDDEN WASTE DEPOTS.
ZZZZTTTT
STEROID ZOMBIES.
WHAT THE HELL WAS THIS TERRIBLE TRIO UP TO?
AND WHERE DID PROFESSOR SEARLES FIT IN?
SIR, WE'VE FOUND THE INTRUDER.
ENOUGH THEORIES.
DISABLE HIM.
TIME FOR ACTIO—
BANG! BANG!

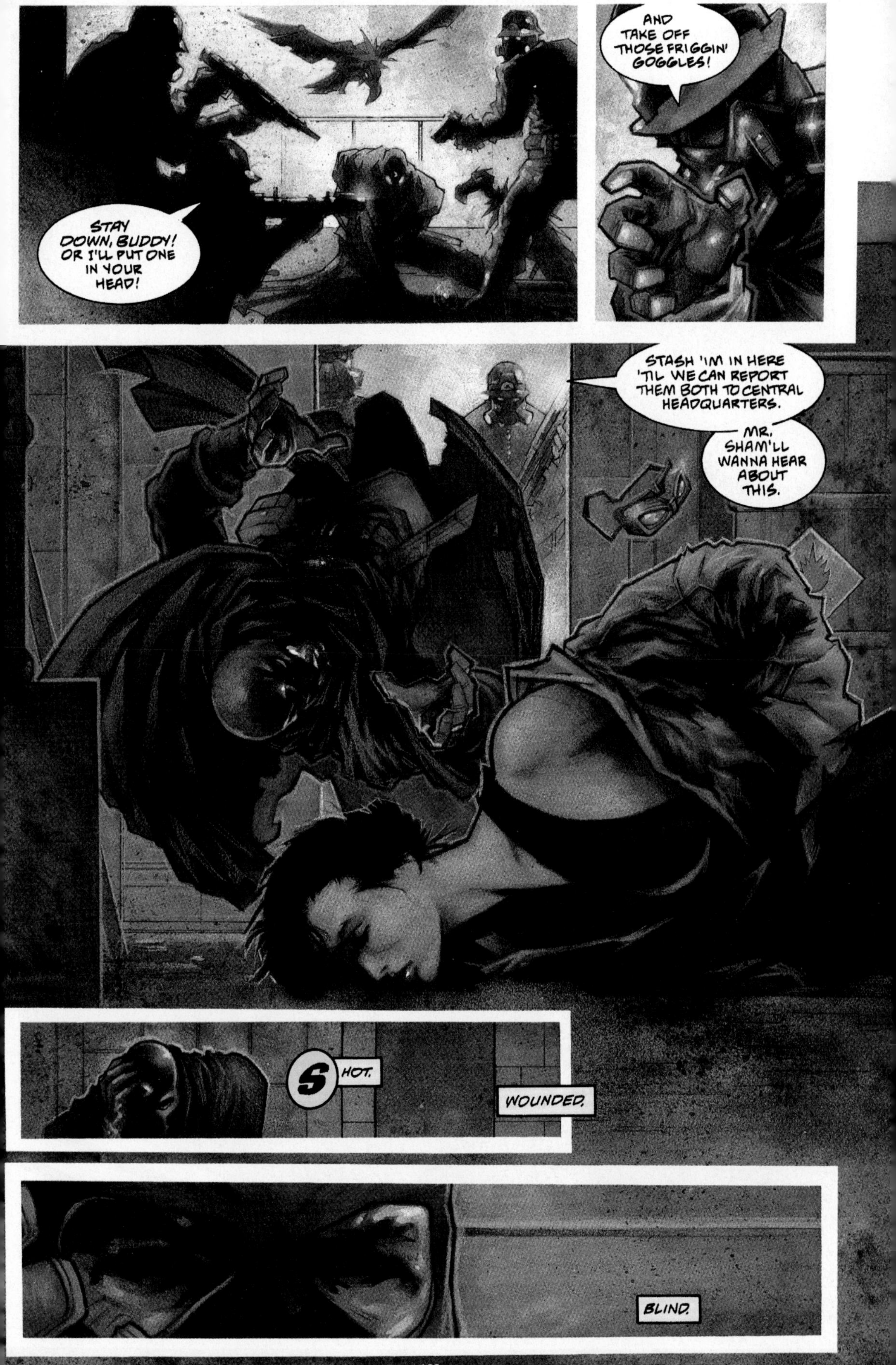
STAY DOWN, BUDDY! OR I'LL PUT ONE IN YOUR HEAD!
AND TAKE OFF THOSE FRIGGIN' GOGGLES!
STASH 'IM IN HERE 'TIL WE CAN REPORT THEM BOTH TO CENTRAL HEADQUARTERS.
MR. SHAM'LL WANNA HEAR ABOUT THIS.
SHOT.
WOUNDED.
BLIND.

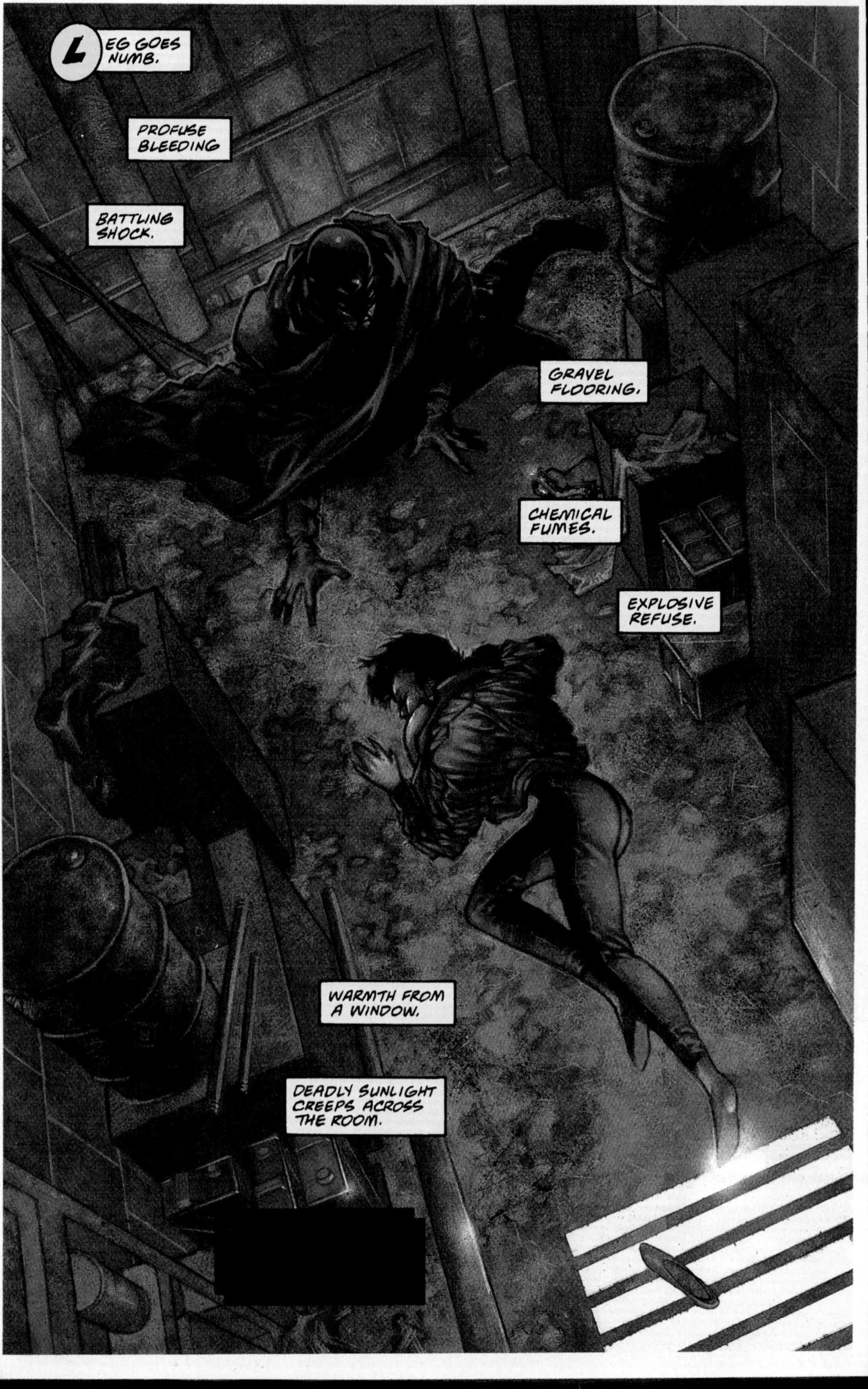
LEG GOES NUMB.
PROFUSE BLEEDING
BATTLING SHOCK.
GRAVEL FLOORING.
CHEMICAL FUMES.
EXPLOSIVE REFUSE.
WARMTH FROM A WINDOW.
DEADLY SUNLIGHT CREEPS ACROSS THE ROOM.
[redacted]

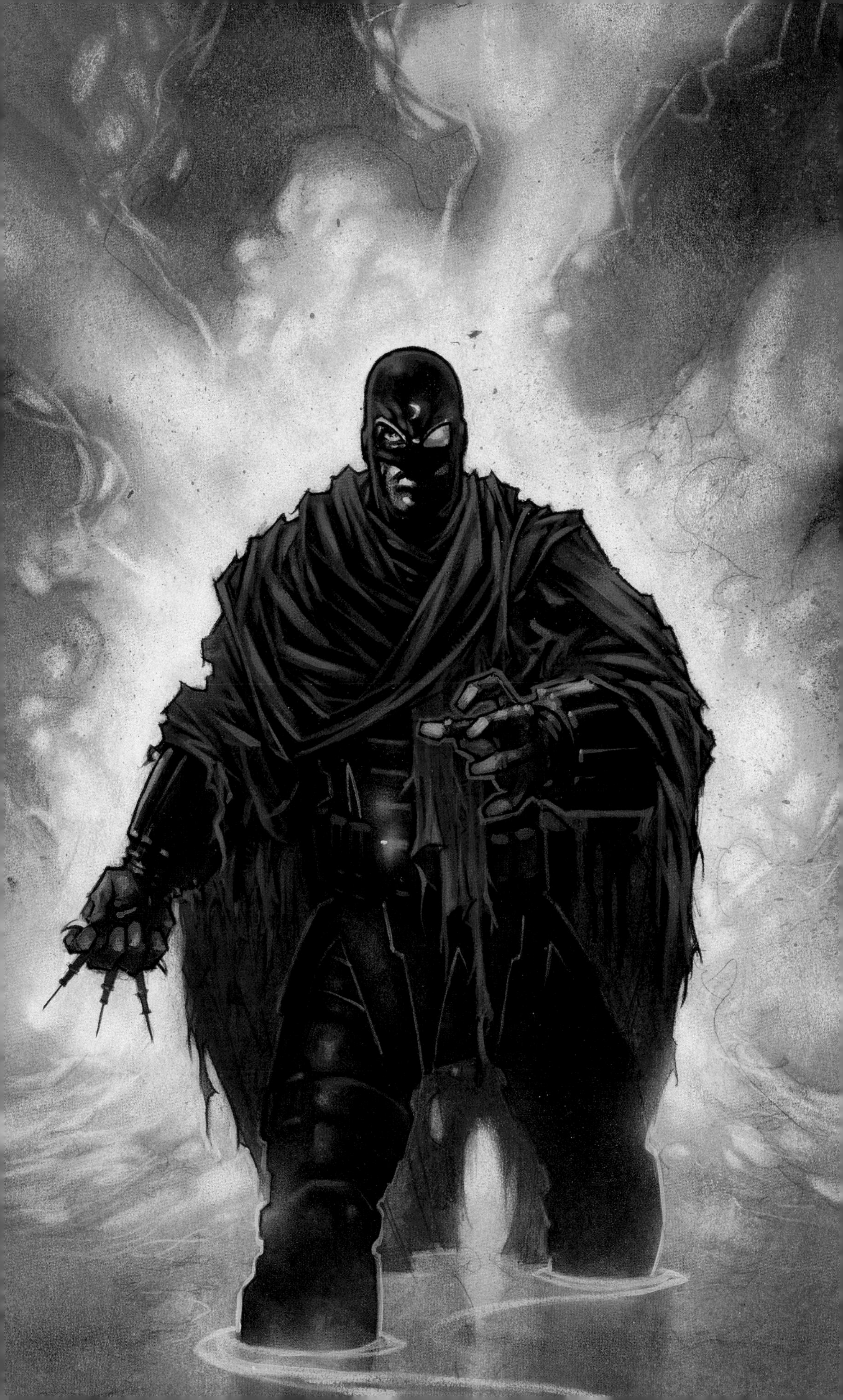

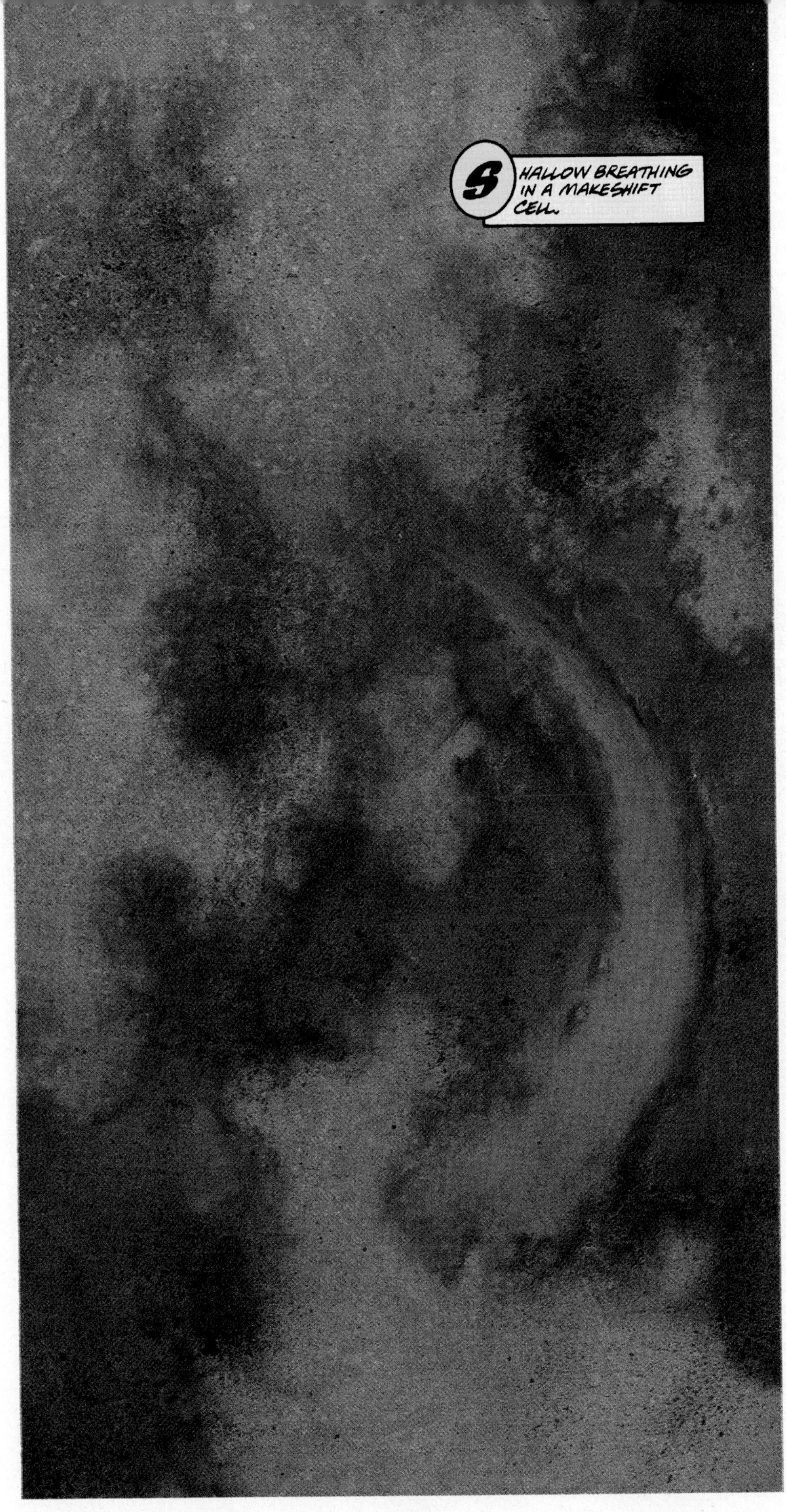
SHALLOW BREATHING IN A MAKESHIFT CELL.

 BOVE THE STENCH OF CHEMICAL FUMES, DOC CAN SMELL MY SHAMPOO.

AS WELL AS THE ACRID SCENT OF HIS OWN BLOOD.

THE GUNSHOT WOUND THROBS IN HIS LEG LIKE A TURBINE.

BENEATH THE SUN'S DEADLY TOUCH, MY SKIN BEGINS TO SCORCH.

NO TIME TO LOSE.

WITHOUT A PAUSE, DOC SETS ABOUT TREATING HIS INJURY.

A SELF-TIGHTENING TOURNIQUET STAUNCHES THE BLOODFLOW.

MORPHINE DEADENS THE PAIN.

THE BLOOD SLACKENS. NO MAJOR ARTERIES DAMAGED.

EVEN THROUGH THE OPIATE, DOC GRIMACES AS HE PROBES DEEP INSIDE HIS OWN LEG.

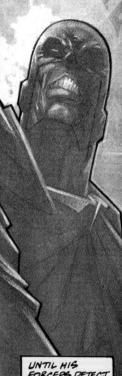

UNTIL HIS FORCEPS DETECT A SCRAPE.

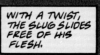 WITH A TWIST, THE SLUG SLIDES FREE OF HIS FLESH.

 BLIND.

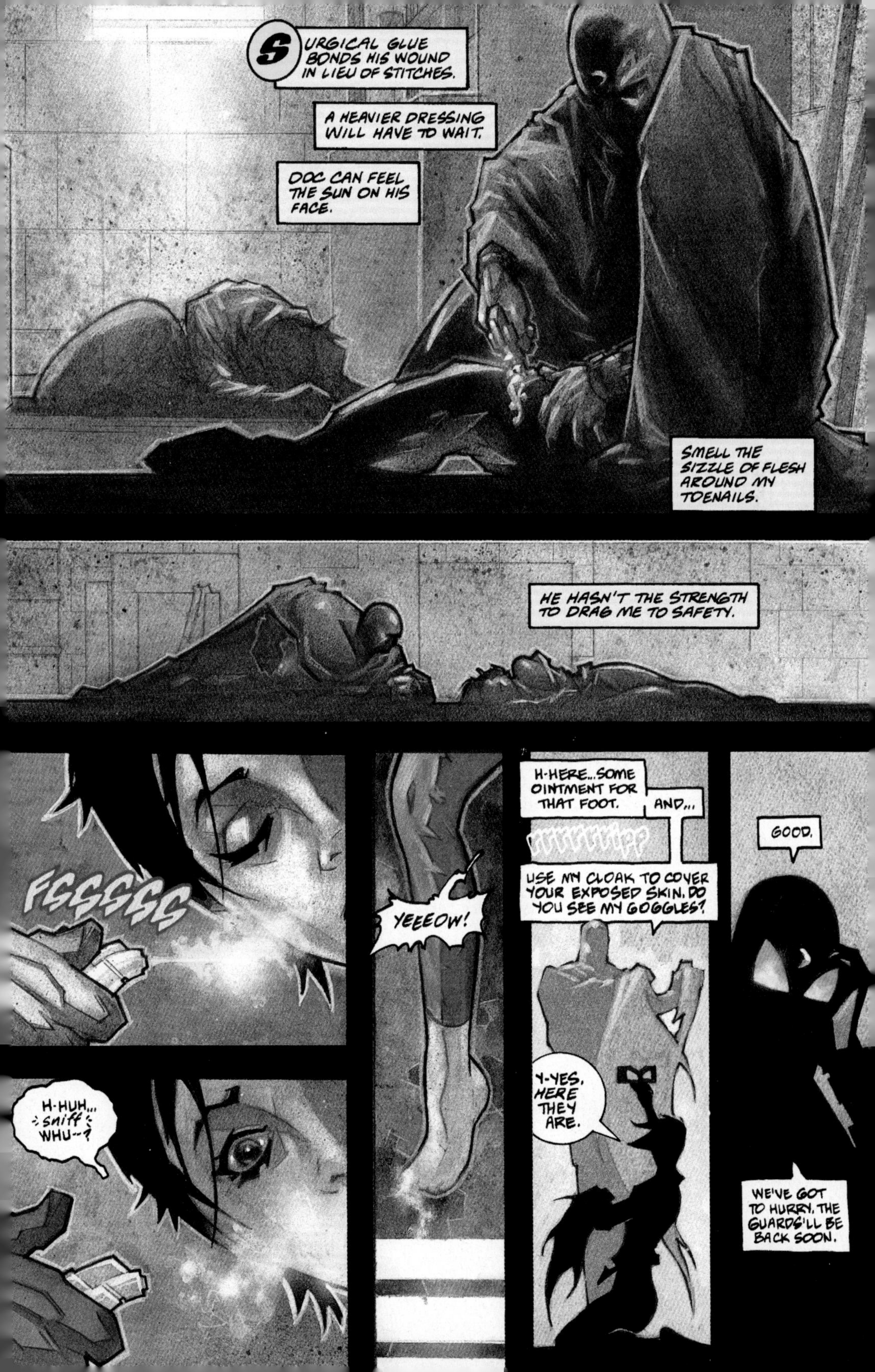
SURGICAL GLUE BONDS HIS WOUND IN LIEU OF STITCHES.
A HEAVIER DRESSING WILL HAVE TO WAIT.
DOC CAN FEEL THE SUN ON HIS FACE.
SMELL THE SIZZLE OF FLESH AROUND MY TOENAILS.
HE HASN'T THE STRENGTH TO DRAG ME TO SAFETY.
FSSSSS
H-HUH... sniff WHU--?
YEEEOW!
H-HERE... SOME OINTMENT FOR THAT FOOT.
AND...
RRRRRRIPP
USE MY CLOAK TO COVER YOUR EXPOSED SKIN. DO YOU SEE MY GOGGLES?
Y-YES, HERE THEY ARE.
GOOD.
WE'VE GOT TO HURRY. THE GUARDS'LL BE BACK SOON.

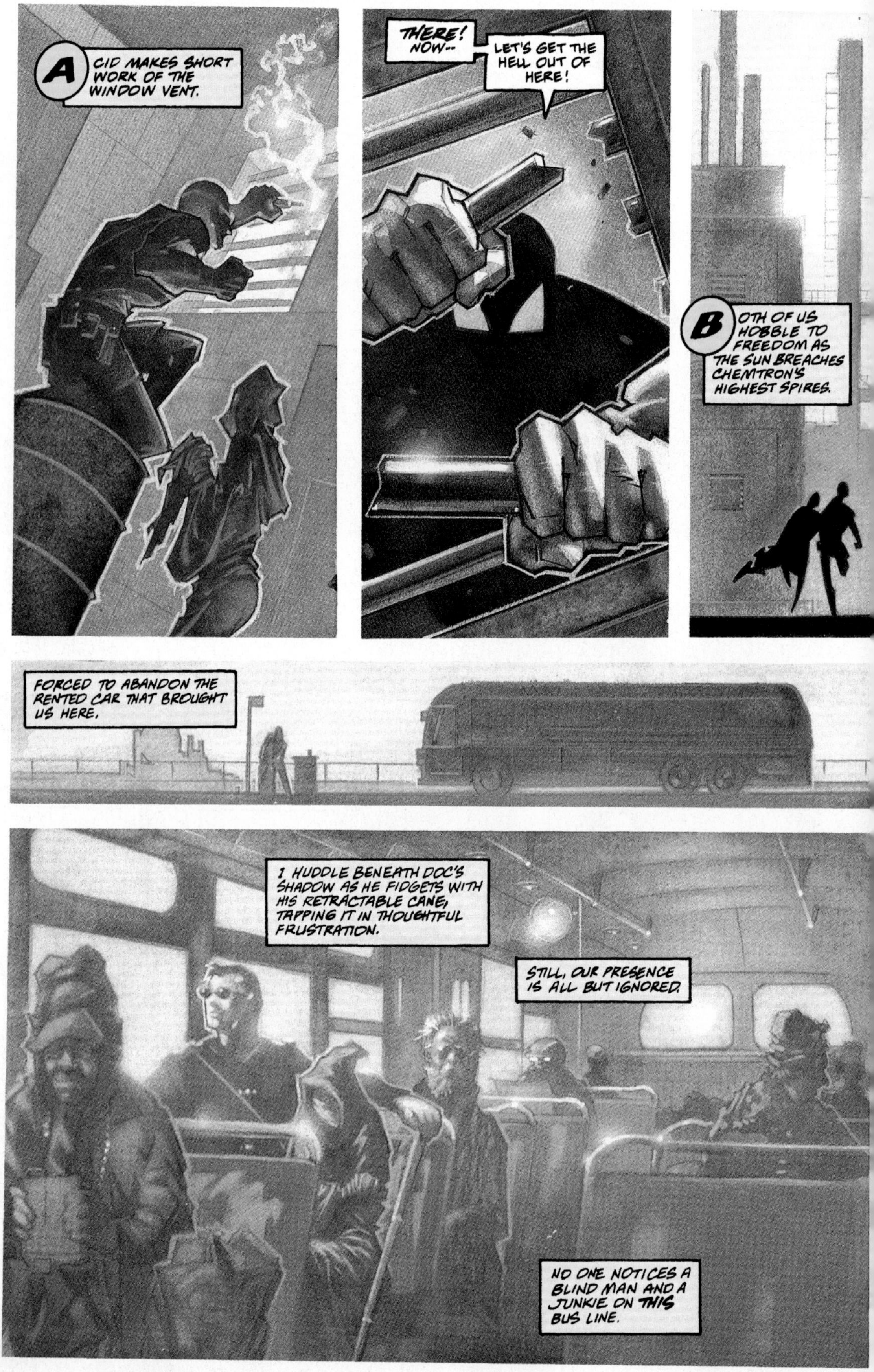
ACID MAKES SHORT WORK OF THE WINDOW VENT.
THERE! NOW--
LET'S GET THE HELL OUT OF HERE!
BOTH OF US HOBBLE TO FREEDOM AS THE SUN BREACHES CHEMTRON'S HIGHEST SPIRES.
FORCED TO ABANDON THE RENTED CAR THAT BROUGHT US HERE.
I HUDDLE BENEATH DOC'S SHADOW AS HE FIDGETS WITH HIS RETRACTABLE CANE, TAPPING IT IN THOUGHTFUL FRUSTRATION.
STILL, OUR PRESENCE IS ALL BUT IGNORED.
NO ONE NOTICES A BLIND MAN AND A JUNKIE ON THIS BUS LINE.

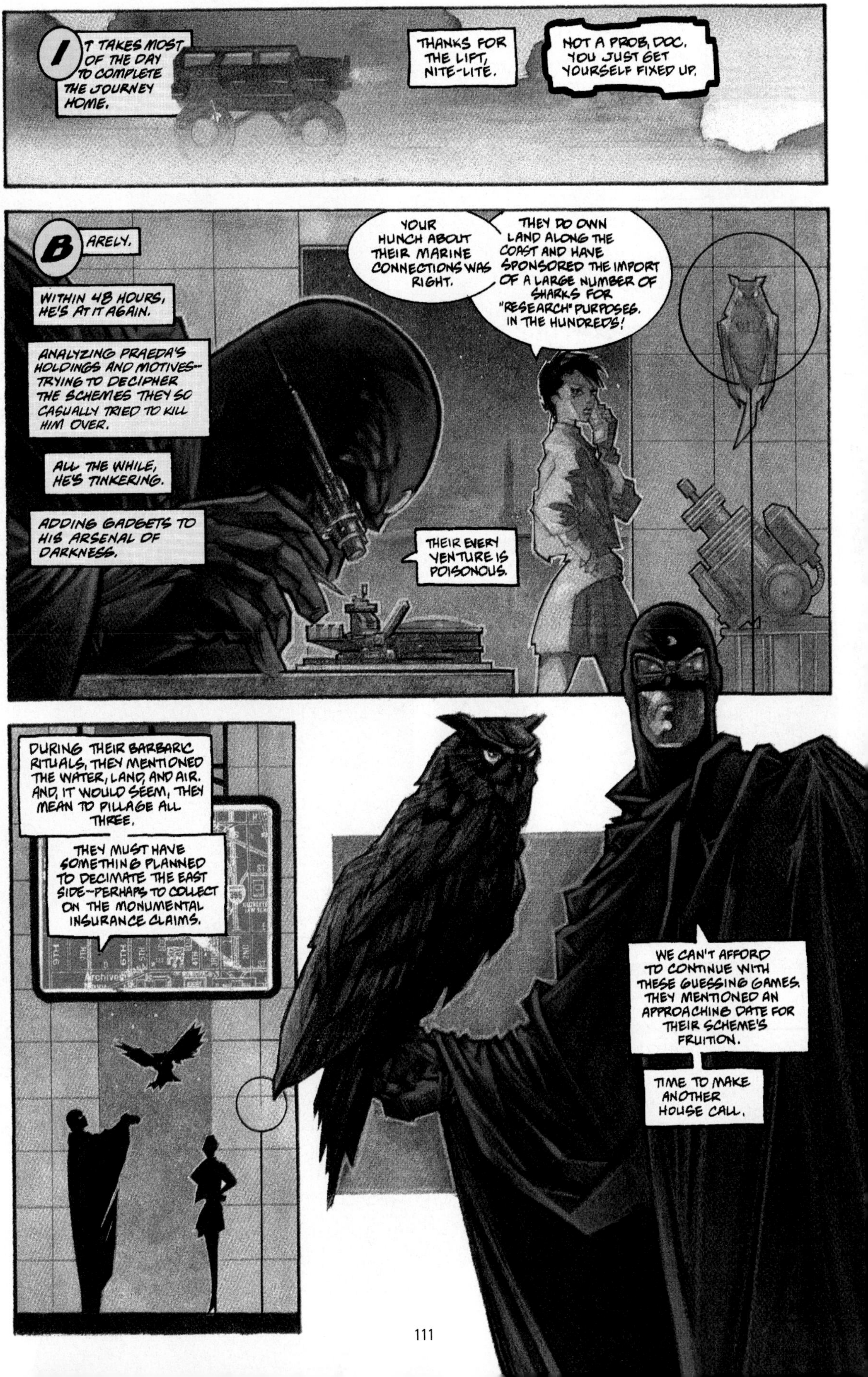
IT TAKES MOST OF THE DAY TO COMPLETE THE JOURNEY HOME.
THANKS FOR THE LIFT, NITE-LITE.
NOT A PROB, DOC. YOU JUST GET YOURSELF FIXED UP.
BARELY.
WITHIN 48 HOURS, HE'S AT IT AGAIN.
ANALYZING PRAEDA'S HOLDINGS AND MOTIVES-- TRYING TO DECIPHER THE SCHEMES THEY SO CASUALLY TRIED TO KILL HIM OVER.
ALL THE WHILE, HE'S TINKERING.
ADDING GADGETS TO HIS ARSENAL OF DARKNESS.
YOUR HUNCH ABOUT THEIR MARINE CONNECTIONS WAS RIGHT.
THEY DO OWN LAND ALONG THE COAST AND HAVE SPONSORED THE IMPORT OF A LARGE NUMBER OF SHARKS FOR "RESEARCH" PURPOSES. IN THE HUNDREDS!
THEIR EVERY VENTURE IS POISONOUS.
DURING THEIR BARBARIC RITUALS, THEY MENTIONED THE WATER, LAND, AND AIR. AND, IT WOULD SEEM, THEY MEAN TO PILLAGE ALL THREE.
THEY MUST HAVE SOMETHING PLANNED TO DECIMATE THE EAST SIDE--PERHAPS TO COLLECT ON THE MONUMENTAL INSURANCE CLAIMS.
WE CAN'T AFFORD TO CONTINUE WITH THESE GUESSING GAMES. THEY MENTIONED AN APPROACHING DATE FOR THEIR SCHEME'S FRUITION.
TIME TO MAKE ANOTHER HOUSE CALL.

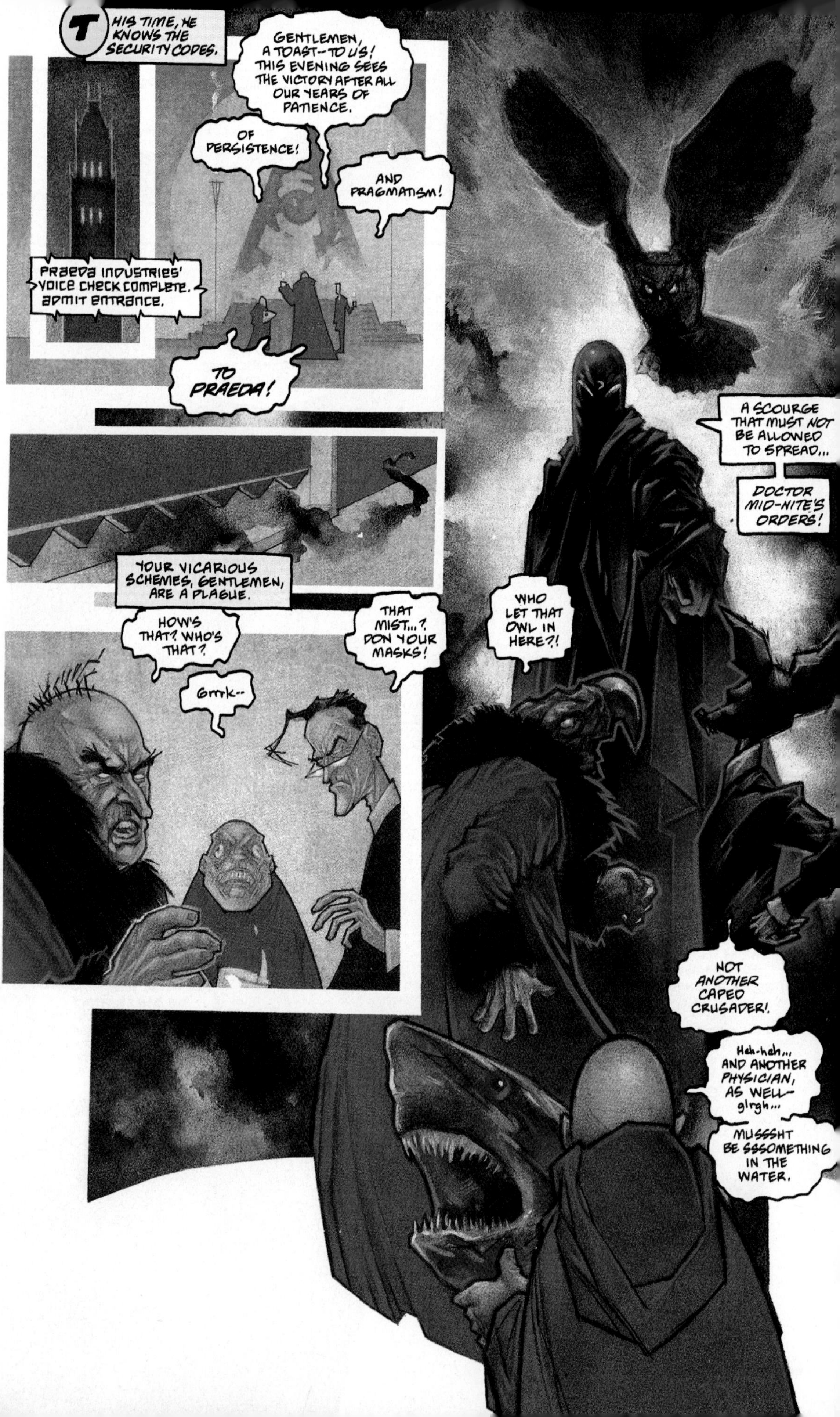
THIS TIME, HE KNOWS THE SECURITY CODES.
GENTLEMEN, A TOAST--TO US! THIS EVENING SEES THE VICTORY AFTER ALL OUR YEARS OF PATIENCE.
OF PERSISTENCE!
AND PRAGMATISM!
PRAEDA INDUSTRIES' VOICE CHECK COMPLETE. ADMIT ENTRANCE.
TO PRAEDA!
YOUR VICARIOUS SCHEMES, GENTLEMEN, ARE A PLAGUE.
HOW'S THAT? WHO'S THAT?
THAT MIST...? DON YOUR MASKS!
Grrrk--
A SCOURGE THAT MUST NOT BE ALLOWED TO SPREAD...
DOCTOR MID-NITE'S ORDERS!
WHO LET THAT OWL IN HERE?!
NOT ANOTHER CAPED CRUSADER!
Heh-heh... AND ANOTHER PHYSICIAN, AS WELL-- glrgh...
MUSSSHT BE SSSOMETHING IN THE WATER.

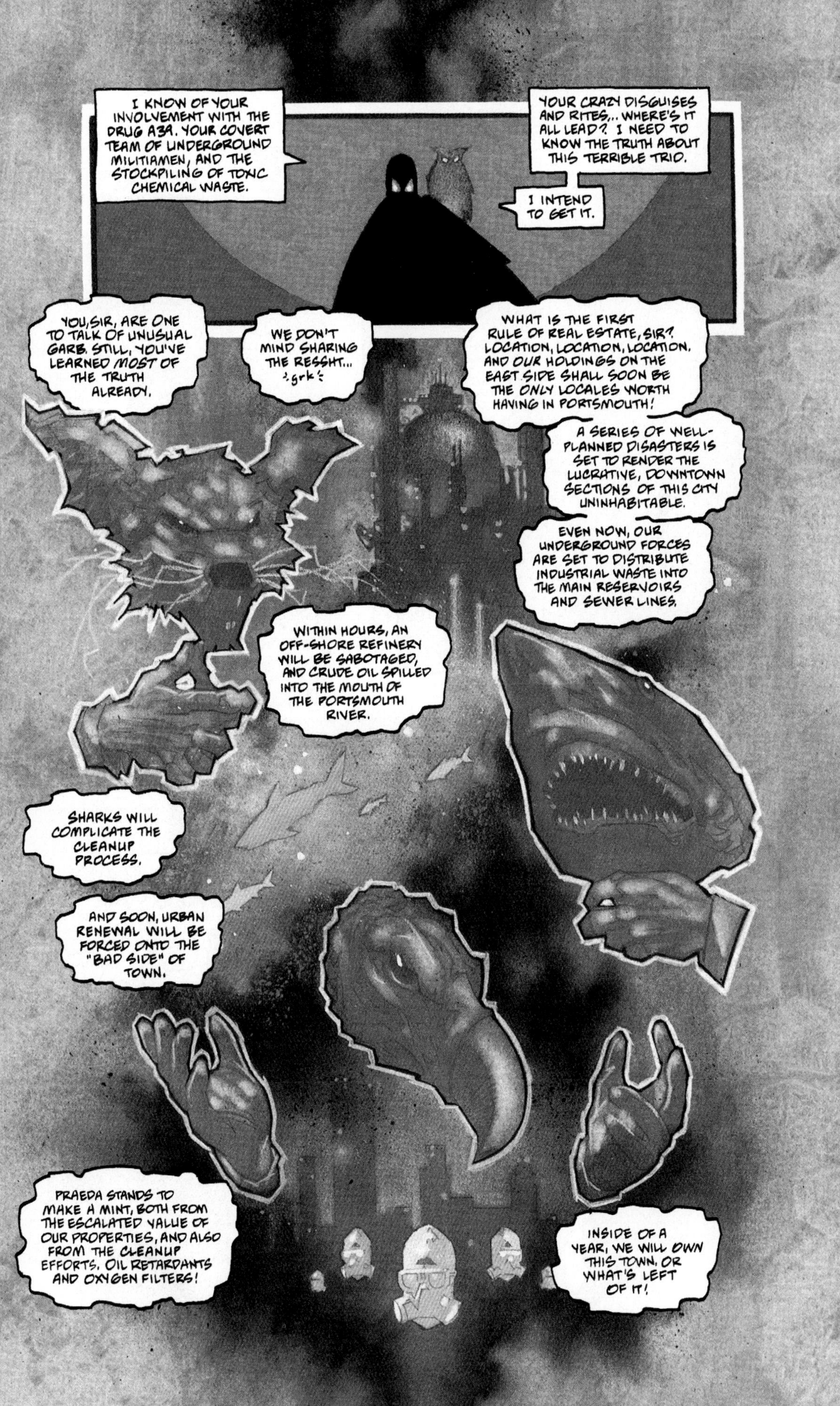
I KNOW OF YOUR INVOLVEMENT WITH THE DRUG A39. YOUR COVERT TEAM OF UNDERGROUND MILITIAMEN, AND THE STOCKPILING OF TOXIC CHEMICAL WASTE.
YOUR CRAZY DISGUISES AND RITES... WHERE'S IT ALL LEAD? I NEED TO KNOW THE TRUTH ABOUT THIS TERRIBLE TRIO.
I INTEND TO GET IT.
YOU, SIR, ARE ONE TO TALK OF UNUSUAL GARB. STILL, YOU'VE LEARNED MOST OF THE TRUTH ALREADY.
WE DON'T MIND SHARING THE RESSHT... grk
WHAT IS THE FIRST RULE OF REAL ESTATE, SIR? LOCATION, LOCATION, LOCATION. AND OUR HOLDINGS ON THE EAST SIDE SHALL SOON BE THE ONLY LOCALES WORTH HAVING IN PORTSMOUTH!
A SERIES OF WELL-PLANNED DISASTERS IS SET TO RENDER THE LUCRATIVE, DOWNTOWN SECTIONS OF THIS CITY UNINHABITABLE.
EVEN NOW, OUR UNDERGROUND FORCES ARE SET TO DISTRIBUTE INDUSTRIAL WASTE INTO THE MAIN RESERVOIRS AND SEWER LINES.
WITHIN HOURS, AN OFF-SHORE REFINERY WILL BE SABOTAGED, AND CRUDE OIL SPILLED INTO THE MOUTH OF THE PORTSMOUTH RIVER.
SHARKS WILL COMPLICATE THE CLEANUP PROCESS.
AND SOON, URBAN RENEWAL WILL BE FORCED ONTO THE "BAD SIDE" OF TOWN.
PRAEDA STANDS TO MAKE A MINT, BOTH FROM THE ESCALATED VALUE OF OUR PROPERTIES, AND ALSO FROM THE CLEANUP EFFORTS, OIL RETARDANTS AND OXYGEN FILTERS!
INSIDE OF A YEAR, WE WILL OWN THIS TOWN, OR WHAT'S LEFT OF IT!

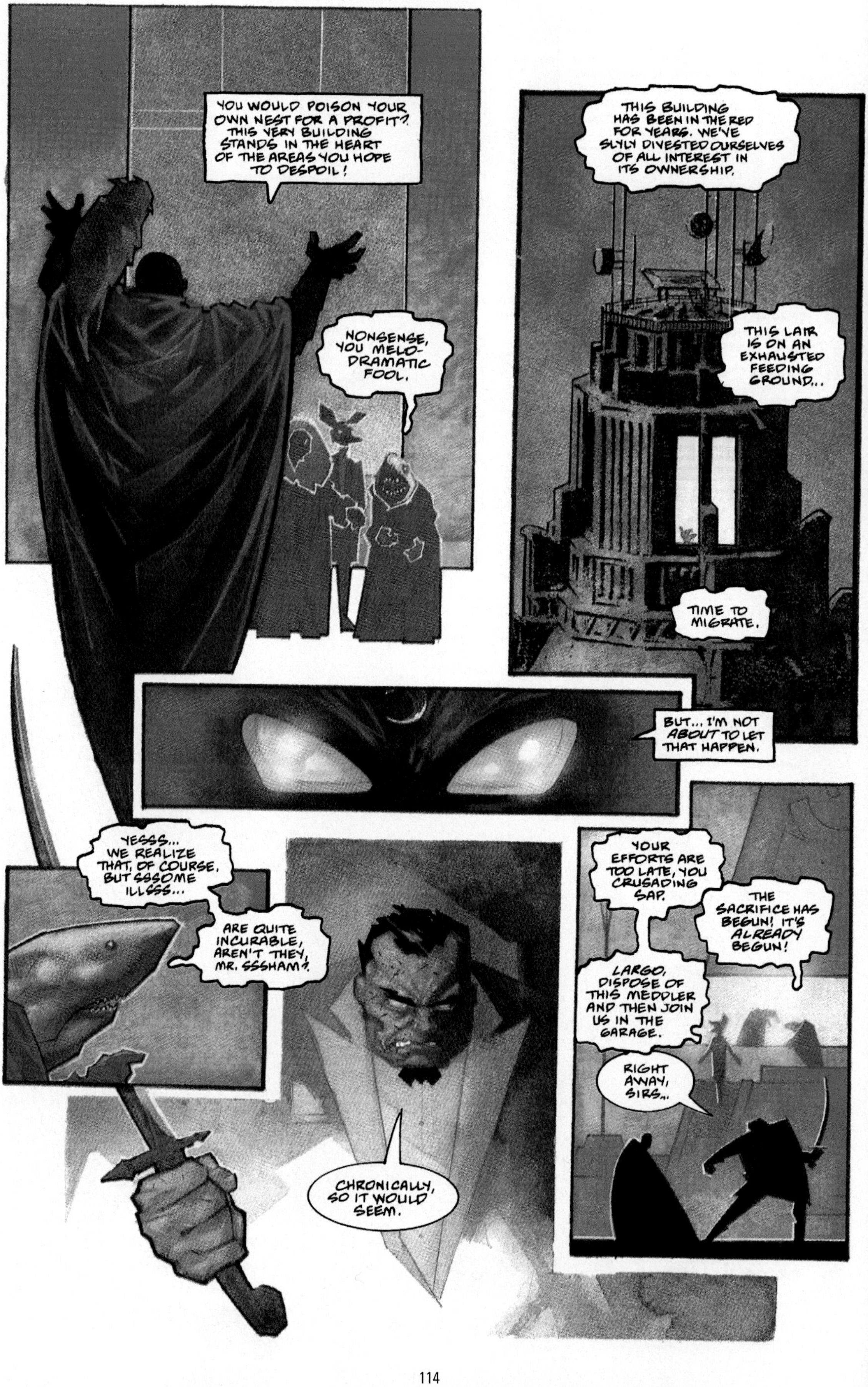
YOU WOULD POISON YOUR OWN NEST FOR A PROFIT? THIS VERY BUILDING STANDS IN THE HEART OF THE AREAS YOU HOPE TO DESPOIL!
NONSENSE, YOU MELODRAMATIC FOOL.
THIS BUILDING HAS BEEN IN THE RED FOR YEARS. WE'VE SLYLY DIVESTED OURSELVES OF ALL INTEREST IN ITS OWNERSHIP.
THIS LAIR IS ON AN EXHAUSTED FEEDING GROUND...
TIME TO MIGRATE.
BUT... I'M NOT ABOUT TO LET THAT HAPPEN.
YESSS... WE REALIZE THAT, OF COURSE, BUT SSSOME ILLSSS...
ARE QUITE INCURABLE, AREN'T THEY, MR. SSSHAM?
CHRONICALLY, SO IT WOULD SEEM.
YOUR EFFORTS ARE TOO LATE, YOU CRUSADING SAP.
THE SACRIFICE HAS BEGUN! IT'S ALREADY BEGUN!
LARGO, DISPOSE OF THIS MEDDLER AND THEN JOIN US IN THE GARAGE.
RIGHT AWAY, SIRS...

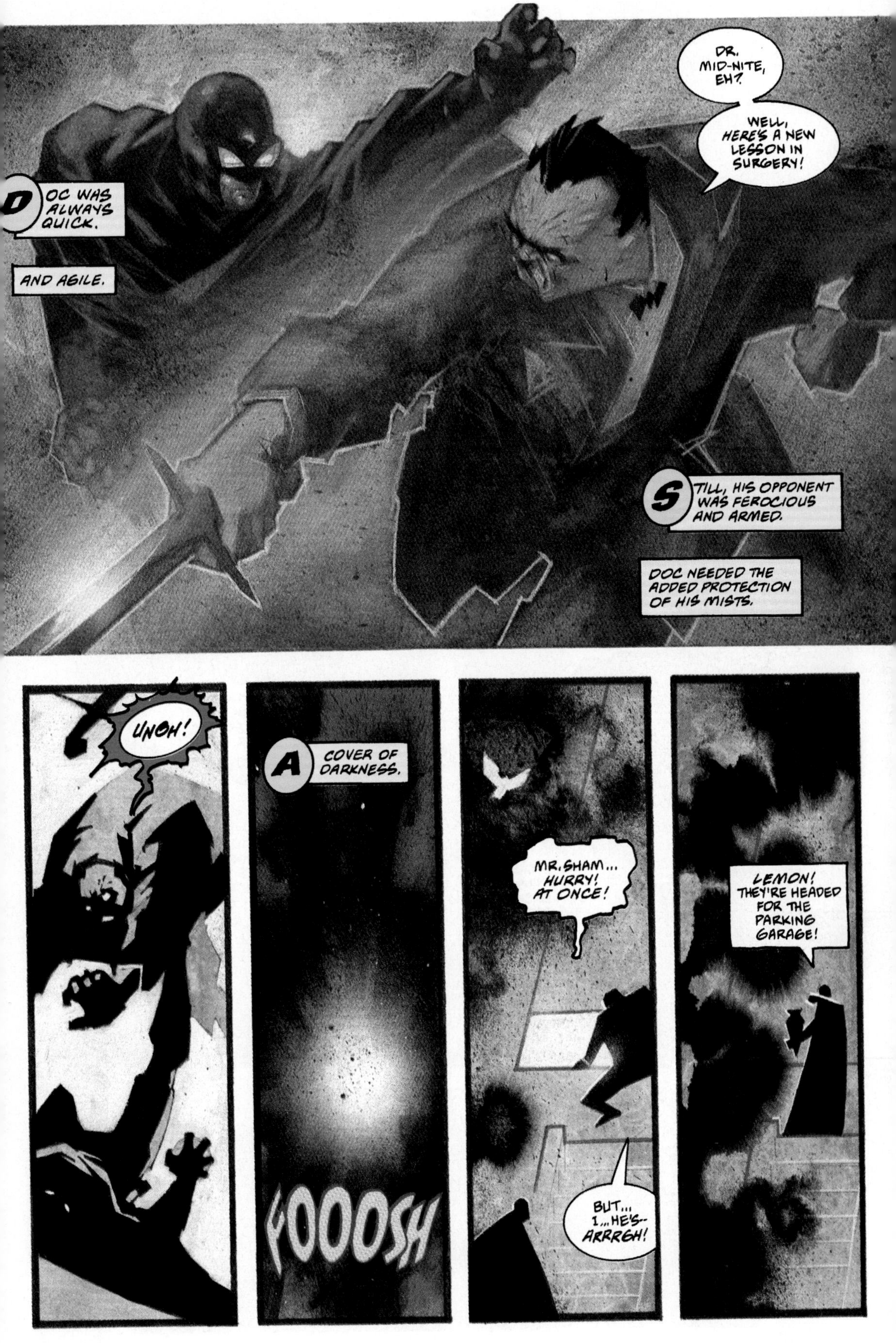
DR. MID-NITE, EH?
WELL, HERE'S A NEW LESSON IN SURGERY!
DOC WAS ALWAYS QUICK.
AND AGILE.
STILL, HIS OPPONENT WAS FEROCIOUS AND ARMED.
DOC NEEDED THE ADDED PROTECTION OF HIS MISTS.
UNGH!
A COVER OF DARKNESS.
FOOOSH
MR. SHAM... HURRY! AT ONCE!
BUT... I... HE'S-- ARRRGH!
LEMON! THEY'RE HEADED FOR THE PARKING GARAGE!

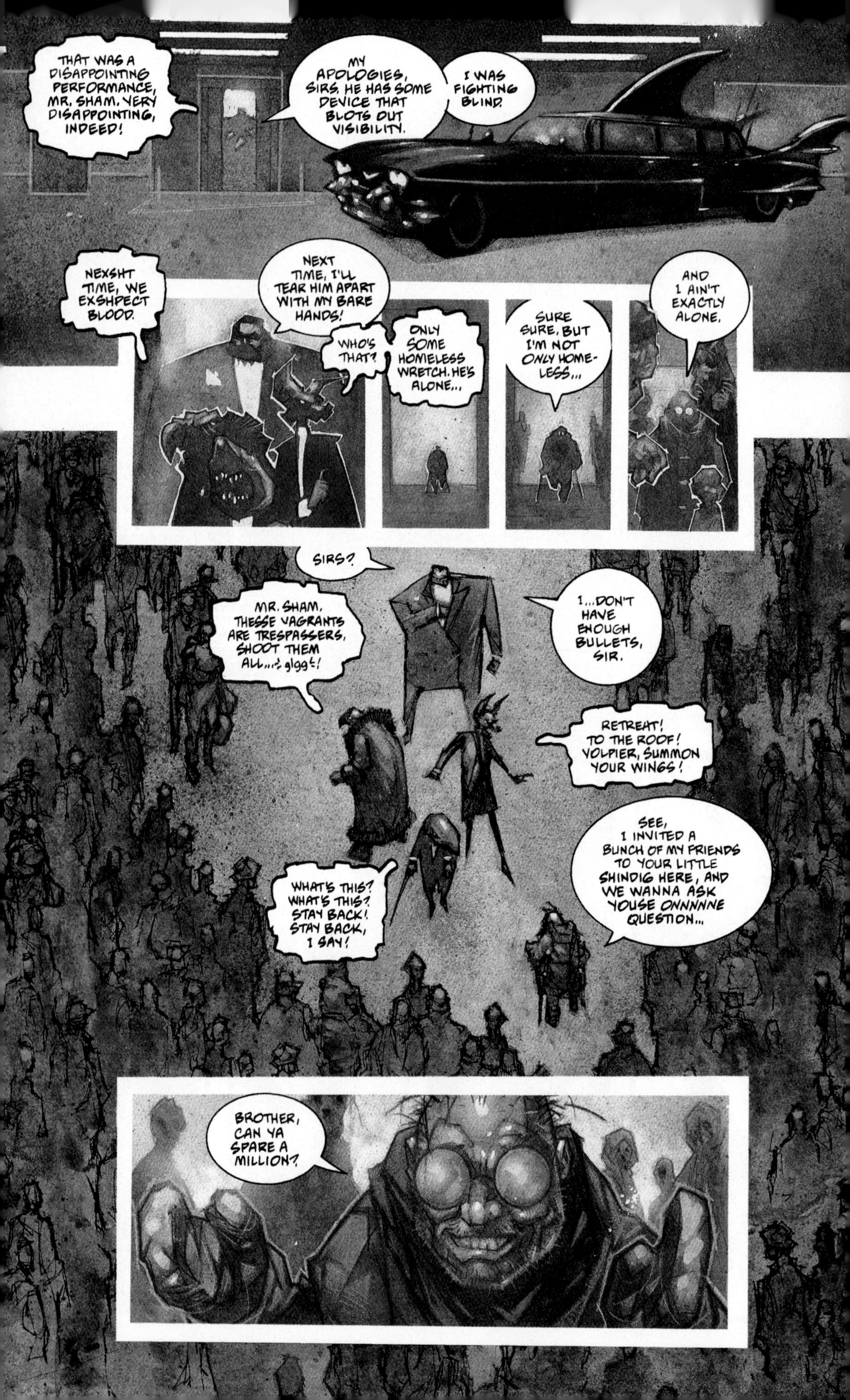
THAT WAS A DISAPPOINTING PERFORMANCE, MR. SHAM. VERY DISAPPOINTING, INDEED!
MY APOLOGIES, SIRS. HE HAS SOME DEVICE THAT BLOTS OUT VISIBILITY.
I WAS FIGHTING BLIND.
NEXSHT TIME, WE EXSHPECT BLOOD.
NEXT TIME, I'LL TEAR HIM APART WITH MY BARE HANDS!
WHO'S THAT?
ONLY SOME HOMELESS WRETCH. HE'S ALONE...
SURE SURE, BUT I'M NOT ONLY HOMELESS...
AND I AIN'T EXACTLY ALONE.
SIRS?
MR. SHAM. THESSE VAGRANTS ARE TRESPASSERS. SHOOT THEM ALL...glgg!
I...DON'T HAVE ENOUGH BULLETS, SIR.
RETREAT! TO THE ROOF! VOLPIER, SUMMON YOUR WINGS!
WHAT'S THIS? WHAT'S THIS? STAY BACK! STAY BACK, I SAY!
SEE, I INVITED A BUNCH OF MY FRIENDS TO YOUR LITTLE SHINDIG HERE, AND WE WANNA ASK YOUSE ONNNNNE QUESTION...
BROTHER, CAN YA SPARE A MILLION?

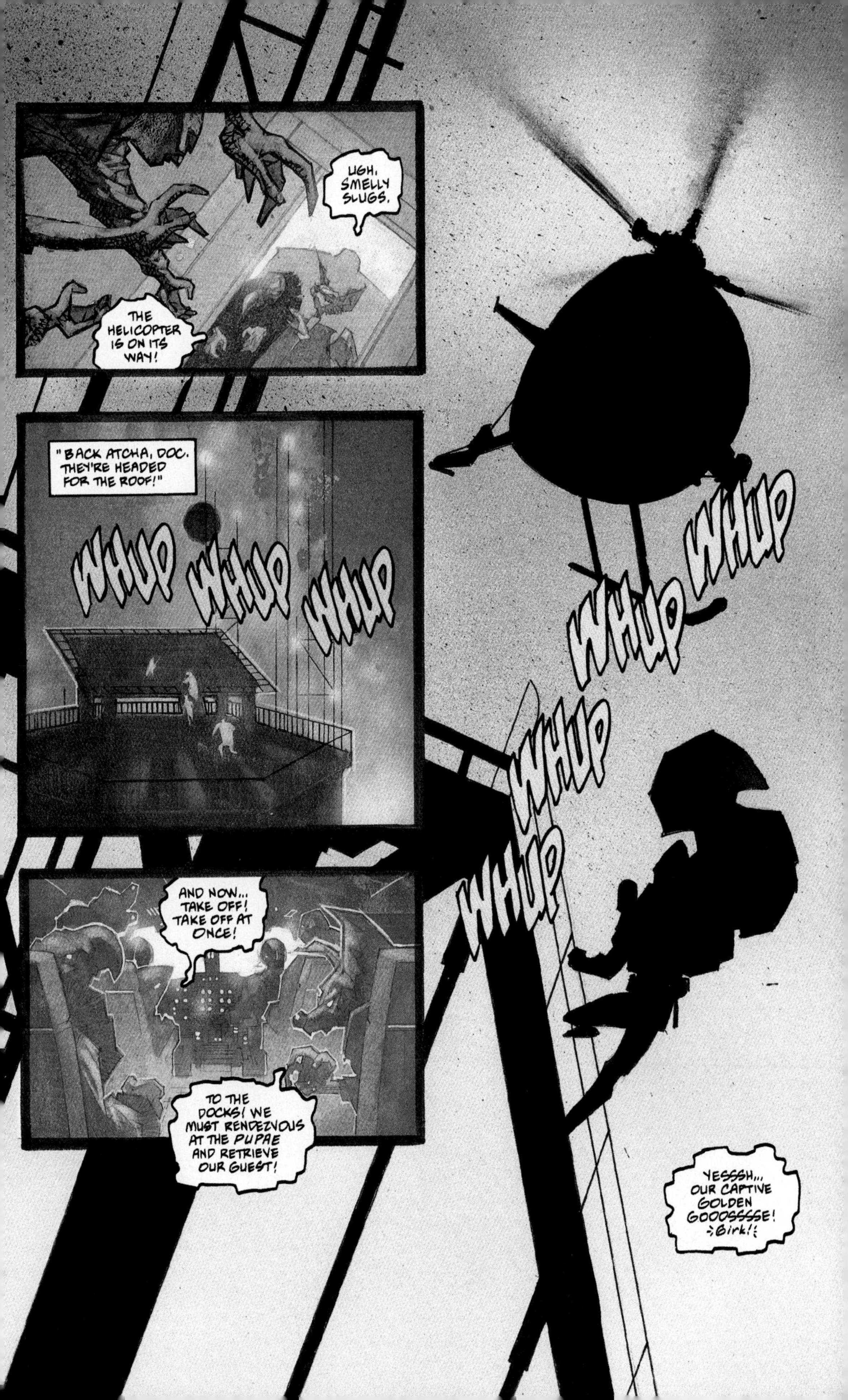
UGH, SMELLY SLUGS.
THE HELICOPTER IS ON ITS WAY!
"BACK ATCHA, DOC. THEY'RE HEADED FOR THE ROOF!"
WHUP WHUP WHUP
WHUP WHUP WHUP WHUP
AND NOW... TAKE OFF! TAKE OFF AT ONCE!
TO THE DOCKS! WE MUST RENDEZVOUS AT THE PUPAE AND RETRIEVE OUR GUEST!
YESSSH... OUR CAPTIVE GOLDEN GOOOSSSSSE! :Birk!:

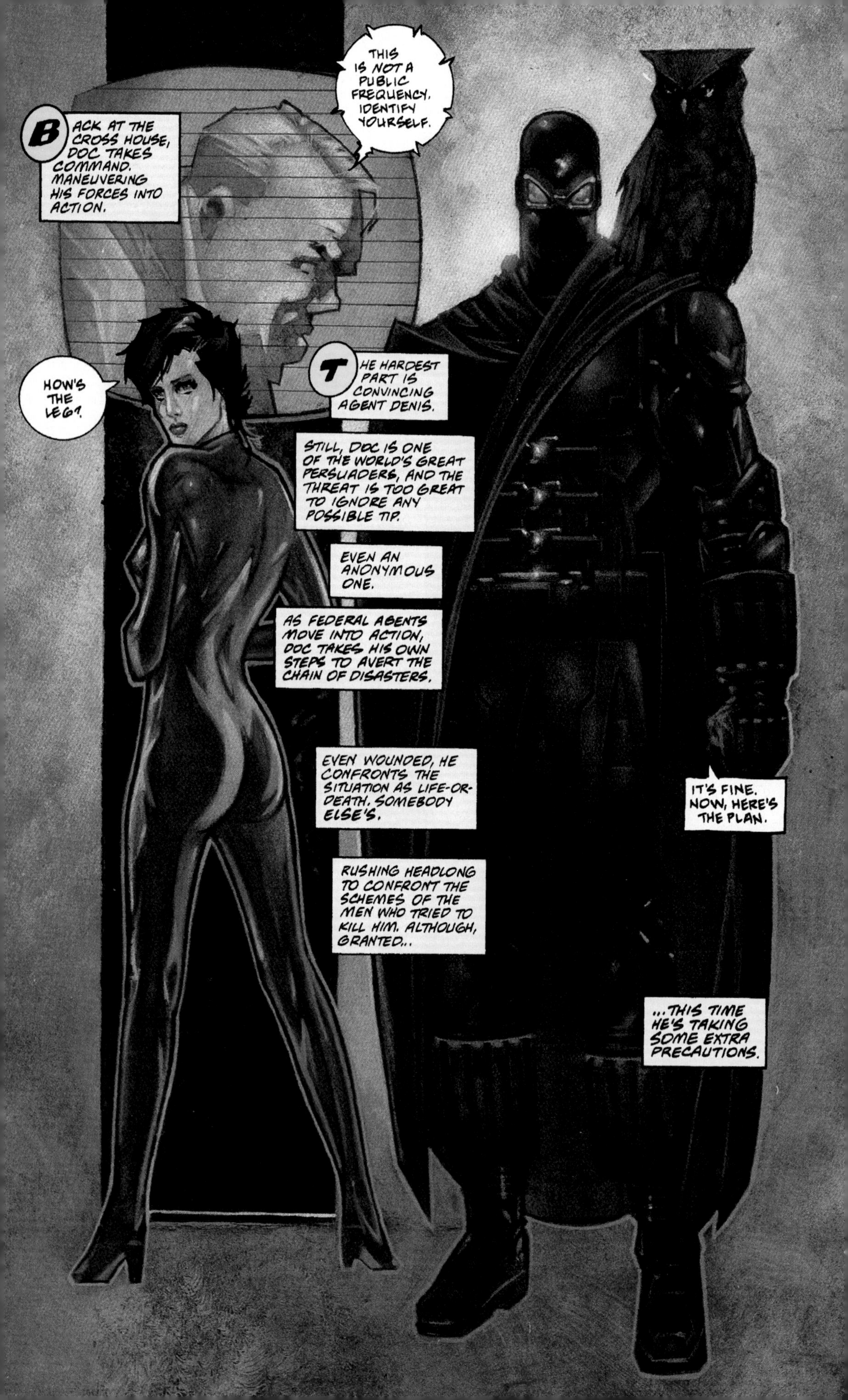
BACK AT THE CROSS HOUSE, DOC TAKES COMMAND. MANEUVERING HIS FORCES INTO ACTION.
THIS IS NOT A PUBLIC FREQUENCY. IDENTIFY YOURSELF.
THE HARDEST PART IS CONVINCING AGENT DENIS.
STILL, DOC IS ONE OF THE WORLD'S GREAT PERSUADERS, AND THE THREAT IS TOO GREAT TO IGNORE ANY POSSIBLE TIP.
EVEN AN ANONYMOUS ONE.
AS FEDERAL AGENTS MOVE INTO ACTION, DOC TAKES HIS OWN STEPS TO AVERT THE CHAIN OF DISASTERS.
HOW'S THE LEG?
EVEN WOUNDED, HE CONFRONTS THE SITUATION AS LIFE-OR-DEATH. SOMEBODY ELSE'S.
IT'S FINE. NOW, HERE'S THE PLAN.
RUSHING HEADLONG TO CONFRONT THE SCHEMES OF THE MEN WHO TRIED TO KILL HIM. ALTHOUGH, GRANTED...
...THIS TIME HE'S TAKING SOME EXTRA PRECAUTIONS.

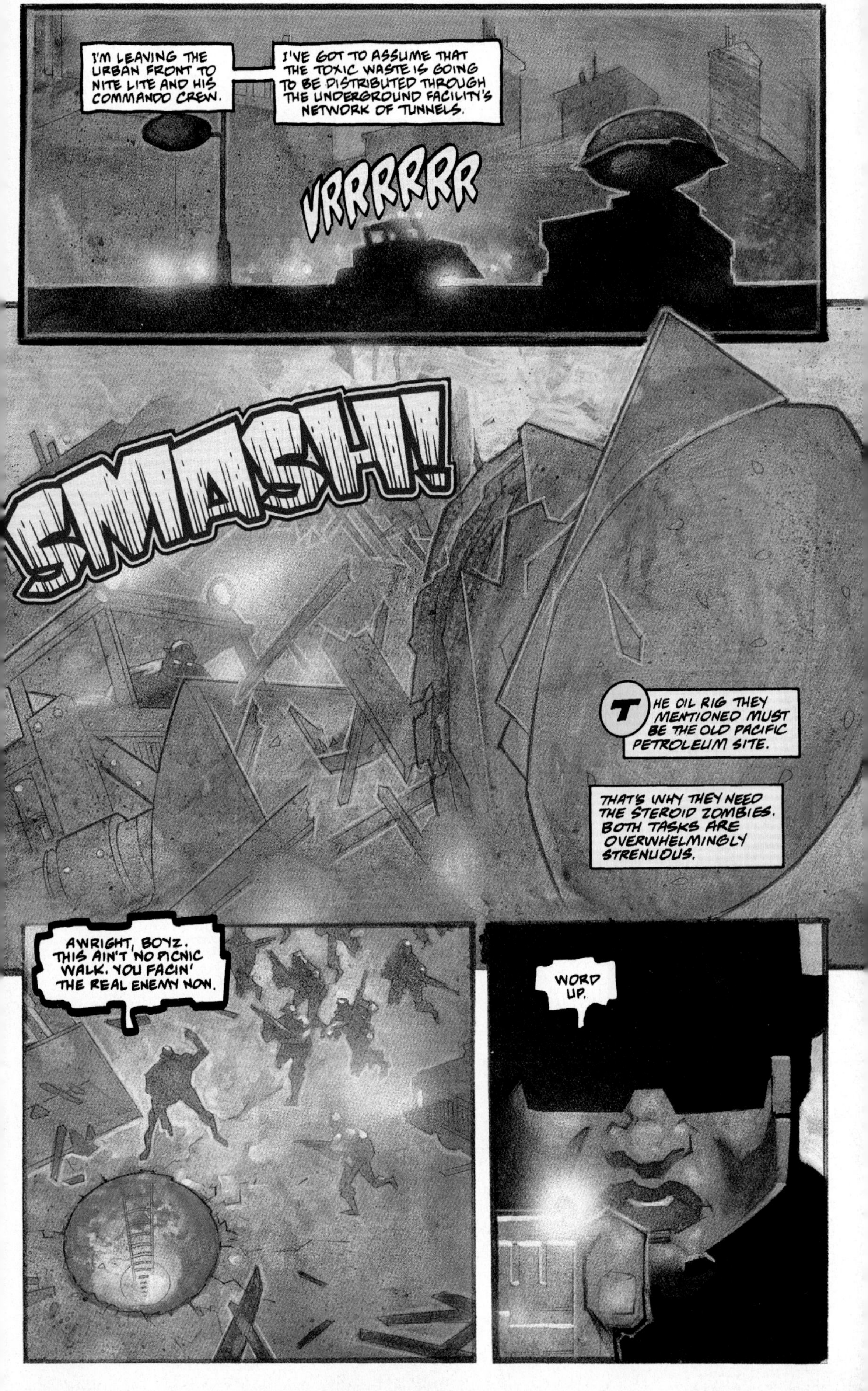

I'M LEAVING THE URBAN FRONT TO NITE LITE AND HIS COMMANDO CREW.
I'VE GOT TO ASSUME THAT THE TOXIC WASTE IS GOING TO BE DISTRIBUTED THROUGH THE UNDERGROUND FACILITY'S NETWORK OF TUNNELS.
VRRRRRR
SMASH!!
THE OIL RIG THEY MENTIONED MUST BE THE OLD PACIFIC PETROLEUM SITE.
THAT'S WHY THEY NEED THE STEROID ZOMBIES. BOTH TASKS ARE OVERWHELMINGLY STRENUOUS.
AWRIGHT, BOYZ. THIS AIN'T 'NO PICNIC WALK. YOU FACIN' THE REAL ENEMY NOW.
WORD UP.

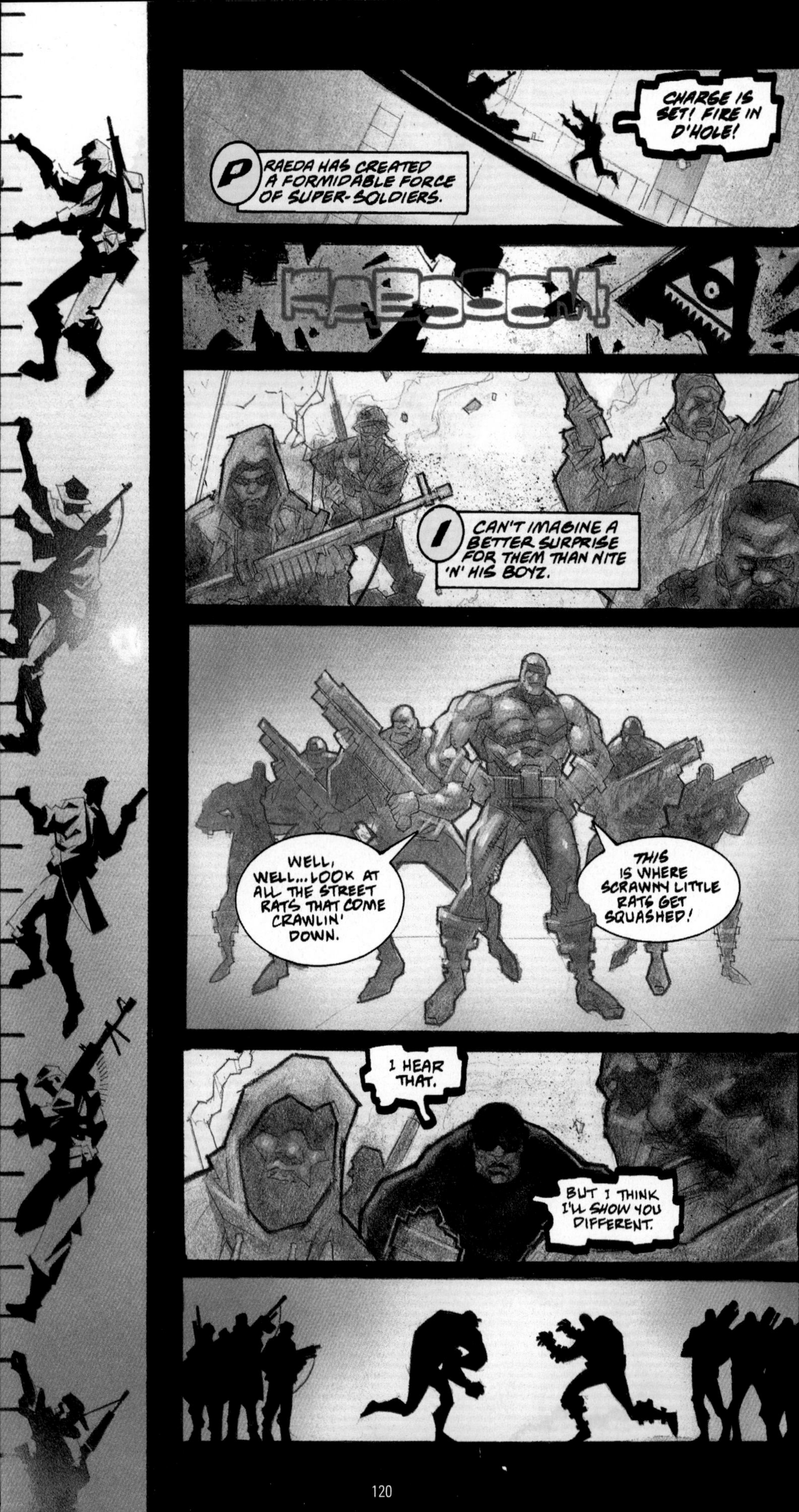
PRAEDA HAS CREATED A FORMIDABLE FORCE OF SUPER-SOLDIERS.
CHARGE IS SET! FIRE IN D'HOLE!
KABOOOM!
I CAN'T IMAGINE A BETTER SURPRISE FOR THEM THAN NITE 'N' HIS BOYZ.
WELL, WELL... LOOK AT ALL THE STREET RATS THAT COME CRAWLIN' DOWN.
THIS IS WHERE SCRAWNY LITTLE RATS GET SQUASHED!
I HEAR THAT.
BUT I THINK I'LL SHOW YOU DIFFERENT.

CHEMTRON MUST BE CRIPPLED.

THE POISONOUS WASTE HAS TO BE CUT OFF AT ITS SOURCE, A FESTERING BOIL THAT NEEDS LANCING.

AT THE OWL'S INTRUSION, ROBOT SENTRIES LAUNCH TO INTERCEPT ITS ENTRY.

BUT OWLS ARE SWIFT, SURE, AND SILENT FLIERS.

BZZ- WHITT

SQUAAA-kik

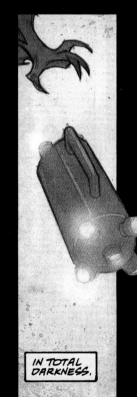

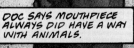

DOC SAYS MOUTHPIECE ALWAYS DID HAVE A WAY WITH ANIMALS.

USED TO NAVIGATING FORESTS FULL OF TREES.

IN TOTAL DARKNESS.

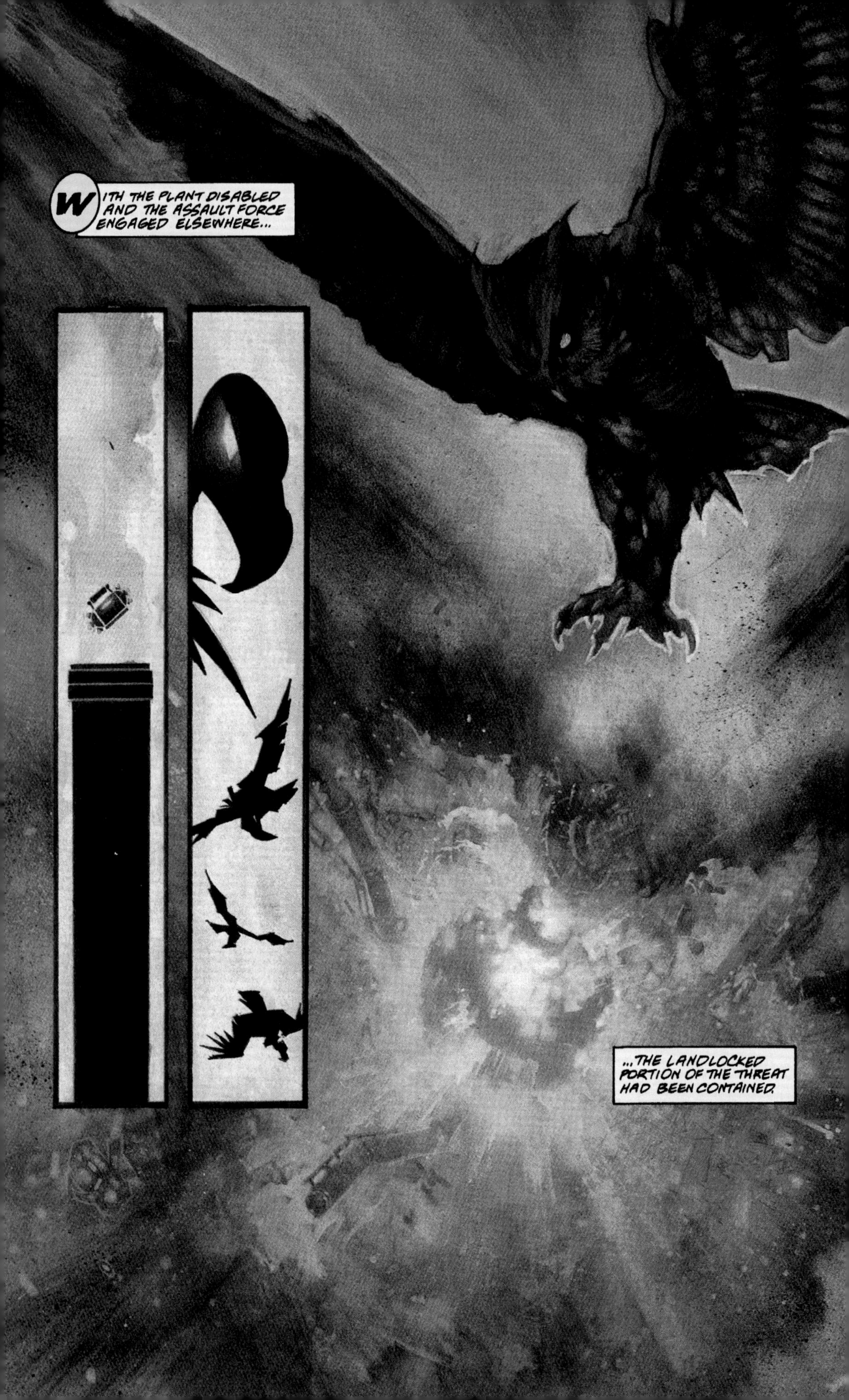
WITH THE PLANT DISABLED AND THE ASSAULT FORCE ENGAGED ELSEWHERE...
...THE LANDLOCKED PORTION OF THE THREAT HAD BEEN CONTAINED.

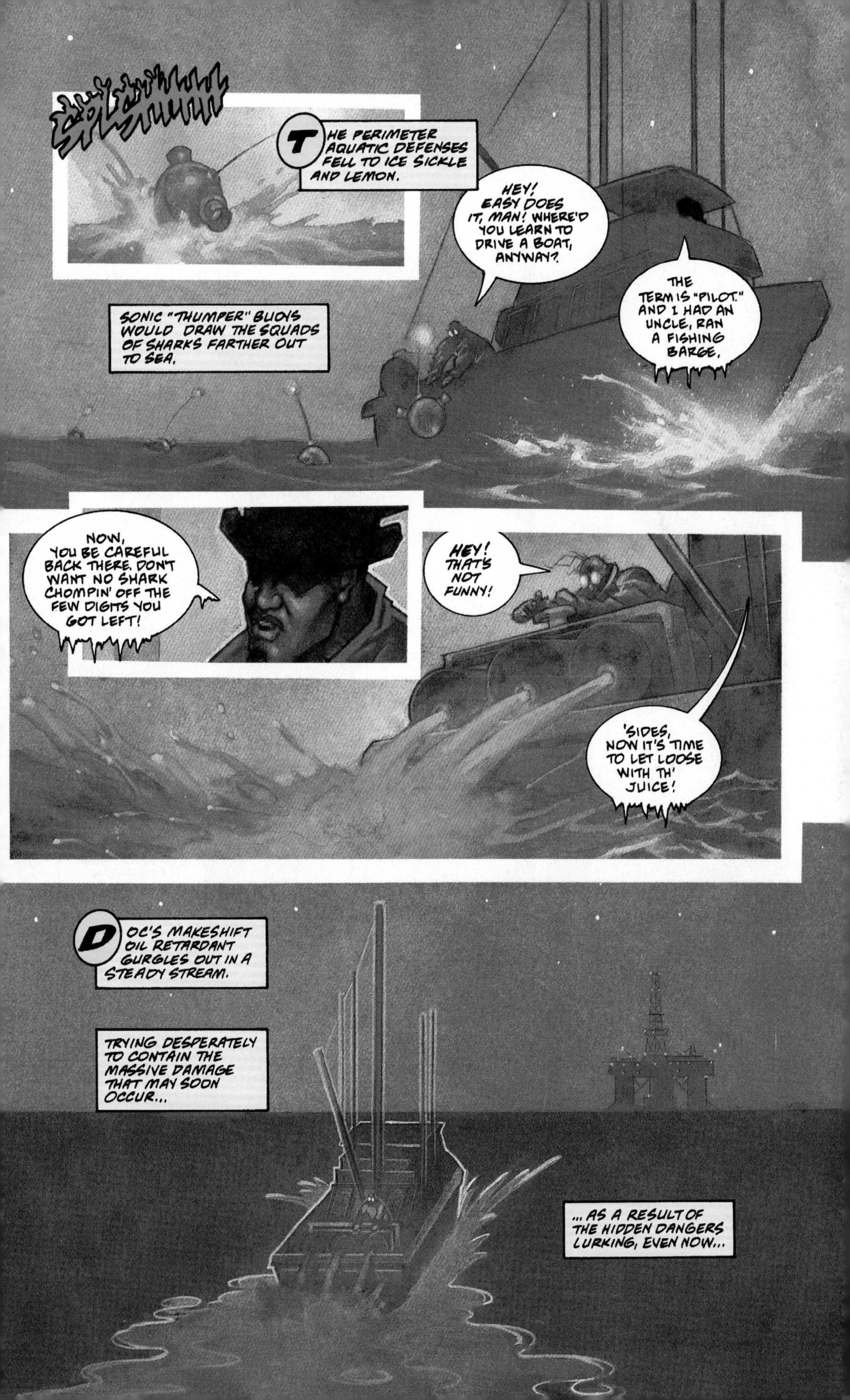
SPLOOSHHHH
THE PERIMETER AQUATIC DEFENSES FELL TO ICE SICKLE AND LEMON.
HEY! EASY DOES IT, MAN! WHERE'D YOU LEARN TO DRIVE A BOAT, ANYWAY?
SONIC "THUMPER" BUOYS WOULD DRAW THE SQUADS OF SHARKS FARTHER OUT TO SEA.
THE TERM IS "PILOT." AND I HAD AN UNCLE, RAN A FISHING BARGE.
NOW, YOU BE CAREFUL BACK THERE. DON'T WANT NO SHARK CHOMPIN' OFF THE FEW DIGITS YOU GOT LEFT!
HEY! THAT'S NOT FUNNY!
'SIDES, NOW IT'S TIME TO LET LOOSE WITH TH' JUICE!
DOC'S MAKESHIFT OIL RETARDANT GURGLES OUT IN A STEADY STREAM.
TRYING DESPERATELY TO CONTAIN THE MASSIVE DAMAGE THAT MAY SOON OCCUR...
...AS A RESULT OF THE HIDDEN DANGERS LURKING, EVEN NOW...

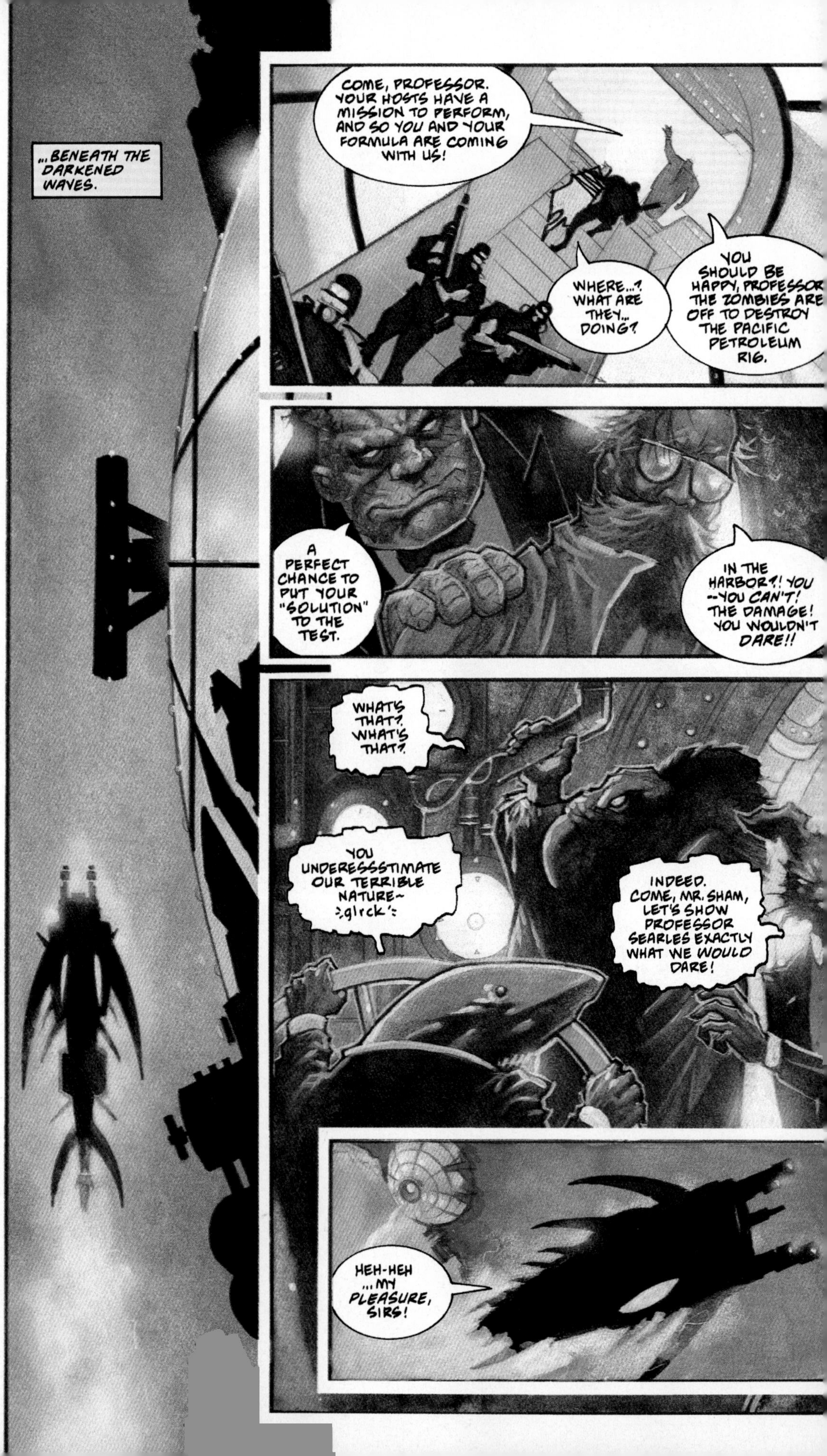
...BENEATH THE DARKENED WAVES.
COME, PROFESSOR. YOUR HOSTS HAVE A MISSION TO PERFORM, AND SO YOU AND YOUR FORMULA ARE COMING WITH US!
WHERE...? WHAT ARE THEY... DOING?
YOU SHOULD BE HAPPY, PROFESSOR. THE ZOMBIES ARE OFF TO DESTROY THE PACIFIC PETROLEUM RIG.
A PERFECT CHANCE TO PUT YOUR "SOLUTION" TO THE TEST.
IN THE HARBOR?! YOU --YOU CAN'T! THE DAMAGE! YOU WOULDN'T DARE!!
WHAT'S THAT? WHAT'S THAT?
YOU UNDERESSSTIMATE OUR TERRIBLE NATURE~ glrck
INDEED. COME, MR. SHAM, LET'S SHOW PROFESSOR SEARLES EXACTLY WHAT WE WOULD DARE!
HEH-HEH ...MY PLEASURE, SIRS!

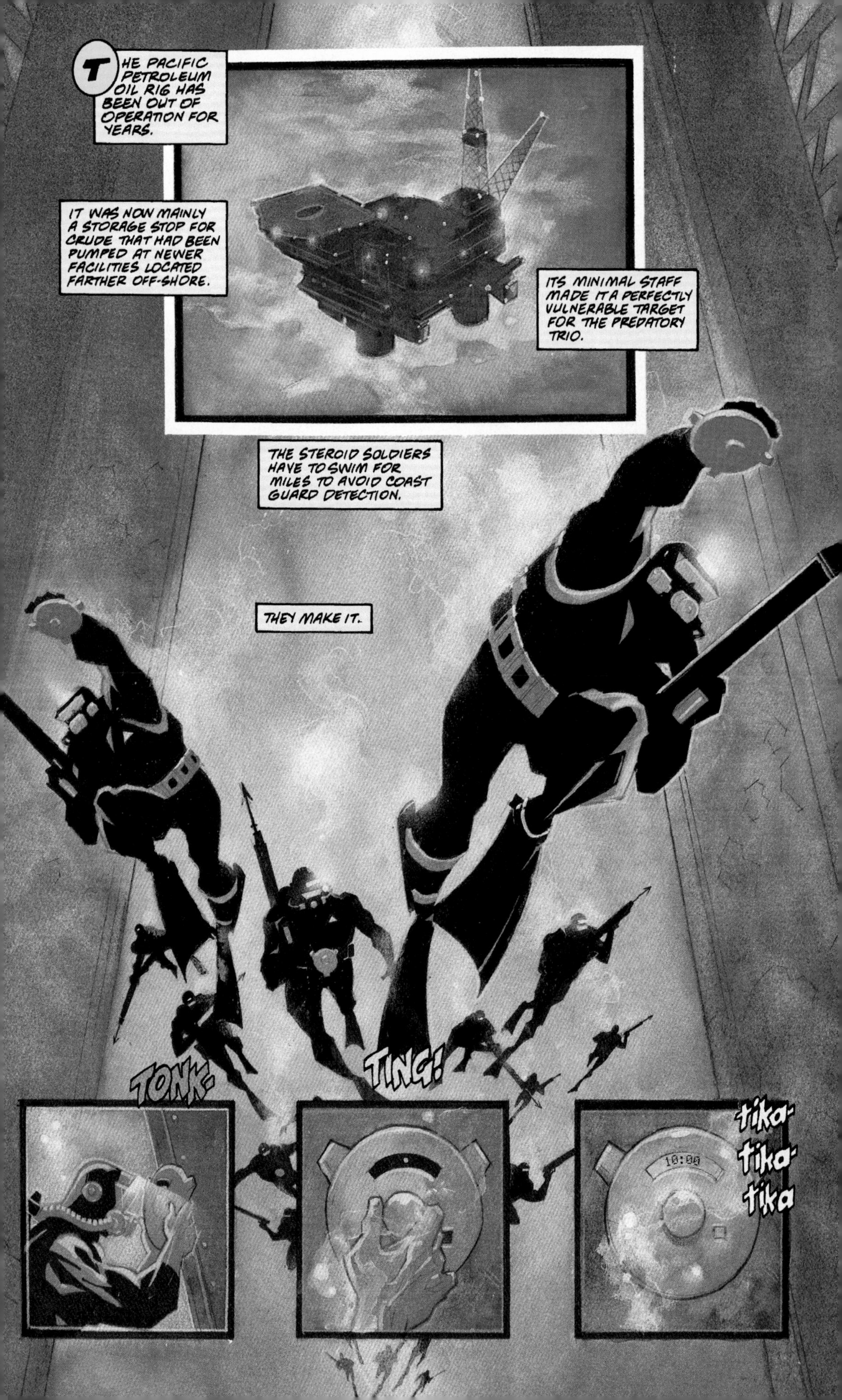
THE PACIFIC PETROLEUM OIL RIG HAS BEEN OUT OF OPERATION FOR YEARS.
IT WAS NOW MAINLY A STORAGE STOP FOR CRUDE THAT HAD BEEN PUMPED AT NEWER FACILITIES LOCATED FARTHER OFF-SHORE.
ITS MINIMAL STAFF MADE IT A PERFECTLY VULNERABLE TARGET FOR THE PREDATORY TRIO.
THE STEROID SOLDIERS HAVE TO SWIM FOR MILES TO AVOID COAST GUARD DETECTION.
THEY MAKE IT.
TONK.
TING!
10:00
tika-
tika-
tika

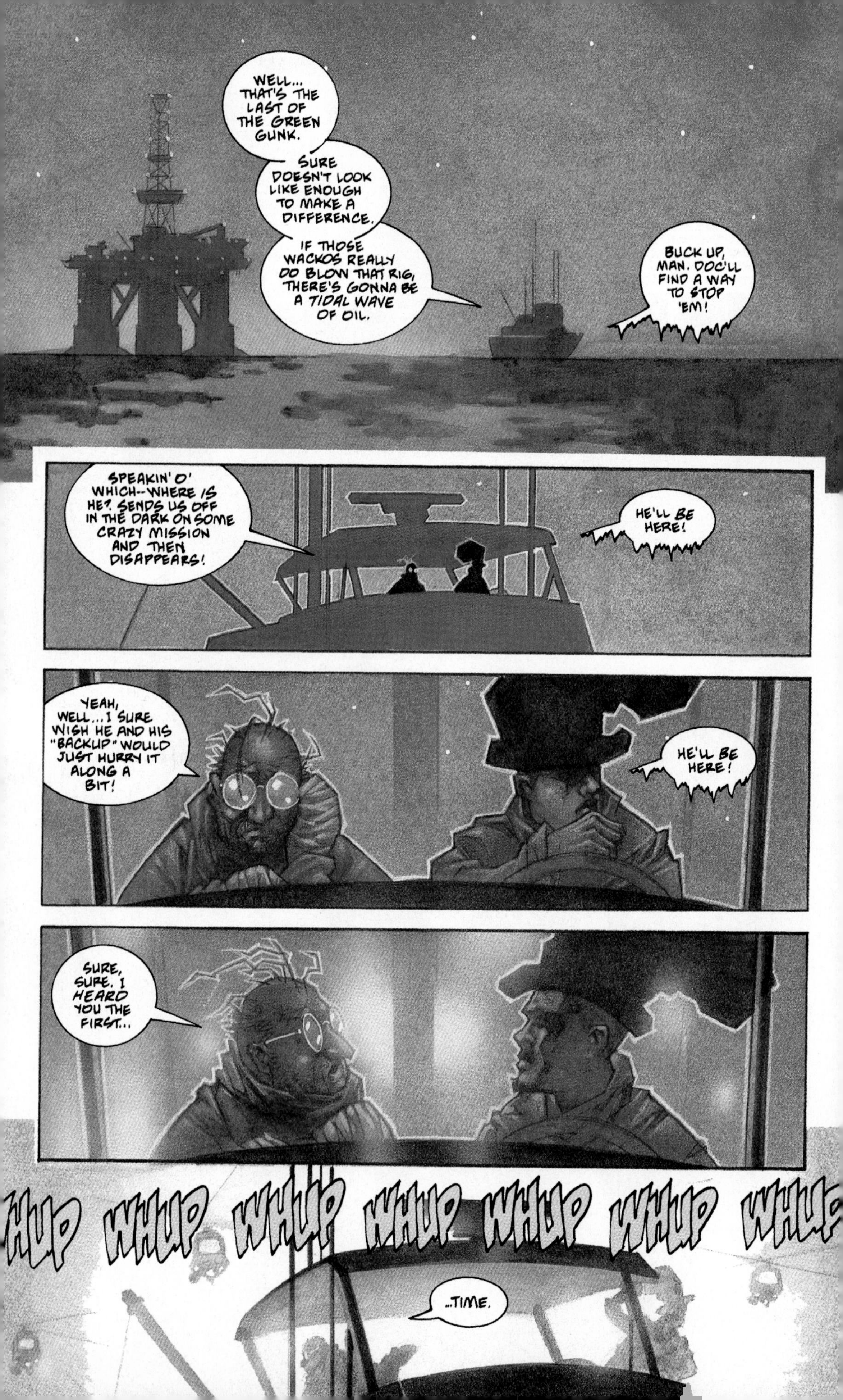
WELL... THAT'S THE LAST OF THE GREEN GUNK.
SURE DOESN'T LOOK LIKE ENOUGH TO MAKE A DIFFERENCE.
IF THOSE WACKOS REALLY DO BLOW THAT RIG, THERE'S GONNA BE A TIDAL WAVE OF OIL.
BUCK UP, MAN. DOC'LL FIND A WAY TO STOP 'EM!
SPEAKIN' O' WHICH--WHERE IS HE? SENDS US OFF IN THE DARK ON SOME CRAZY MISSION AND THEN DISAPPEARS!
HE'LL BE HERE!
YEAH, WELL... I SURE WISH HE AND HIS "BACKUP" WOULD JUST HURRY IT ALONG A BIT!
HE'LL BE HERE!
SURE, SURE. I HEARD YOU THE FIRST...
HUP WHUP WHUP WHUP WHUP WHUP WHU
...TIME.

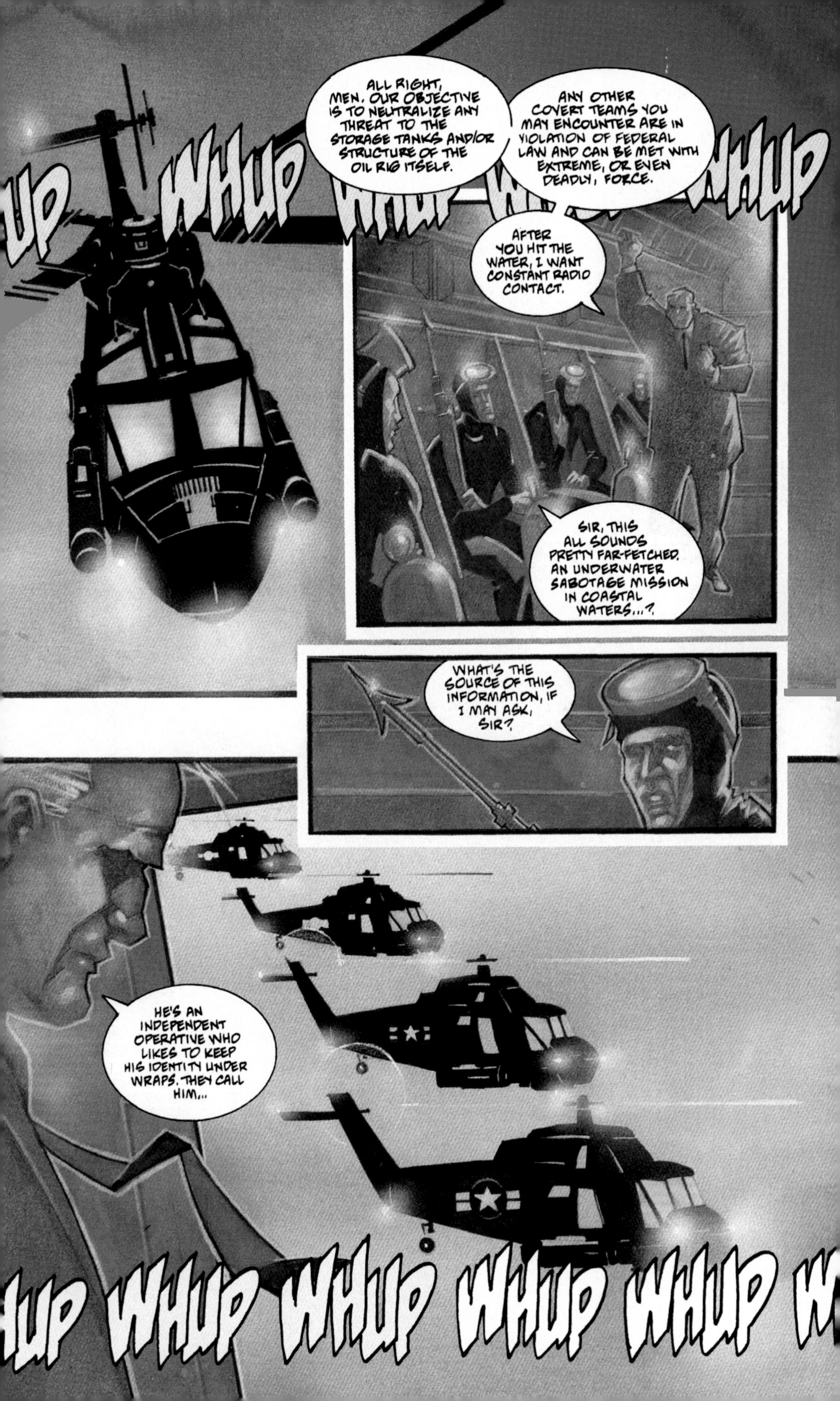
WHUP WHUP WHUP WHUP
ALL RIGHT, MEN. OUR OBJECTIVE IS TO NEUTRALIZE ANY THREAT TO THE STORAGE TANKS AND/OR STRUCTURE OF THE OIL RIG ITSELF.
ANY OTHER COVERT TEAMS YOU MAY ENCOUNTER ARE IN VIOLATION OF FEDERAL LAW AND CAN BE MET WITH EXTREME, OR EVEN DEADLY, FORCE.
AFTER YOU HIT THE WATER, I WANT CONSTANT RADIO CONTACT.
SIR, THIS ALL SOUNDS PRETTY FAR-FETCHED. AN UNDERWATER SABOTAGE MISSION IN COASTAL WATERS...?
WHAT'S THE SOURCE OF THIS INFORMATION, IF I MAY ASK, SIR?
HE'S AN INDEPENDENT OPERATIVE WHO LIKES TO KEEP HIS IDENTITY UNDER WRAPS. THEY CALL HIM...
WHUP WHUP WHUP WHUP WHUP

"DR. MID-NITE!"
WHUP WHUP
WHUP WH
WHUP
WHUP WHUP
THE OCEAN SPRAY IS COLD AND FIERCE AGAINST MY SKIN.
YA2698TT
OUR BOAT DASHES ACROSS THE SURF, KEEPING PACE WITH THE RESCUE TEAM VEHICLES.
BESIDE ME, DOC STANDS RIGID AGAINST THE BATTERING WIND..
...DETERMINED TO BE ON HAND AS CASUALTIES ARE INCURRED.

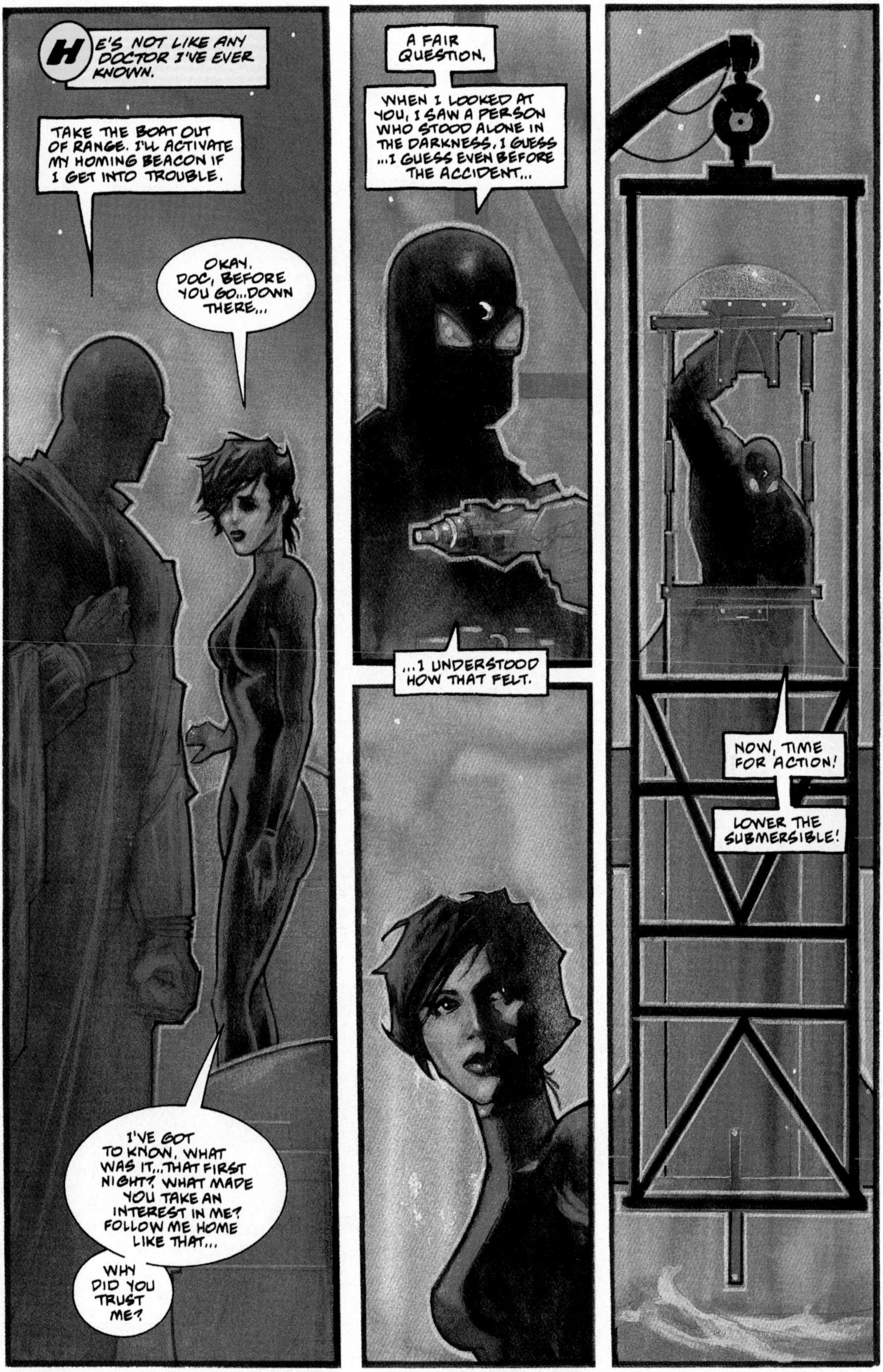
HE'S NOT LIKE ANY DOCTOR I'VE EVER KNOWN.
TAKE THE BOAT OUT OF RANGE. I'LL ACTIVATE MY HOMING BEACON IF I GET INTO TROUBLE.
OKAY. DOC, BEFORE YOU GO...DOWN THERE...
I'VE GOT TO KNOW. WHAT WAS IT...THAT FIRST NIGHT? WHAT MADE YOU TAKE AN INTEREST IN ME? FOLLOW ME HOME LIKE THAT...
WHY DID YOU TRUST ME?
A FAIR QUESTION.
WHEN I LOOKED AT YOU, I SAW A PERSON WHO STOOD ALONE IN THE DARKNESS, I GUESS ...I GUESS EVEN BEFORE THE ACCIDENT...
...I UNDERSTOOD HOW THAT FELT.
NOW, TIME FOR ACTION!
LOWER THE SUBMERSIBLE!

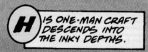**IS ONE-MAN CRAFT DESCENDS INTO THE INKY DEPTHS.**

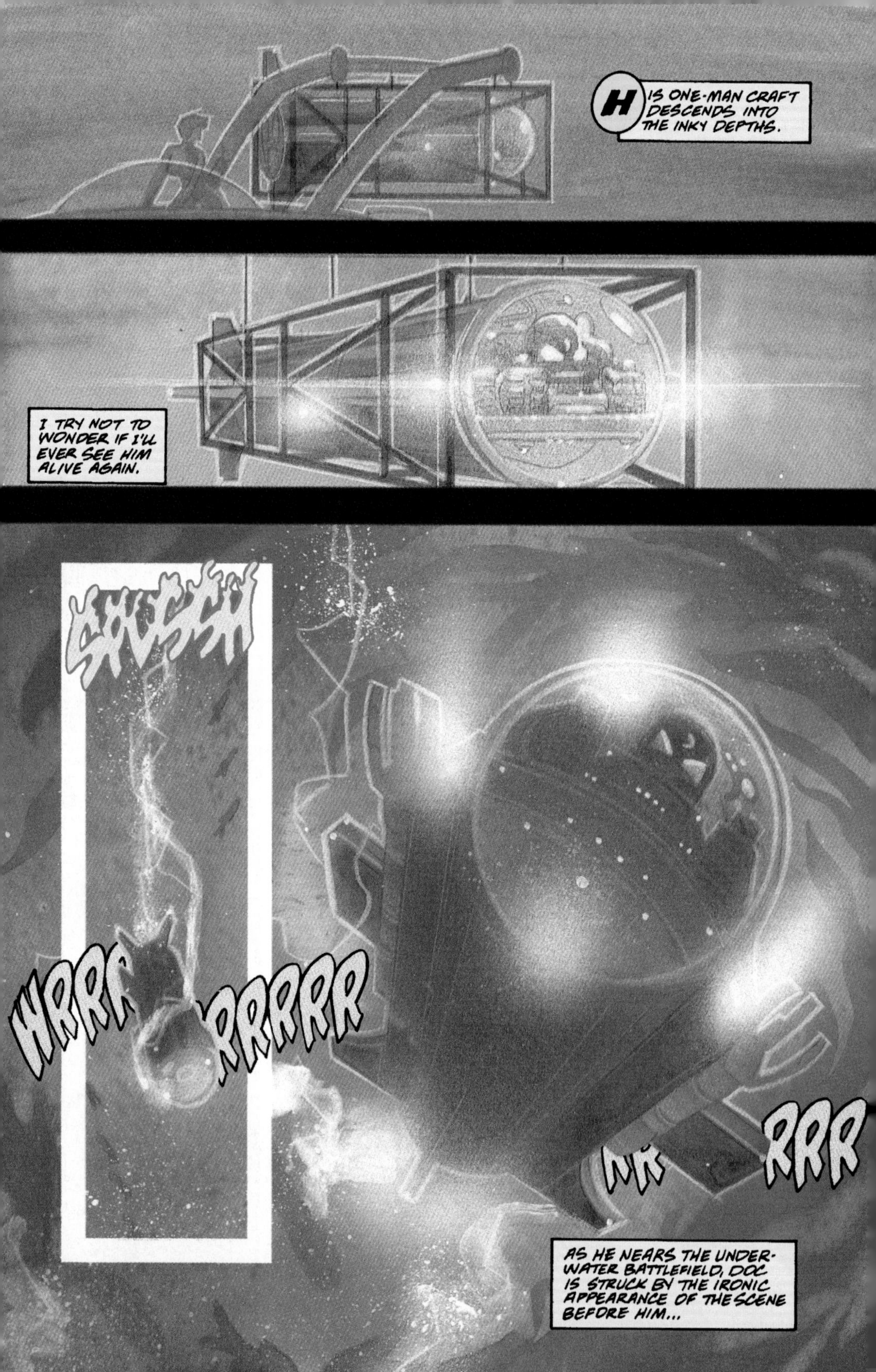

I TRY NOT TO WONDER IF I'LL EVER SEE HIM ALIVE AGAIN.

SHOOM

HRRR RRRRR

HR RRR

AS HE NEARS THE UNDER-WATER BATTLEFIELD, DOC IS STRUCK BY THE IRONIC APPEARANCE OF THE SCENE BEFORE HIM...

LIKE A SWARMING MASS OF DELICATE FIREFLIES.

HE GRIMACES AS THE REALITY BECOMES CLEAR.

WARILY, HE CIRCLES THE UNDERWATER CARNAGE.

PRAYING THAT LEMON AND ICE-SICKLE HAVE DISPERSED ALL THE SHARK THUMPERS.

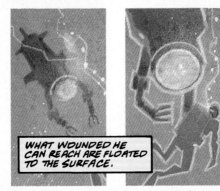

WHAT WOUNDED HE CAN REACH ARE FLOATED TO THE SURFACE.

THE SUB'S ROBOTIC ARMS, SO MUCH LIKE MICROSURGERY.

W HERE HE CAN...

...DOC LENDS A HAND TO THE FLAILING COMBAT.

FSSSSHH-

A LIQUID VERSION OF HIS BLACKOUT FORMULA.

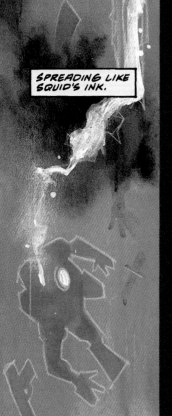

SPREADING LIKE SQUID'S INK.

BUT, EVENTUALLY, HIS FRINGE ACTIVITIES...

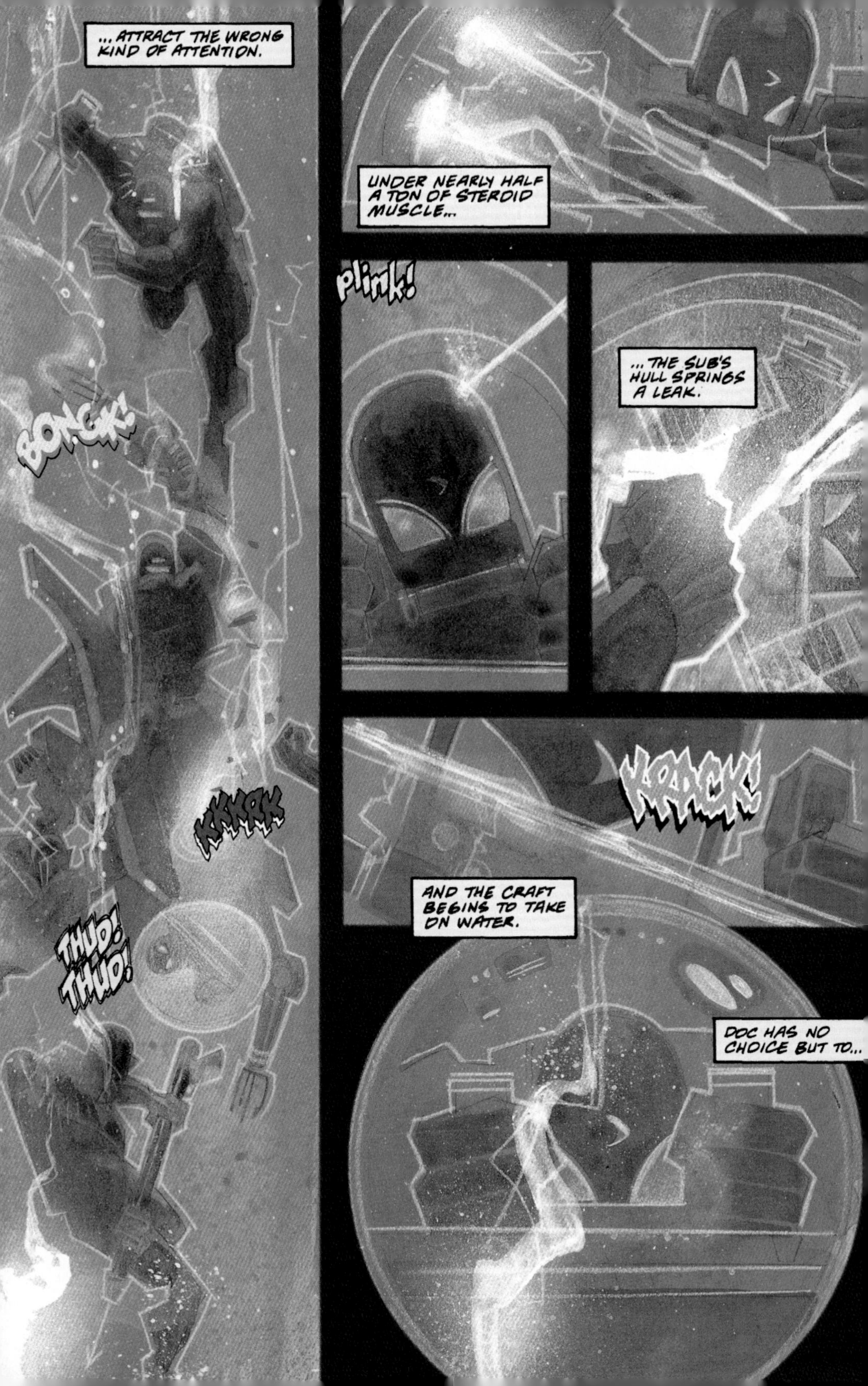
...ATTRACT THE WRONG KIND OF ATTENTION.
BONGK!
KKKRK
THUD! THUD!
UNDER NEARLY HALF A TON OF STEROID MUSCLE...
plink!
...THE SUB'S HULL SPRINGS A LEAK.
KRACK!
AND THE CRAFT BEGINS TO TAKE ON WATER.
DOC HAS NO CHOICE BUT TO...

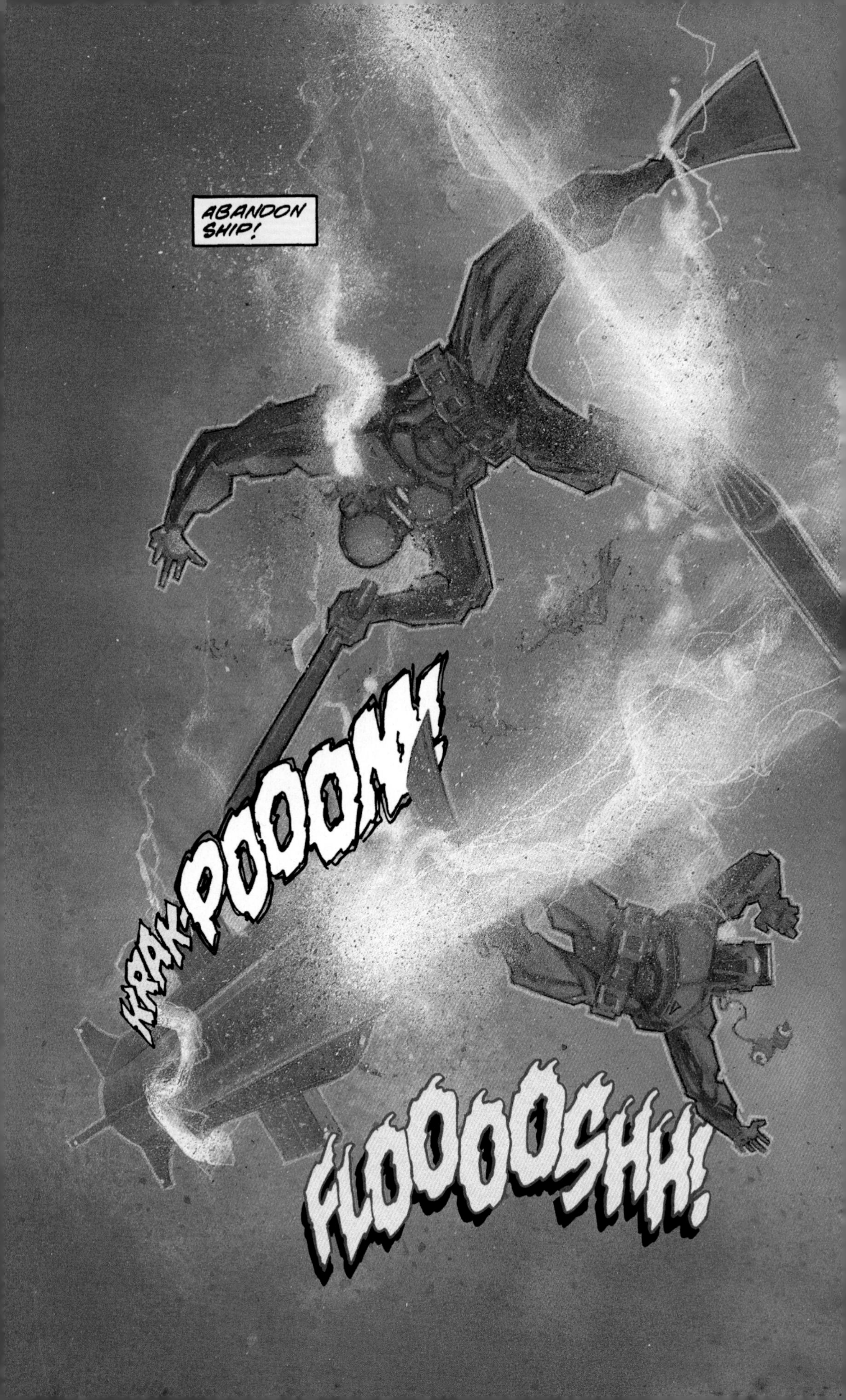
ABANDON SHIP!
KRAK-POOOM!
FLOOOOSHH!

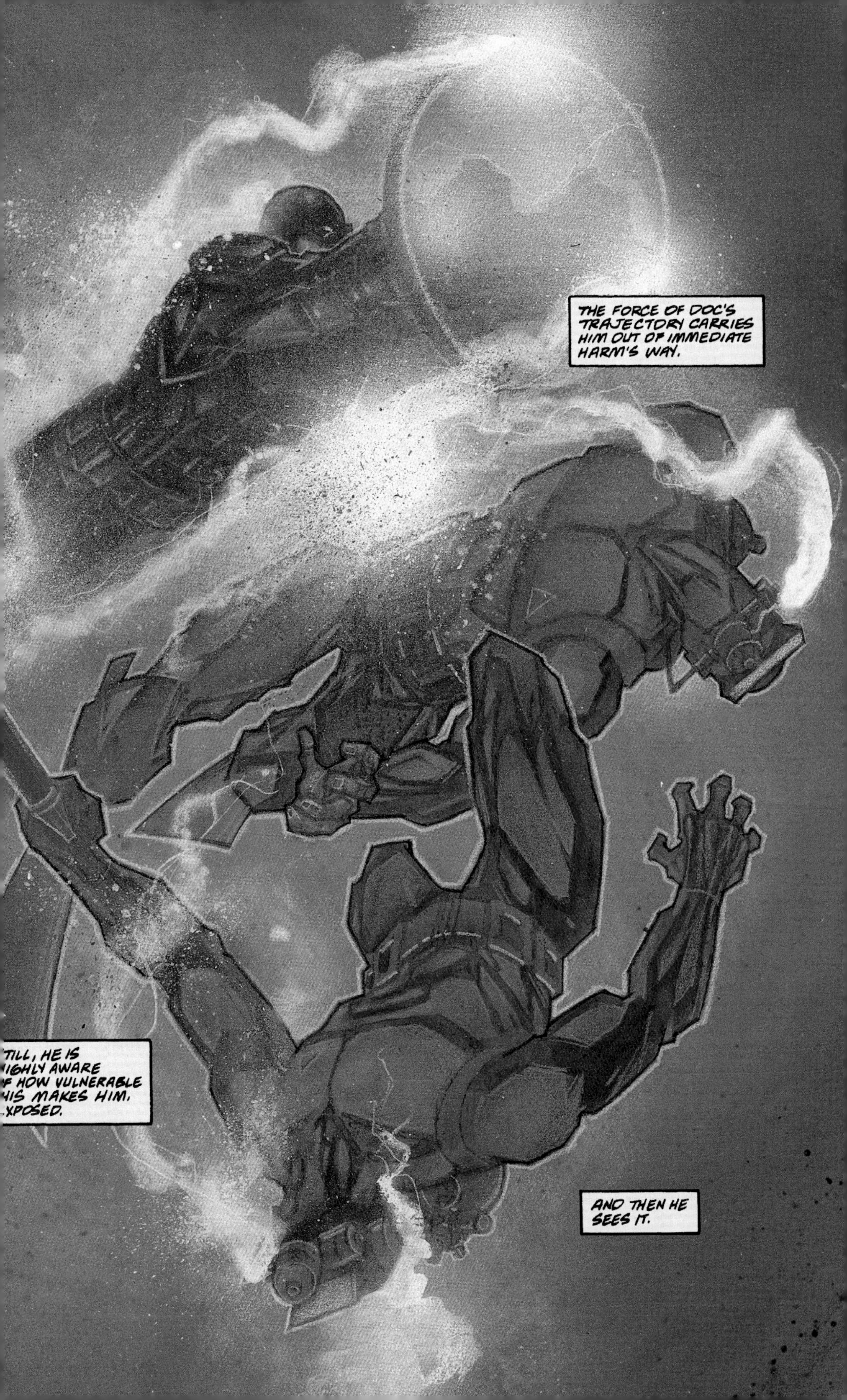
THE FORCE OF DOC'S TRAJECTORY CARRIES HIM OUT OF IMMEDIATE HARM'S WAY.
TILL, HE IS IGHLY AWARE F HOW VULNERABLE HIS MAKES HIM. XPOSED.
AND THEN HE SEES IT.

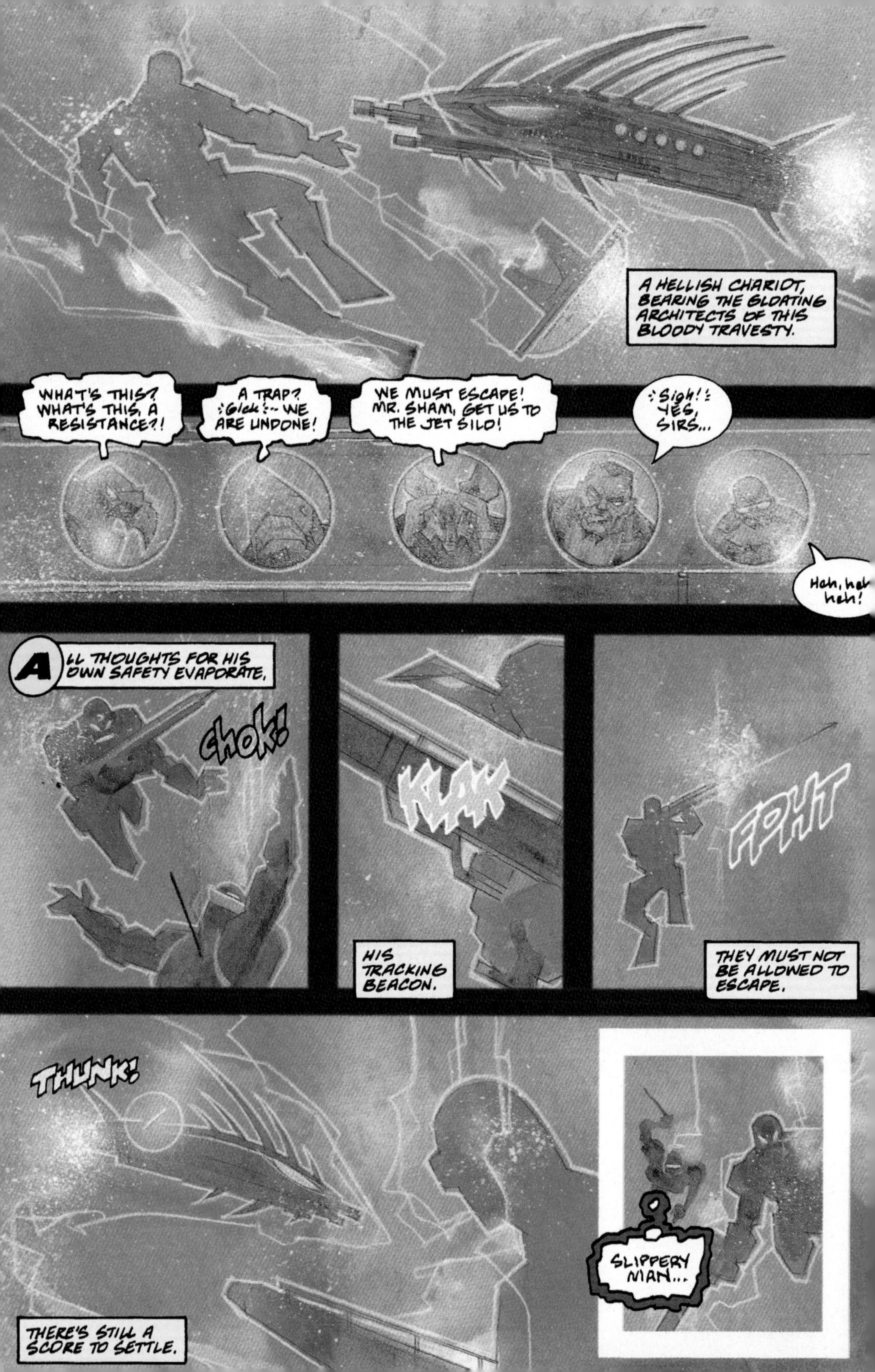
A HELLISH CHARIOT, BEARING THE GLOATING ARCHITECTS OF THIS BLOODY TRAVESTY.
WHAT'S THIS? WHAT'S THIS, A RESISTANCE?!
A TRAP? :Gick!:-- WE ARE UNDONE!
WE MUST ESCAPE! MR. SHAM, GET US TO THE JET SILO!
:Sigh!: YES, SIRS...
Heh, heh heh!
ALL THOUGHTS FOR HIS OWN SAFETY EVAPORATE.
CHOK!
KLAK
HIS TRACKING BEACON.
FDHT
THEY MUST NOT BE ALLOWED TO ESCAPE.
THUNK!
SLIPPERY MAN...
THERE'S STILL A SCORE TO SETTLE.

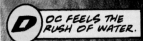
DOC FEELS THE RUSH OF WATER.

BARELY IN TIME.

I'VE GOT A BONE TO PICK WITH YOU!

DOC FAILS TO FREE HIMSELF.

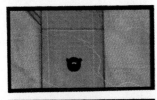

PAYBACKS ARE HELL!

KNOWS HE'S NO MATCH FOR THE ZOMBIE'S ENHANCED STRENGTH.

0:07

ALL THE WHILE, IN THE BACK OF HIS HEAD, HE CAN HEAR THE DEPTH CHARGES— COUNTING DOWN.

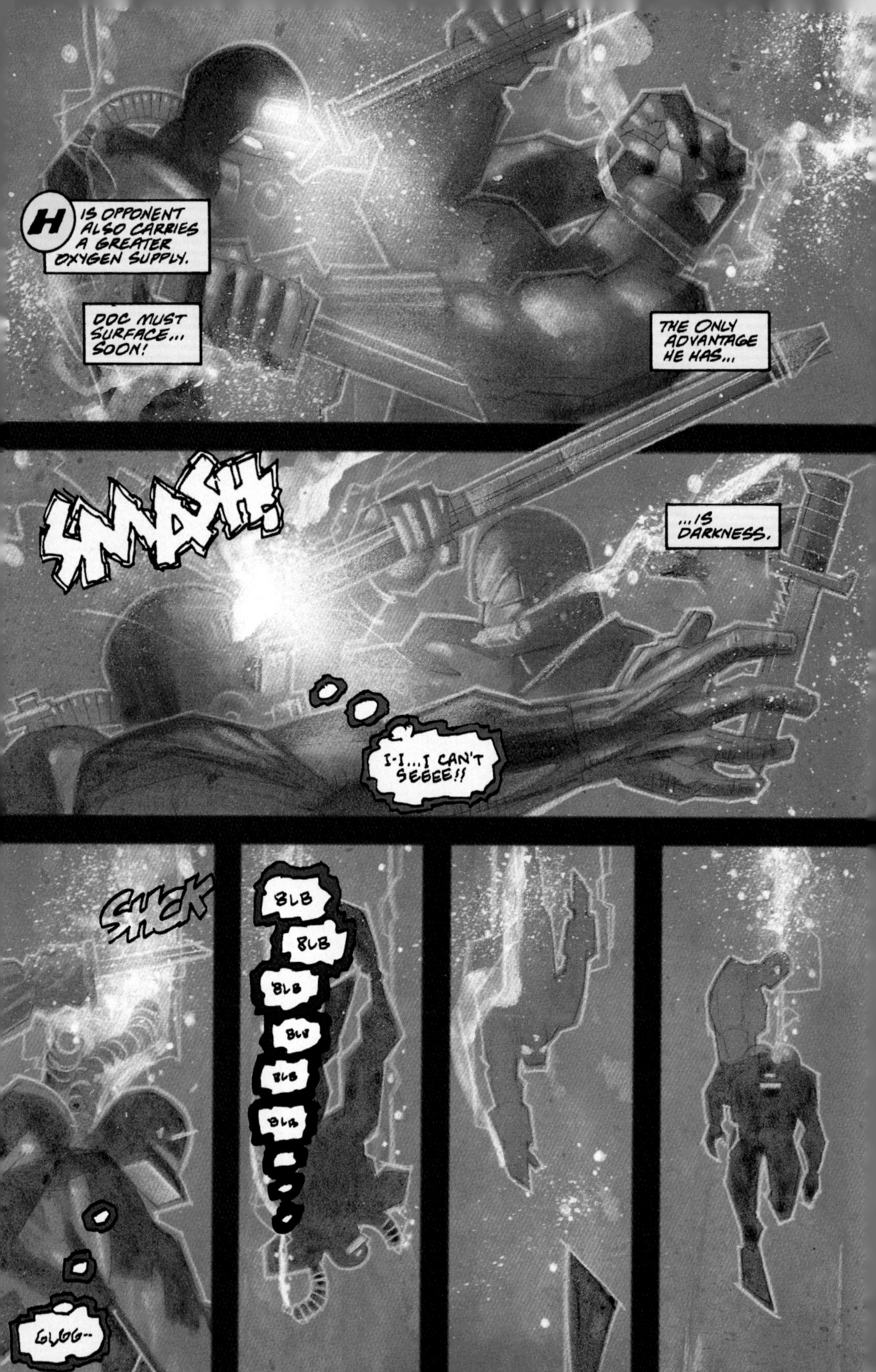
HIS OPPONENT ALSO CARRIES A GREATER OXYGEN SUPPLY.
DOC MUST SURFACE... SOON!
THE ONLY ADVANTAGE HE HAS...
SMASH!
...IS DARKNESS.
I-I...I CAN'T SEEEE!!
SHICK
GLUG--
BLB
BLB
BLB
BLB
BLB
BLB

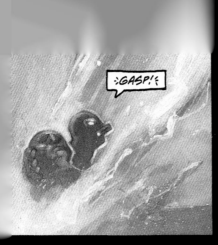

:<GASP!>:

WHAT HAPPENED? I'VE BEEN CIRCLING EVER SINCE YOUR BEACON SIGNALED--

QUICKLY, WE'VE GOT TO--

B-BOOM!

B-BOOM!

B-BOOM!

AND THEN, DESPITE SO MANY VALIANT EFFORTS TO THE CONTRARY...

...THE PACIFIC PETROLEUM STORAGE STATION CRUMBLES AND FALLS INTO THE SEA.

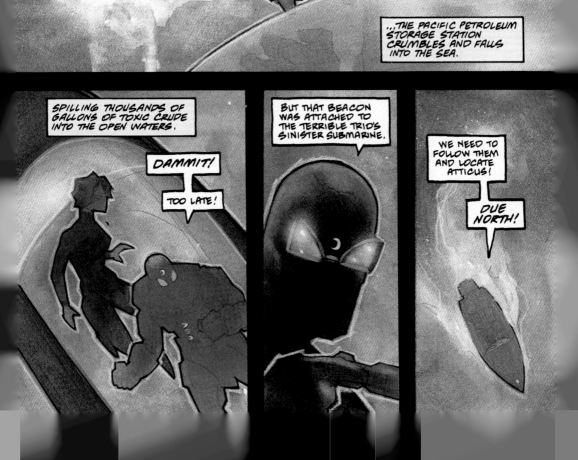

SPILLING THOUSANDS OF GALLONS OF TOXIC CRUDE INTO THE OPEN WATERS.

DAMMIT!

TOO LATE!

BUT THAT BEACON WAS ATTACHED TO THE TERRIBLE TRIO'S SINISTER SUBMARINE.

WE NEED TO FOLLOW THEM AND LOCATE ATTICUS!

DUE NORTH!

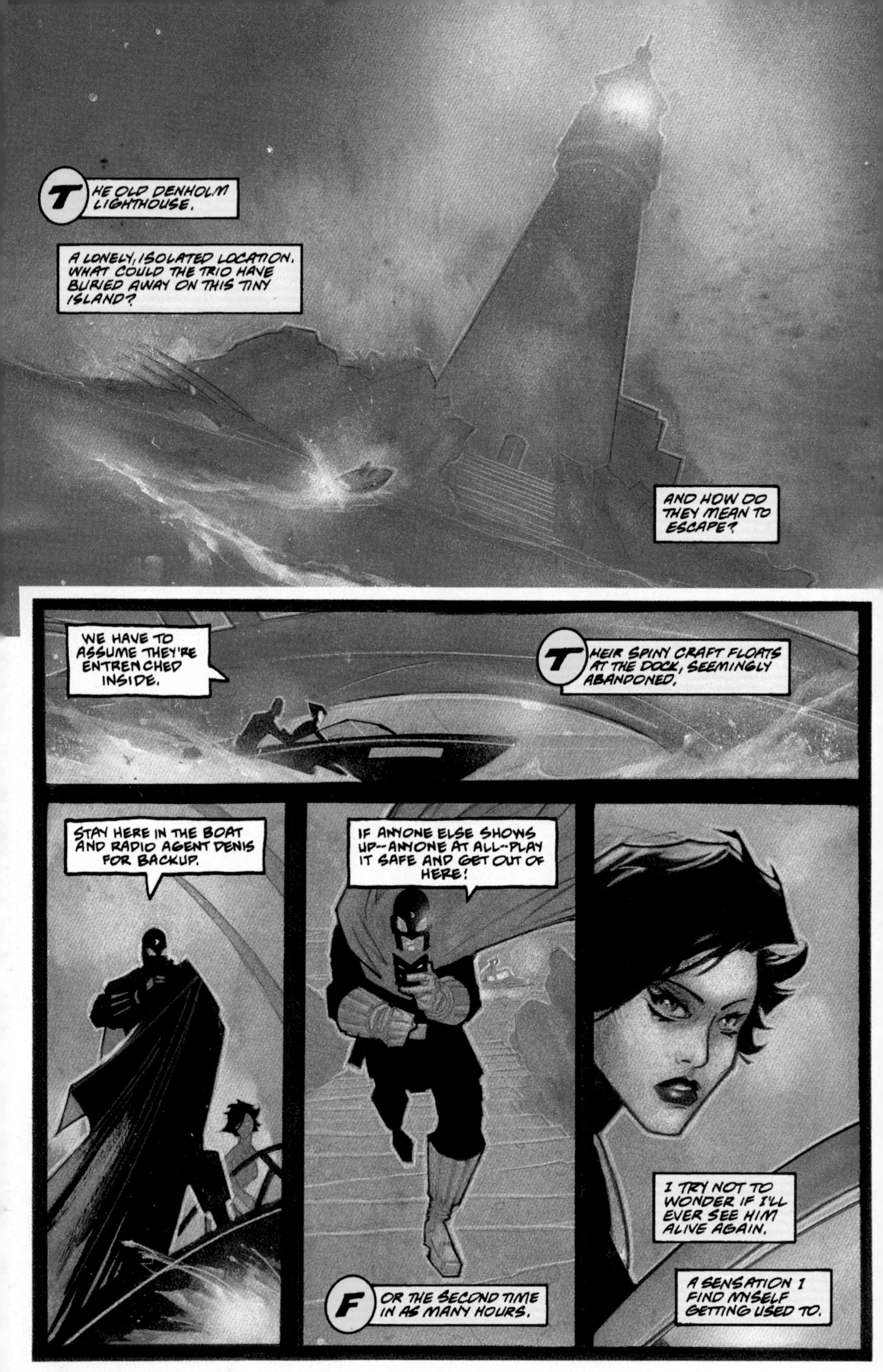
THE OLD DENHOLM LIGHTHOUSE.
A LONELY, ISOLATED LOCATION. WHAT COULD THE TRIO HAVE BURIED AWAY ON THIS TINY ISLAND?
AND HOW DO THEY MEAN TO ESCAPE?
WE HAVE TO ASSUME THEY'RE ENTRENCHED INSIDE.
THEIR SPINY CRAFT FLOATS AT THE DOCK, SEEMINGLY ABANDONED.
STAY HERE IN THE BOAT AND RADIO AGENT DENIS FOR BACKUP.
IF ANYONE ELSE SHOWS UP--ANYONE AT ALL--PLAY IT SAFE AND GET OUT OF HERE!
FOR THE SECOND TIME IN AS MANY HOURS.
I TRY NOT TO WONDER IF I'LL EVER SEE HIM ALIVE AGAIN.
A SENSATION I FIND MYSELF GETTING USED TO.

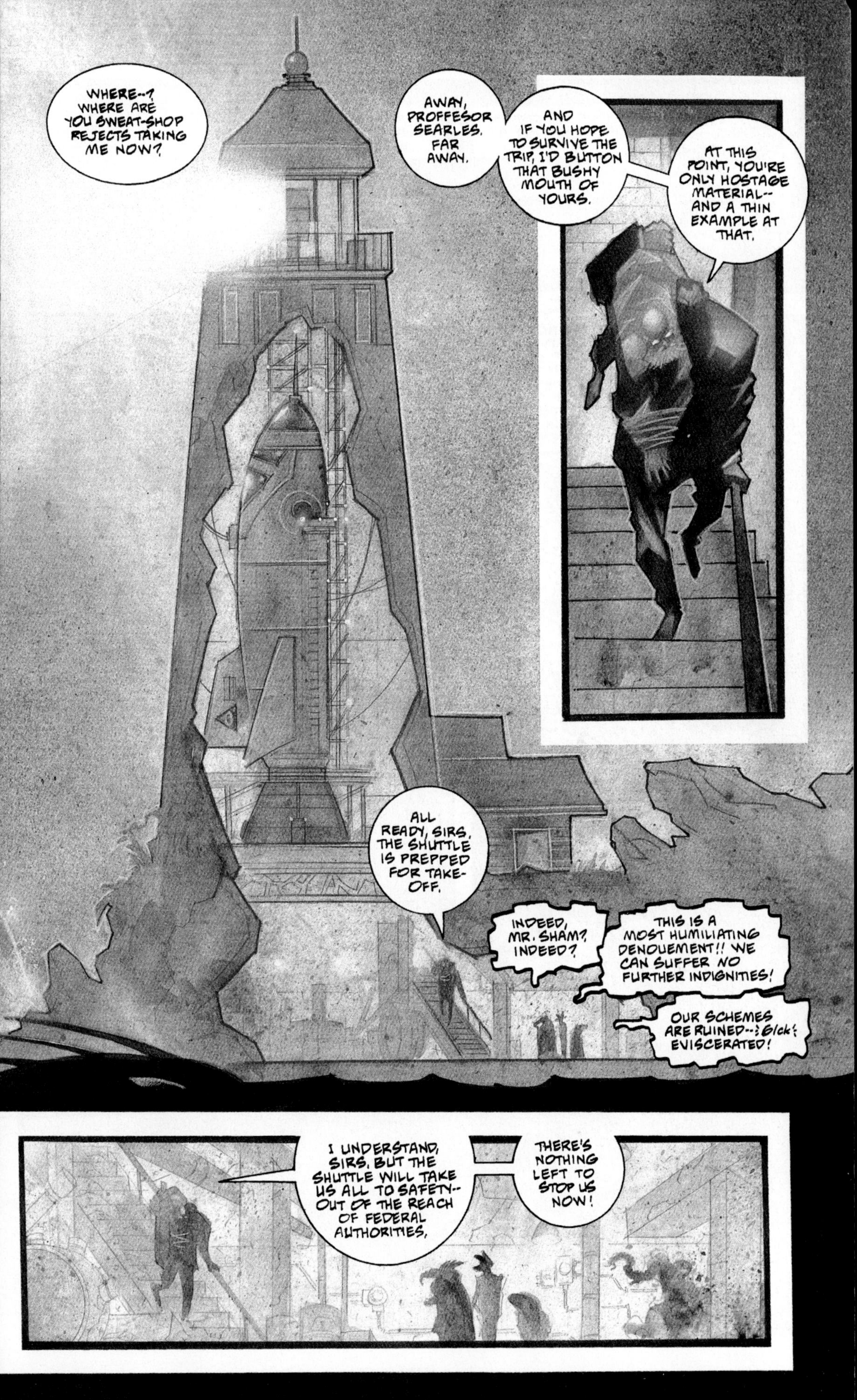
WHERE--? WHERE ARE YOU SWEAT-SHOP REJECTS TAKING ME NOW?
AWAY, PROFFESOR SEARLES. FAR AWAY.
AND IF YOU HOPE TO SURVIVE THE TRIP, I'D BUTTON THAT BUSHY MOUTH OF YOURS.
AT THIS POINT, YOU'RE ONLY HOSTAGE MATERIAL--AND A THIN EXAMPLE AT THAT.
ALL READY, SIRS. THE SHUTTLE IS PREPPED FOR TAKE-OFF.
INDEED, MR. SHAM? INDEED?
THIS IS A MOST HUMILIATING DENOUEMENT!! WE CAN SUFFER NO FURTHER INDIGNITIES!
OUR SCHEMES ARE RUINED--¡Glck¡ EVISCERATED!
I UNDERSTAND, SIRS, BUT THE SHUTTLE WILL TAKE US ALL TO SAFETY--OUT OF THE REACH OF FEDERAL AUTHORITIES.
THERE'S NOTHING LEFT TO STOP US NOW!

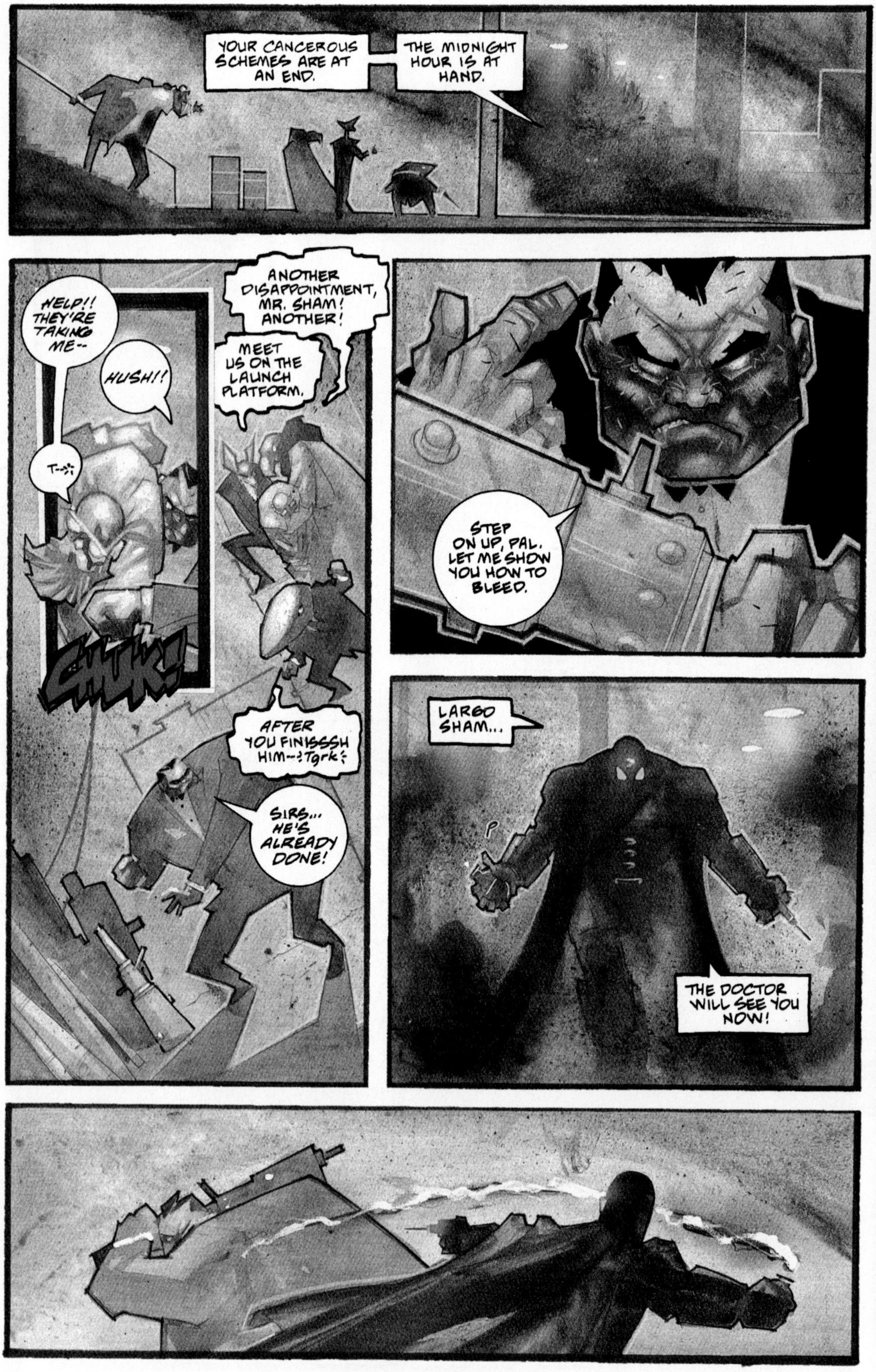
YOUR CANCEROUS SCHEMES ARE AT AN END.
THE MIDNIGHT HOUR IS AT HAND.
HELP!! THEY'RE TAKING ME--
HUSH!!
T--
ANOTHER DISAPPOINTMENT, MR. SHAM! ANOTHER!
MEET US ON THE LAUNCH PLATFORM.
CHUK!
AFTER YOU FINISSSH HIM-- Tgrk
SIRS... HE'S ALREADY DONE!
STEP ON UP, PAL. LET ME SHOW YOU HOW TO BLEED.
LARGO SHAM...
THE DOCTOR WILL SEE YOU NOW!

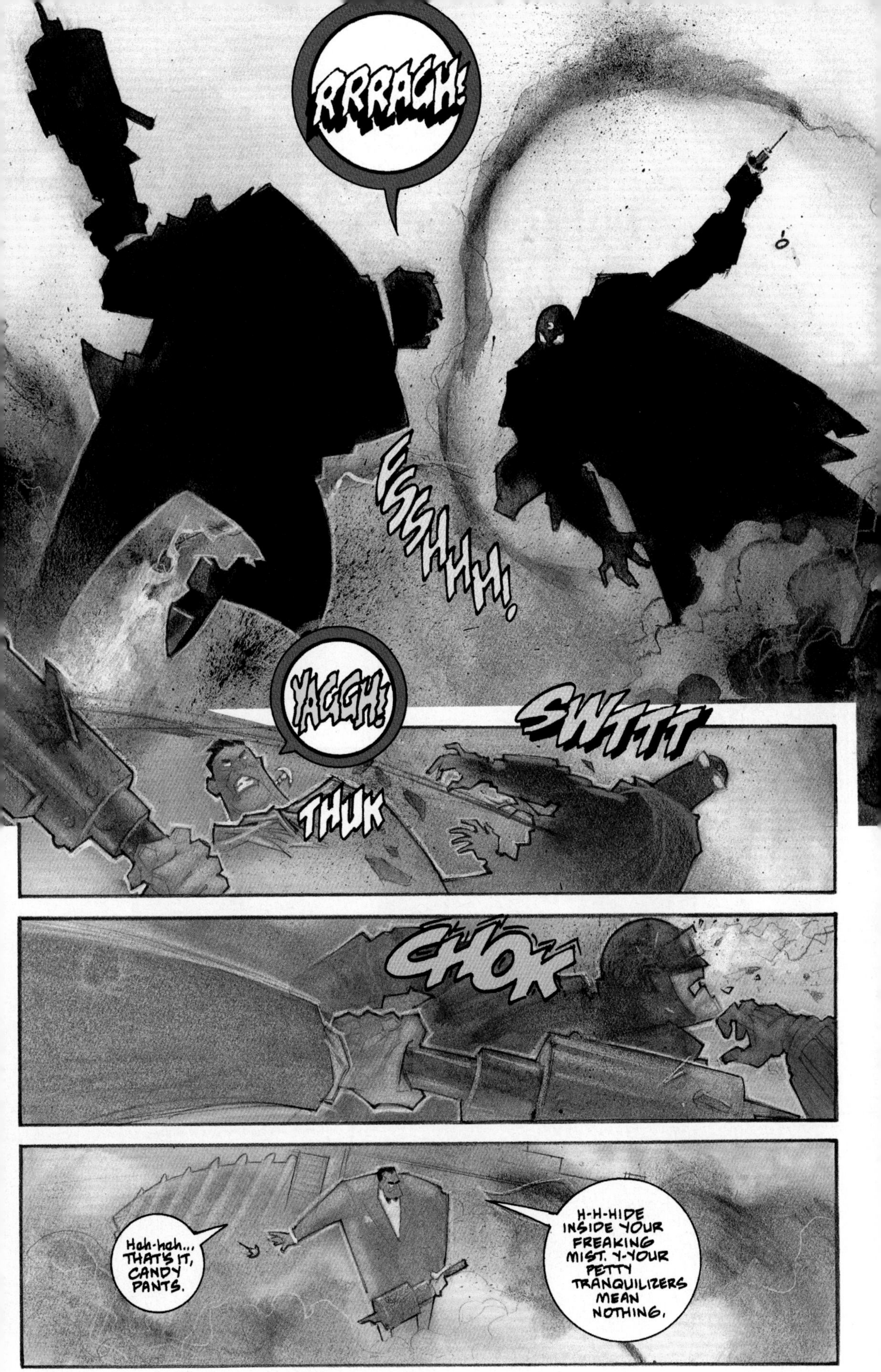
RRRACH!
FSSHHH!
YAGGH!
SWTTT
THUK
CHOK
Hah-hah... THAT'S IT, CANDY PANTS.
H-H-HIDE INSIDE YOUR FREAKING MIST. Y-YOUR PETTY TRANQUILIZERS MEAN NOTHING.

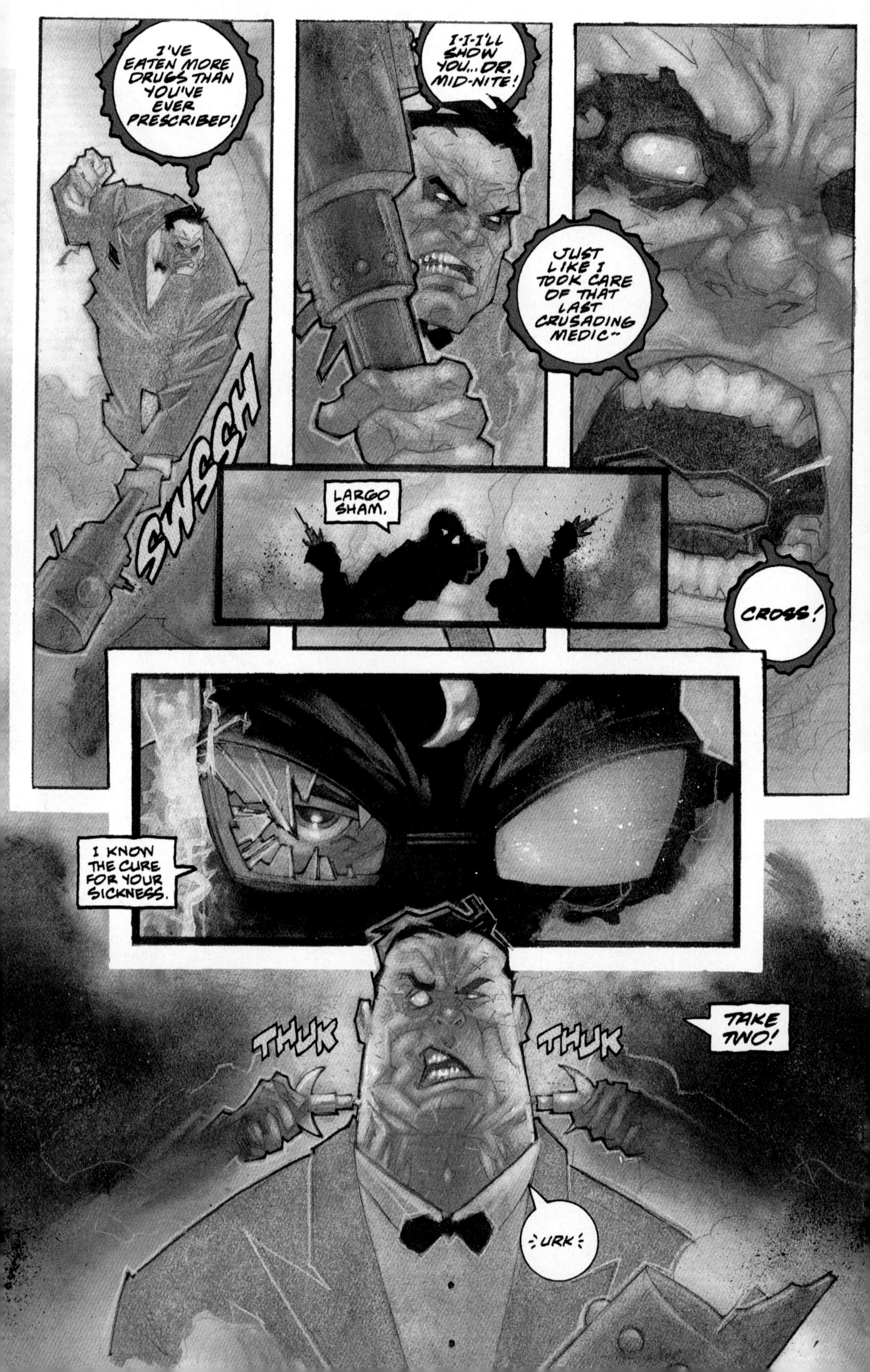
I'VE EATEN MORE DRUGS THAN YOU'VE EVER PRESCRIBED!
SWSSH
I-I-I'LL SHOW YOU... DR. MID-NITE!
JUST LIKE I TOOK CARE OF THAT LAST CRUSADING MEDIC--
LARGO SHAM.
CROSS!
I KNOW THE CURE FOR YOUR SICKNESS.
THUK
THUK
TAKE TWO!
URK

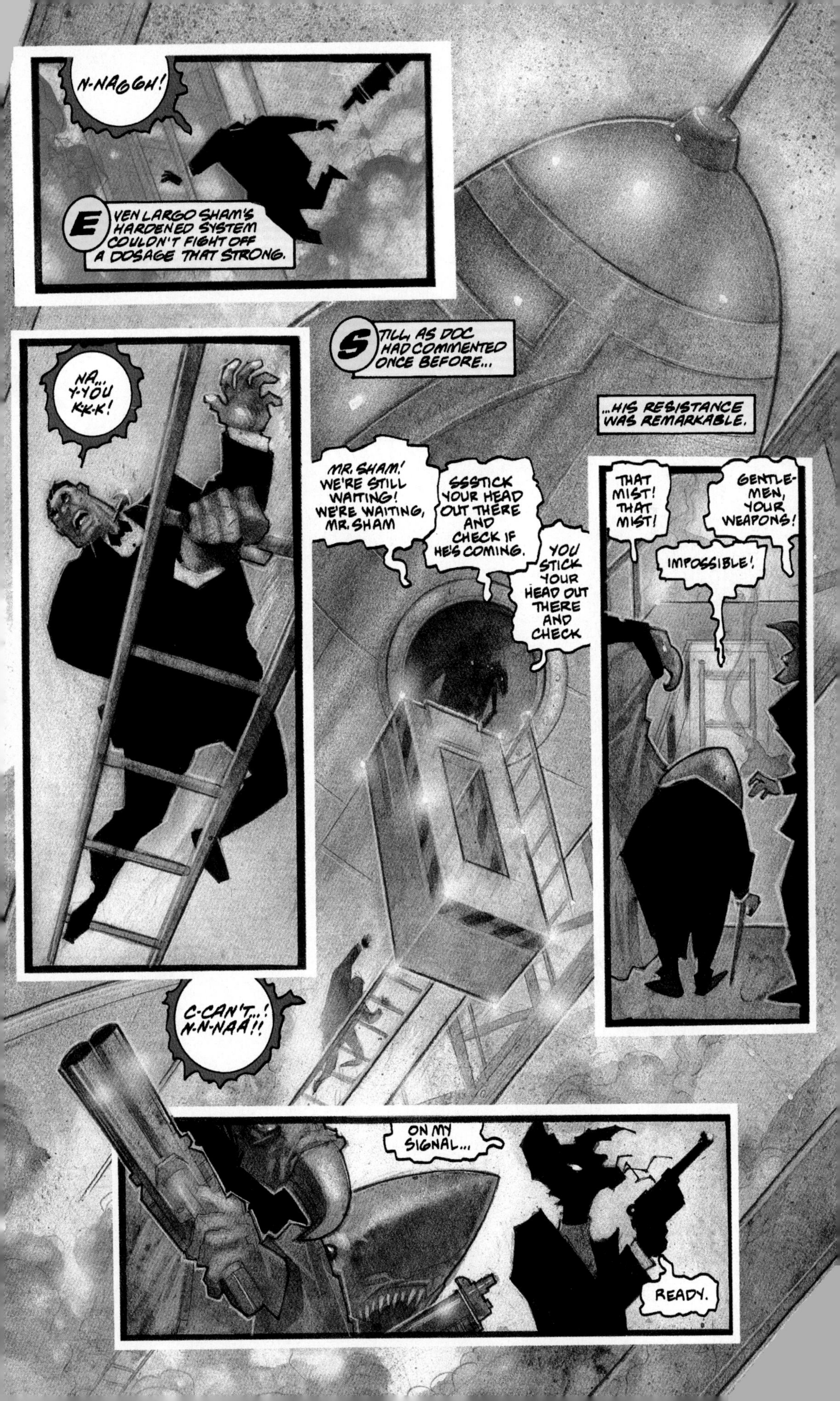

N-NAGGH!
EVEN LARGO SHAM'S HARDENED SYSTEM COULDN'T FIGHT OFF A DOSAGE THAT STRONG.
NA... Y-YOU K-K-K!
STILL, AS DOC HAD COMMENTED ONCE BEFORE...
...HIS RESISTANCE WAS REMARKABLE.
MR. SHAM! WE'RE STILL WAITING! WE'RE WAITING, MR. SHAM
SSSTICK YOUR HEAD OUT THERE AND CHECK IF HE'S COMING.
YOU STICK YOUR HEAD OUT THERE AND CHECK
THAT MIST! THAT MIST!
GENTLE-MEN, YOUR WEAPONS!
IMPOSSIBLE!
C-CAN'T...! N-N-NAA!!
ON MY SIGNAL...
READY.

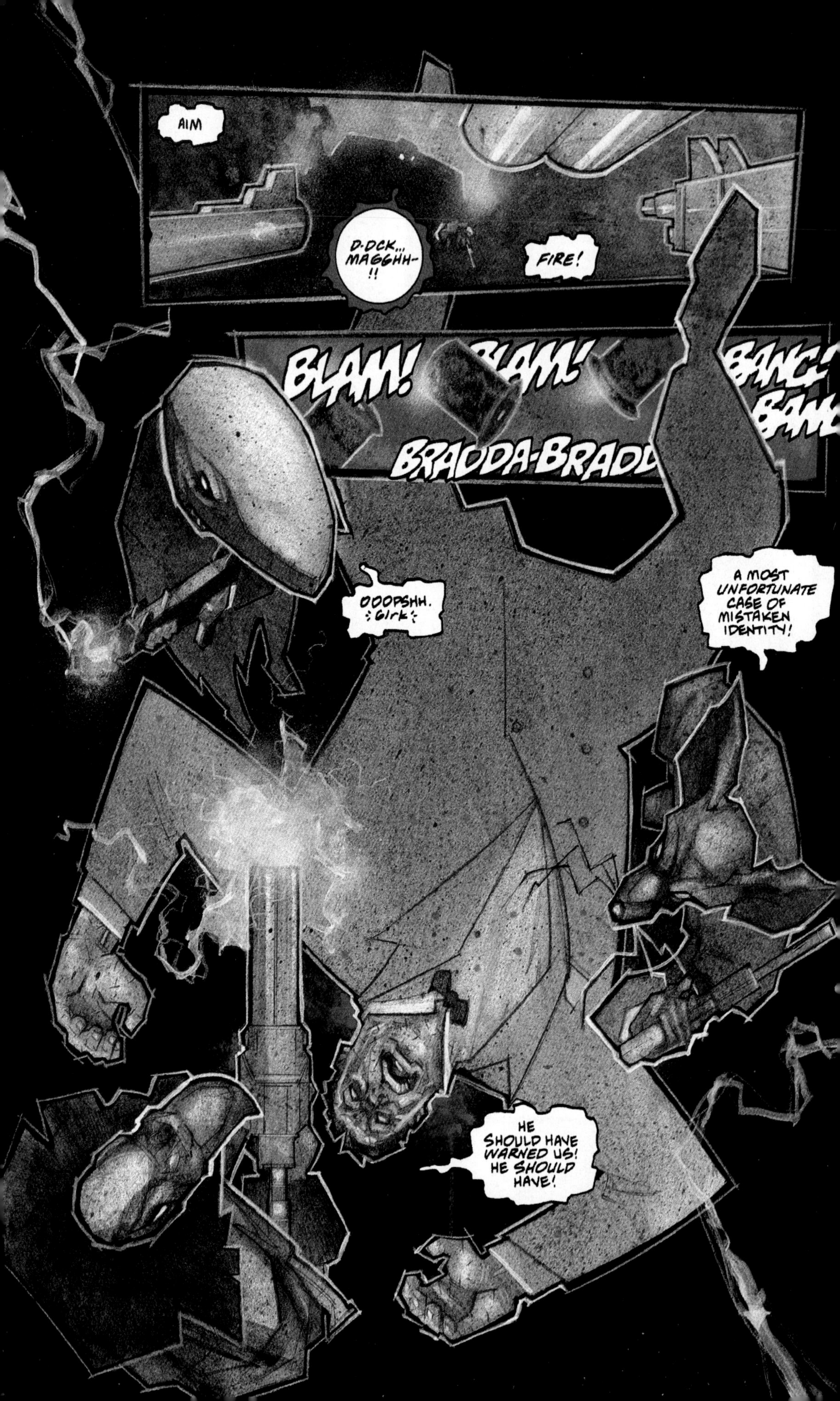
AIM
D-DCK... MAGGHH-!!
FIRE!
BLAM! BLAM!
BANG! BAM
BRADDA-BRADD
OOOPSHH. Glrk
A MOST UNFORTUNATE CASE OF MISTAKEN IDENTITY!
HE SHOULD HAVE WARNED US! HE SHOULD HAVE!

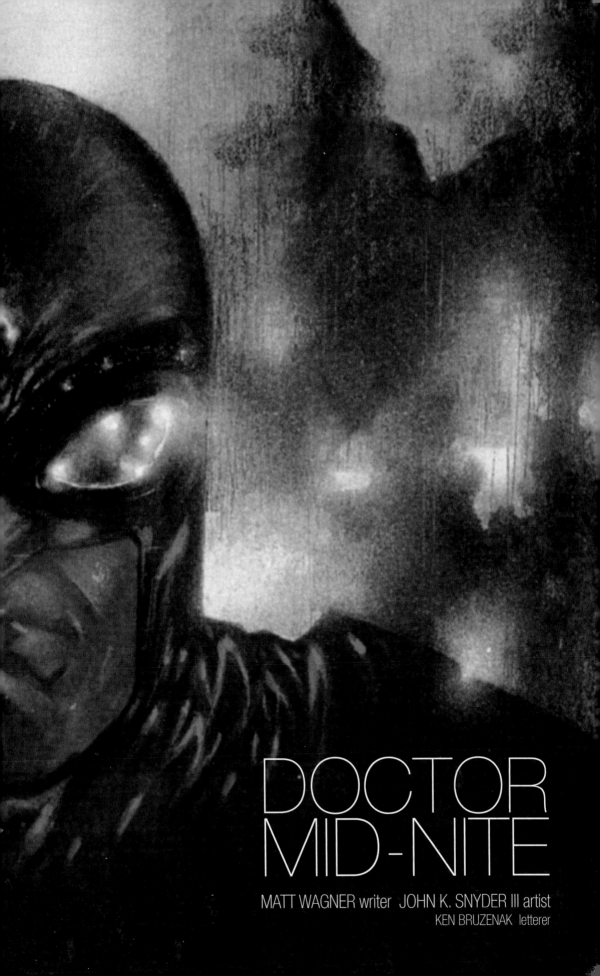

DOCTOR MID-NITE

MATT WAGNER writer JOHN K. SNYDER III artist

KEN BRUZENAK letterer

Dan Raspler Editor – Original Series
Alisande Morales Assistant Editor-Original Series
Robin Wildman Editor
Robbin Brosterman Design Director – Books
Louis Prandi Publication Design

Bob Harras Senior VP – Editor-in-Chief, DC Comics

Diane Nelson President
Dan DiDio and Jim Lee Co-Publishers
Geoff Johns Chief Creative Officer
John Rood Executive VP – Sales, Marketing & Business Development
Amy Genkins Senior VP – Business & Legal Affairs
Nairi Gardiner Senior VP – Finance
Jeff Boison VP – Publishing Planning
Mark Chiarello VP – Art Direction & Design
John Cunningham VP – Marketing
Terri Cunningham VP – Editorial Administration
Alison Gill Senior VP – Manufacturing & Operations
Hank Kanalz Senior VP – Vertigo & Integrated Publishing
Jay Kogan VP – Business & Legal Affairs, Publishing
Jack Mahan VP – Business Affairs, Talent
Nick Napolitano VP – Manufacturing Administration
Sue Pohja VP – Book Sales
Courtney Simmons Senior VP – Publicity
Bob Wayne Senior VP – Sales

DOCTOR MID-NITE
Published by DC Comics. Copyright © 2013 DC Comics. All Rights Reserved.
Originally published in single magazine form as DOCTOR MID-NITE 1-3 ©
1999 DC Comics. All Rights Reserved. All characters, their distinctive like-
nesses and related elements featured in this publication are trademarks of
DC Comics. The stories, characters and incidents featured in this publication
are entirely fictional. DC Comics does not read or accept unsolicited ideas,
stories or artwork.
DC Comics, 1700 Broadway, New York, NY 10019
A Warner Bros. Entertainment Company.
Printed by RR Donnelley, Salem, VA, USA. 11/08/13. First Printing.
ISBN: 978-1-4012-4325-8

Library of Congress Cataloging-in-Publication Data

Wagner, Matt, author.
  Doctor Mid-Nite / Matt Wagner, John K. Snyder. -- New edition.
    pages cm
  Summary: "Matt Wagner, creator of indy comics favorites GRENDEL and
MAGE and the writer and artist of SUPERMAN/BATMAN/WONDER WOMAN:
TRINITY, creates a new vision of a classic DC hero. When Dr. Pieter Cross lost
his sight during a terrible accident, he thought his life was over. But after a
chance encounter with an owl showed the Doctor that he could now see in
the dark, his existence gained new meaning. Using his scientific genius and
acquired wealth, Cross assumes the identity of vigilante Doctor Mid-Nite to
protect the downtrodden from the vermin that prey on them. But in order to
fulfill his mission, Doctor Mid-Nite must take down an evil criminal triumvirate bent on profiting from the demise of his city. Collects DOCTOR MID-NITE
#1-3"-- Provided by publisher.
  ISBN 978-1-4012-4325-8 (pbk.)
1. Graphic novels. I. Snyder, John K., 1961- illustrator. II. Title.
  PN6728.D57W343 2013
  741.5'973—dc23
                              2013031438

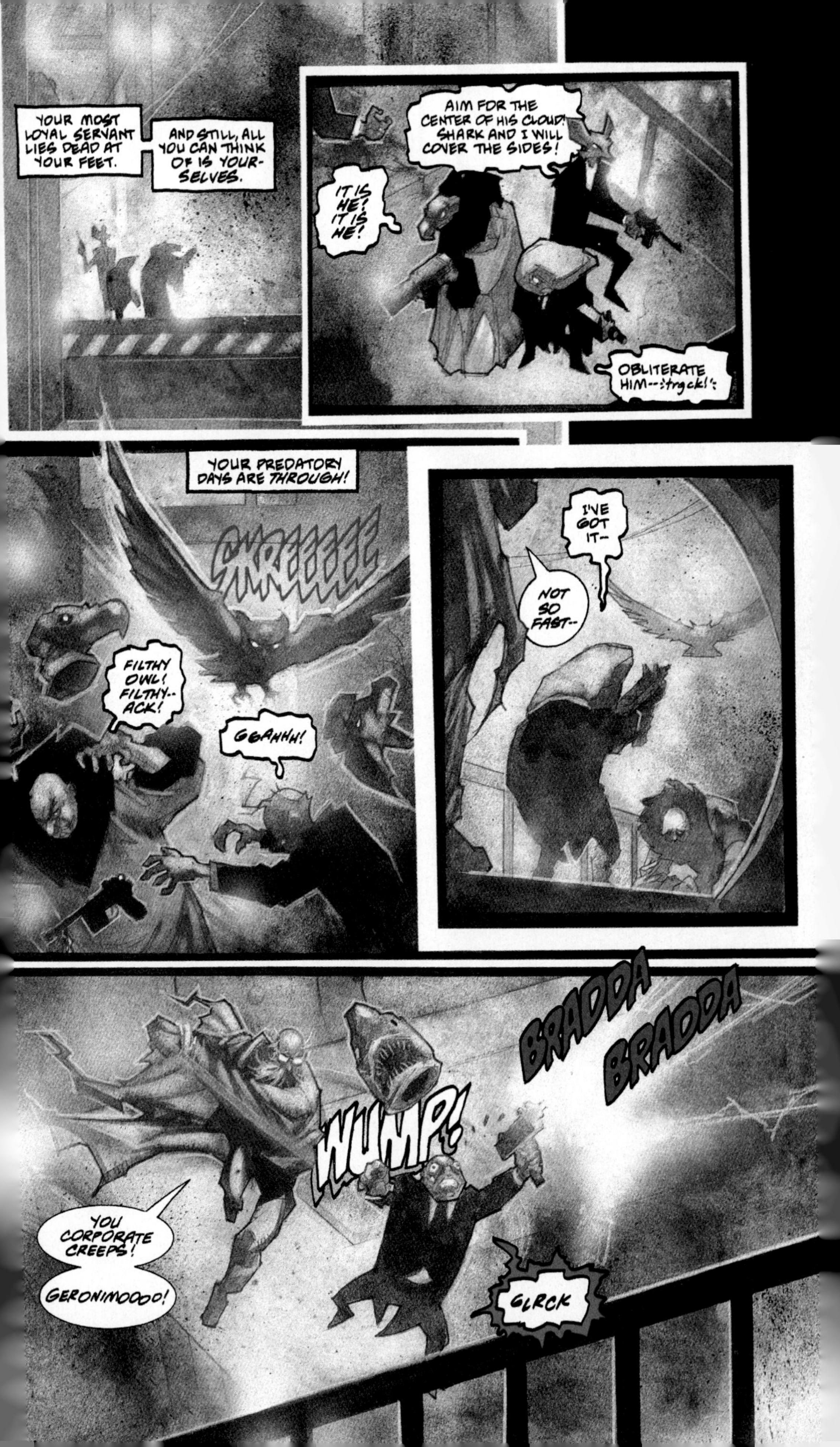
YOUR MOST LOYAL SERVANT LIES DEAD AT YOUR FEET.
AND STILL, ALL YOU CAN THINK OF IS YOUR-SELVES.
AIM FOR THE CENTER OF HIS CLOUD! SHARK AND I WILL COVER THE SIDES!
IT IS HE! IT IS HE!
OBLITERATE HIM--
YOUR PREDATORY DAYS ARE THROUGH!
SKREEEEE
FILTHY OWL! FILTHY-- ACK!
GGAHHH!
I'VE GOT IT--
NOT SO FAST--
BRADDA BRADDA
WUMP!
YOU CORPORATE CREEPS!
GERONIMOOOO!
GLRCK

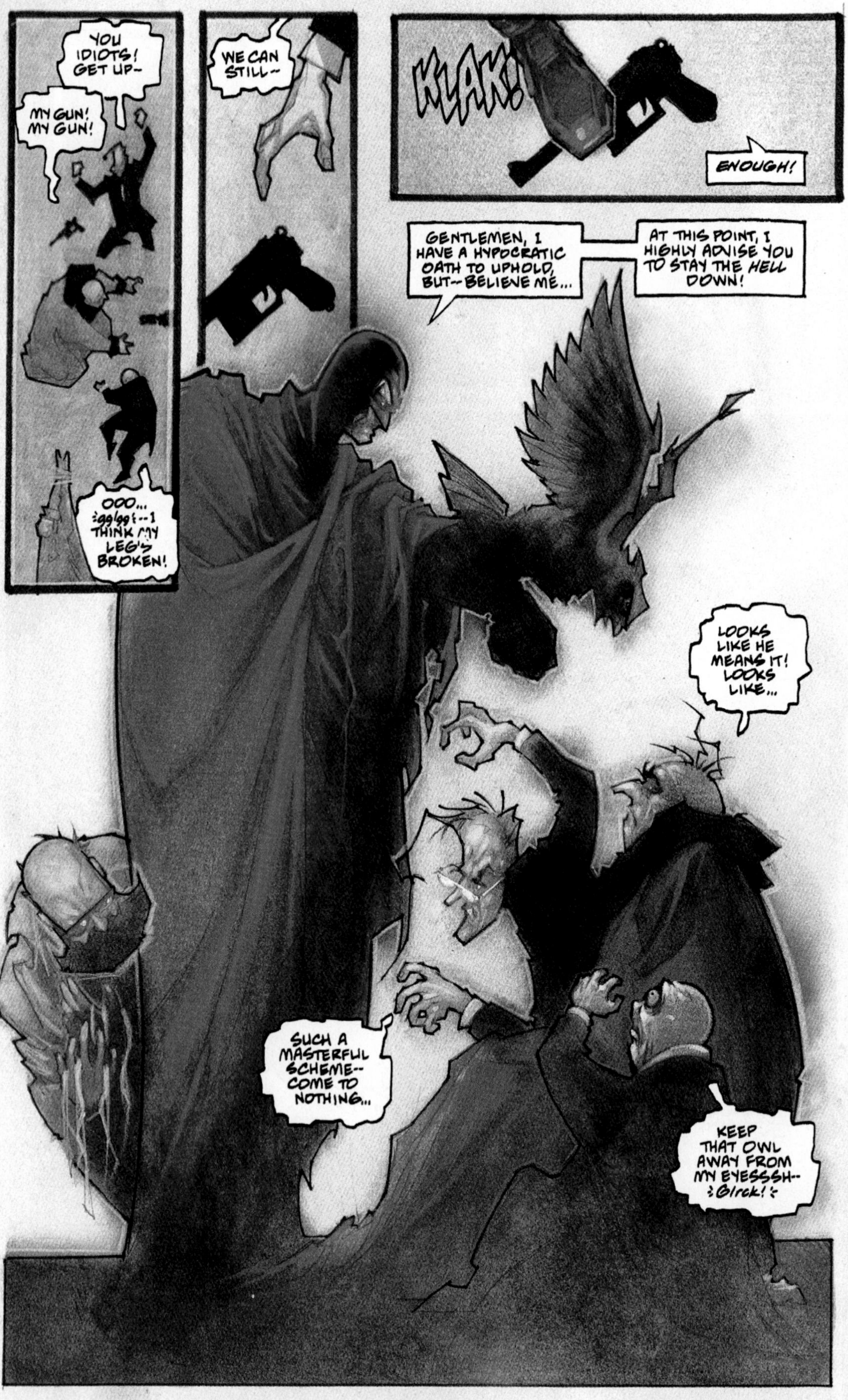
YOU IDIOTS! GET UP--
MY GUN! MY GUN!
OOO... :gg/gg:--I THINK MY LEG'S BROKEN!
WE CAN STILL--
KLAK!
ENOUGH!
GENTLEMEN, I HAVE A HYPOCRATIC OATH TO UPHOLD, BUT--BELIEVE ME...
AT THIS POINT, I HIGHLY ADVISE YOU TO STAY THE HELL DOWN!
LOOKS LIKE HE MEANS IT! LOOKS LIKE...
SUCH A MASTERFUL SCHEME-- COME TO NOTHING...
KEEP THAT OWL AWAY FROM MY EYESSSH-- :Glrck!:

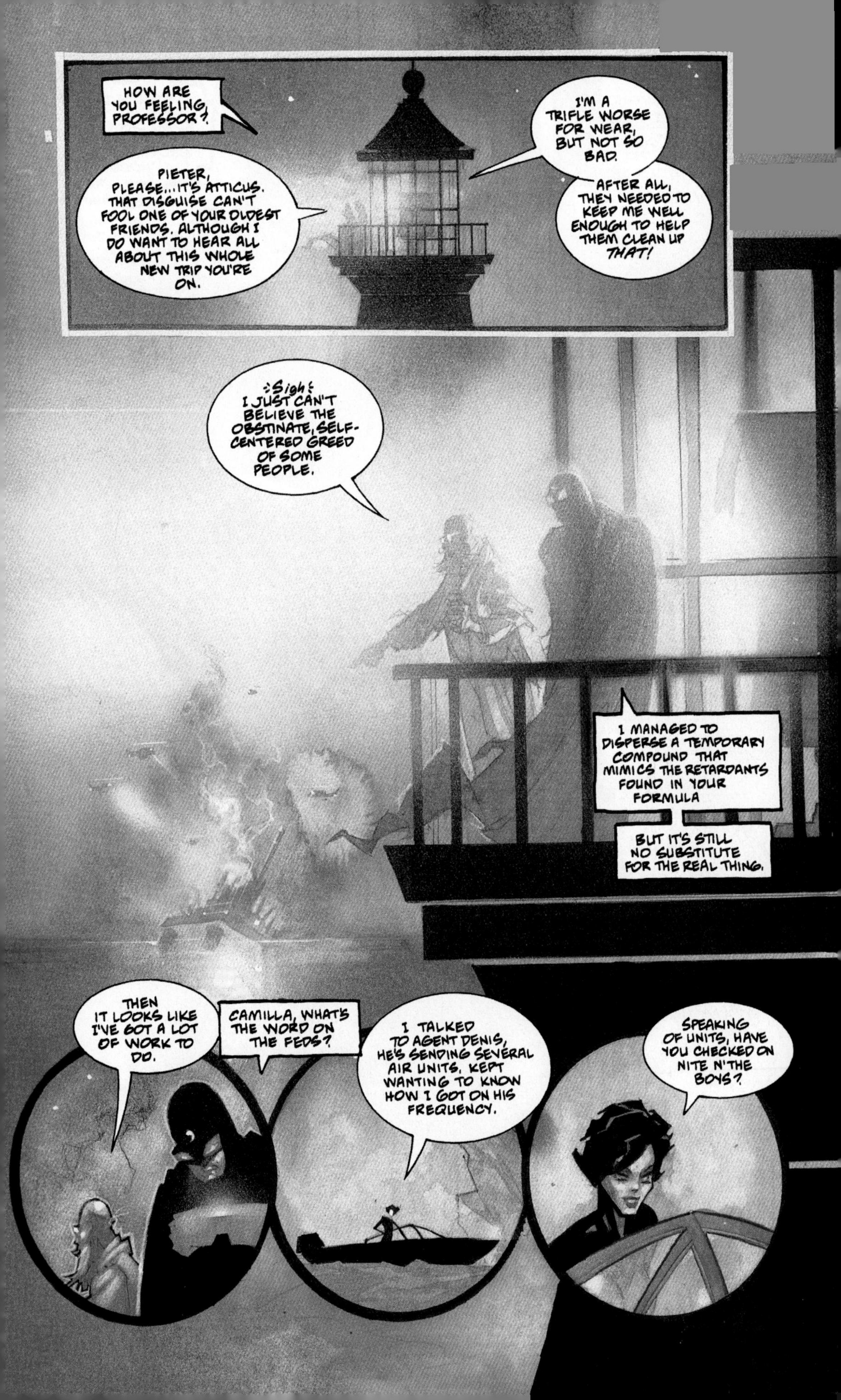

HOW ARE YOU FEELING, PROFESSOR?
PIETER, PLEASE... IT'S ATTICUS. THAT DISGUISE CAN'T FOOL ONE OF YOUR OLDEST FRIENDS. ALTHOUGH I DO WANT TO HEAR ALL ABOUT THIS WHOLE NEW TRIP YOU'RE ON.
I'M A TRIFLE WORSE FOR WEAR, BUT NOT SO BAD.
AFTER ALL, THEY NEEDED TO KEEP ME WELL ENOUGH TO HELP THEM CLEAN UP THAT!
:Sigh: I JUST CAN'T BELIEVE THE OBSTINATE, SELF-CENTERED GREED OF SOME PEOPLE.
I MANAGED TO DISPERSE A TEMPORARY COMPOUND THAT MIMICS THE RETARDANTS FOUND IN YOUR FORMULA
BUT IT'S STILL NO SUBSTITUTE FOR THE REAL THING.
THEN IT LOOKS LIKE I'VE GOT A LOT OF WORK TO DO.
CAMILLA, WHAT'S THE WORD ON THE FEDS?
I TALKED TO AGENT DENIS, HE'S SENDING SEVERAL AIR UNITS, KEPT WANTING TO KNOW HOW I GOT ON HIS FREQUENCY.
SPEAKING OF UNITS, HAVE YOU CHECKED ON NITE N' THE BOYS?

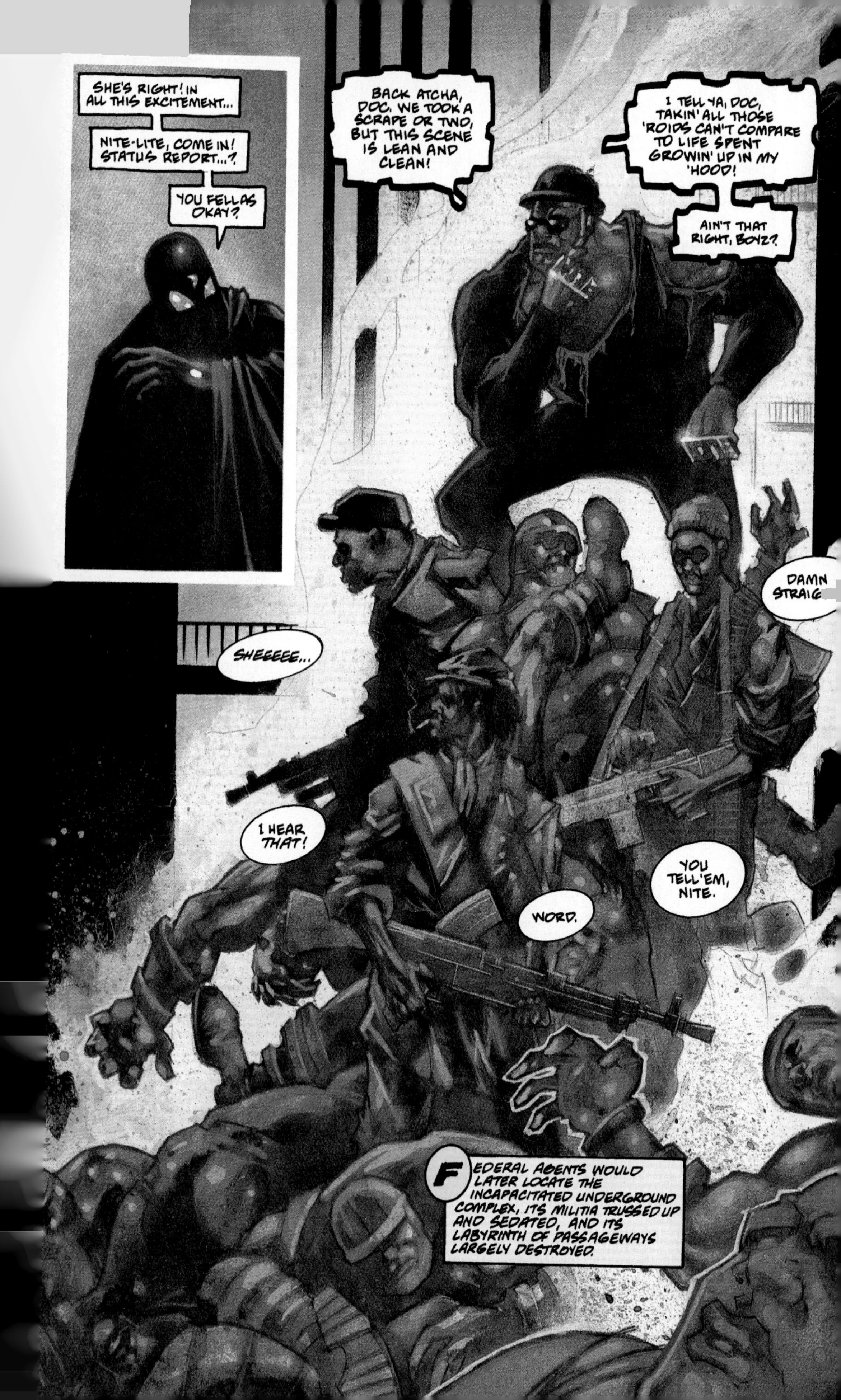

SHE'S RIGHT! IN ALL THIS EXCITEMENT...
NITE-LITE, COME IN! STATUS REPORT...?
YOU FELLAS OKAY?
BACK ATCHA, DOC. WE TOOK A SCRAPE OR TWO, BUT THIS SCENE IS LEAN AND CLEAN!
I TELL YA, DOC, TAKIN' ALL THOSE 'ROIDS CAN'T COMPARE TO LIFE SPENT GROWIN' UP IN MY 'HOOD!
AIN'T THAT RIGHT, BOYZ?
SHEEEEE...
DAMN STRAIG
I HEAR THAT!
YOU TELL'EM, NITE.
WORD.
FEDERAL AGENTS WOULD LATER LOCATE THE INCAPACITATED UNDERGROUND COMPLEX, ITS MILITIA TRUSSED UP AND SEDATED, AND ITS LABYRINTH OF PASSAGEWAYS LARGELY DESTROYED.

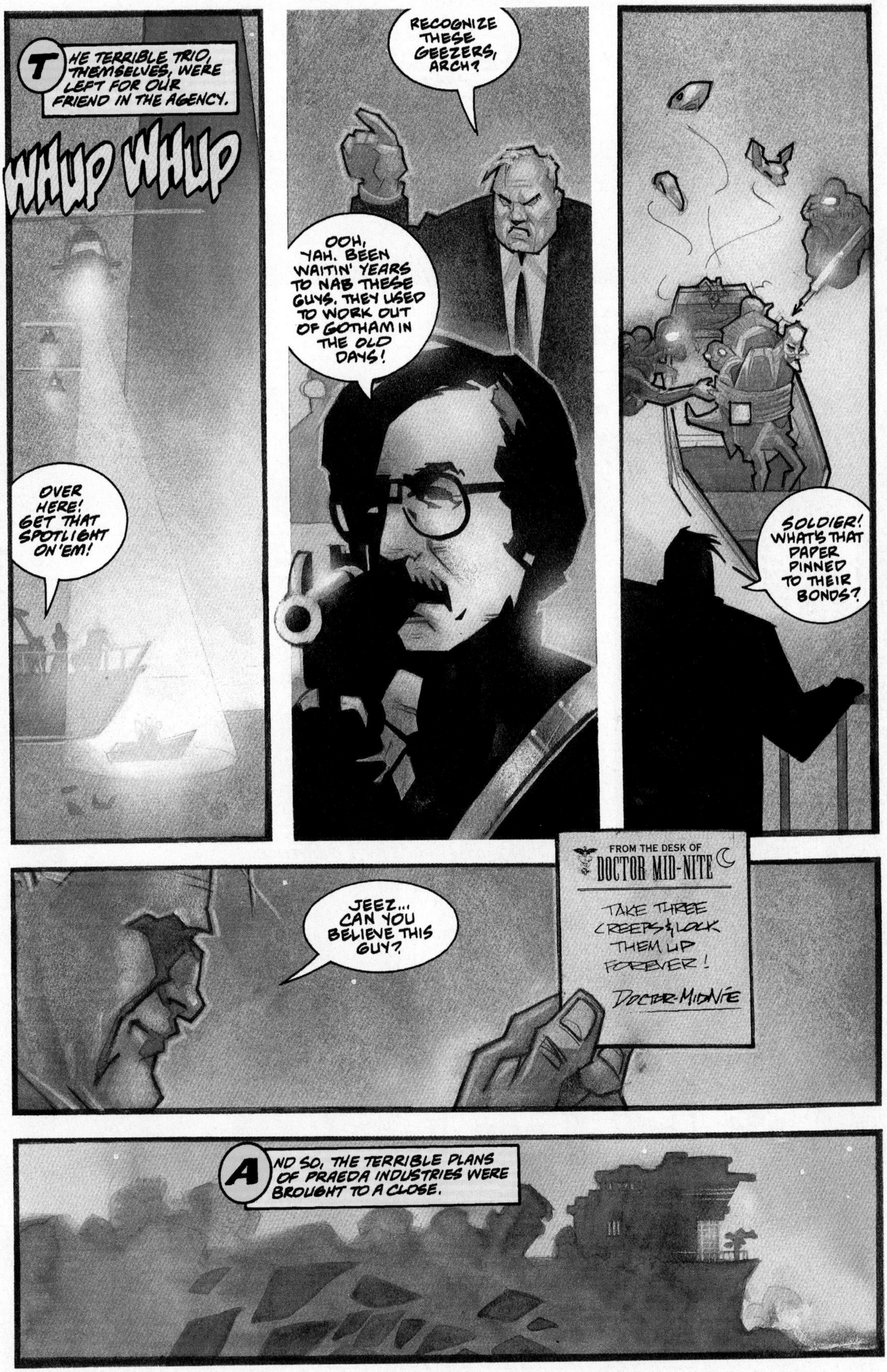
THE TERRIBLE TRIO, THEMSELVES, WERE LEFT FOR OUR FRIEND IN THE AGENCY.
WHUP WHUP
OVER HERE! GET THAT SPOTLIGHT ON'EM!
RECOGNIZE THESE GEEZERS, ARCH?
OOH, YAH. BEEN WAITIN' YEARS TO NAB THESE GUYS. THEY USED TO WORK OUT OF GOTHAM IN THE OLD DAYS!
SOLDIER! WHAT'S THAT PAPER PINNED TO THEIR BONDS?
JEEZ... CAN YOU BELIEVE THIS GUY?
FROM THE DESK OF DOCTOR MID-NITE
TAKE THREE CREEPS & LOCK THEM UP FOREVER!
DOCTOR MIDNITE
AND SO, THE TERRIBLE PLANS OF PRAEDA INDUSTRIES WERE BROUGHT TO A CLOSE.

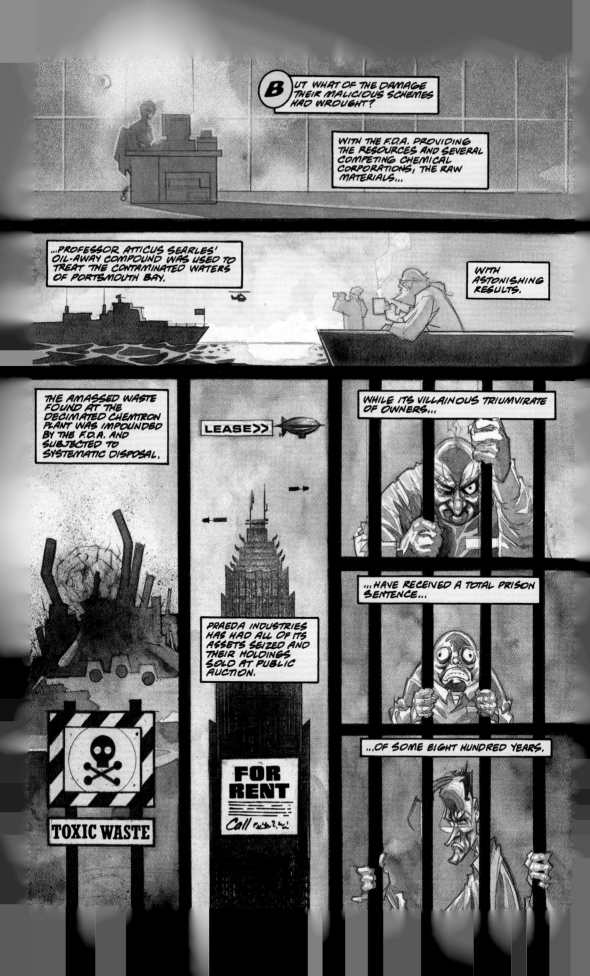

BUT WHAT OF THE DAMAGE THEIR MALICIOUS SCHEMES HAD WROUGHT?

WITH THE F.D.A. PROVIDING THE RESOURCES AND SEVERAL COMPETING CHEMICAL CORPORATIONS, THE RAW MATERIALS...

...PROFESSOR ATTICUS SEARLES' OIL-AWAY COMPOUND WAS USED TO TREAT THE CONTAMINATED WATERS OF PORTSMOUTH BAY.

WITH ASTONISHING RESULTS.

THE AMASSED WASTE FOUND AT THE DECIMATED CHEMTRON PLANT WAS IMPOUNDED BY THE F.D.A. AND SUBJECTED TO SYSTEMATIC DISPOSAL.

LEASE>>

PRAEDA INDUSTRIES HAS HAD ALL OF ITS ASSETS SEIZED AND THEIR HOLDINGS SOLD AT PUBLIC AUCTION.

WHILE ITS VILLAINOUS TRIUMVIRATE OF OWNERS...

...HAVE RECEIVED A TOTAL PRISON SENTENCE...

...OF SOME HUNDRED YEARS.

TOXIC WASTE

FOR RENT
Call

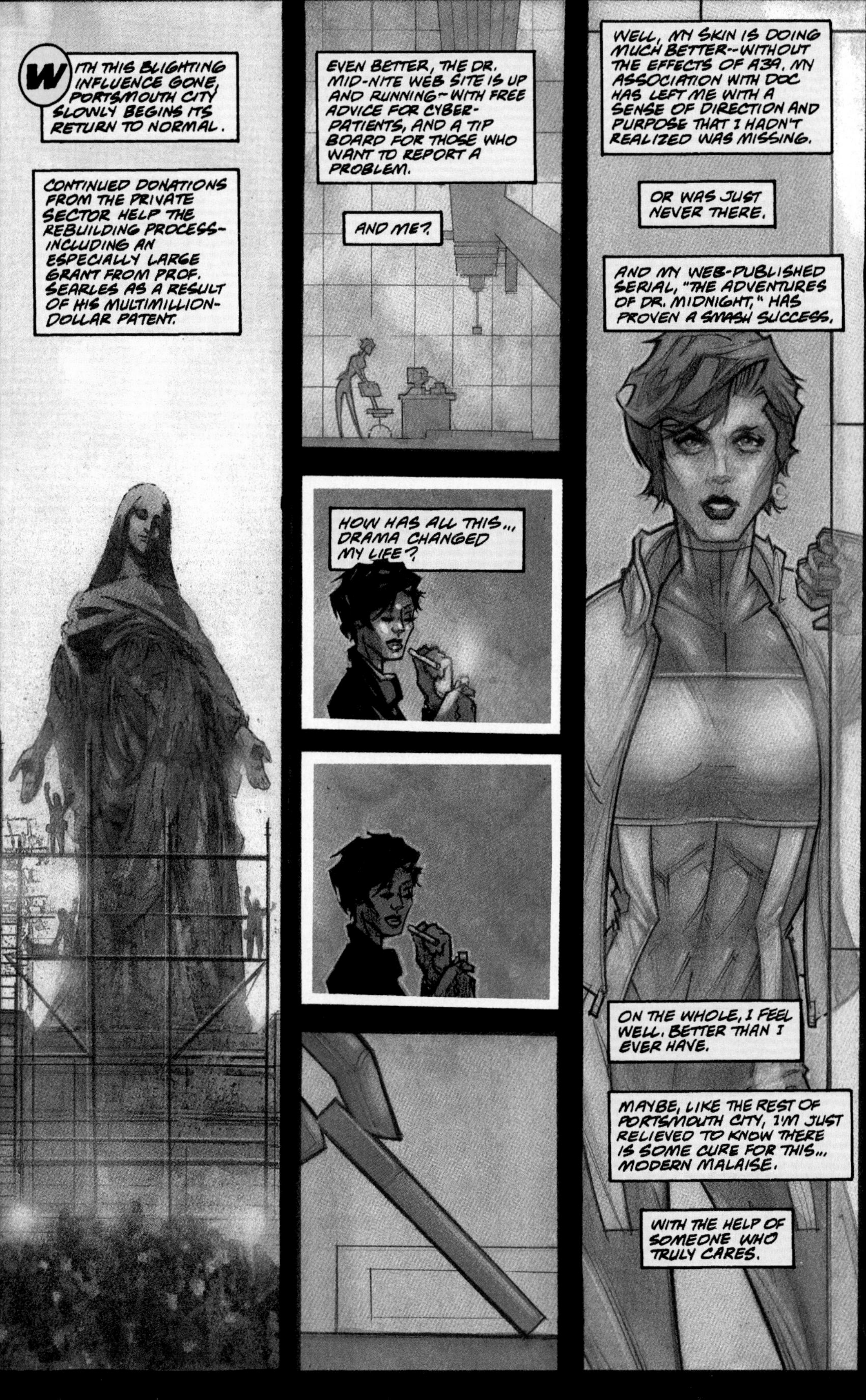
WITH THIS BLIGHTING INFLUENCE GONE, PORTSMOUTH CITY SLOWLY BEGINS ITS RETURN TO NORMAL.
CONTINUED DONATIONS FROM THE PRIVATE SECTOR HELP THE REBUILDING PROCESS-- INCLUDING AN ESPECIALLY LARGE GRANT FROM PROF. SEARLES AS A RESULT OF HIS MULTIMILLION-DOLLAR PATENT.
EVEN BETTER, THE DR. MID-NITE WEB SITE IS UP AND RUNNING--WITH FREE ADVICE FOR CYBER-PATIENTS, AND A TIP BOARD FOR THOSE WHO WANT TO REPORT A PROBLEM.
AND ME?
HOW HAS ALL THIS... DRAMA CHANGED MY LIFE?
WELL, MY SKIN IS DOING MUCH BETTER--WITHOUT THE EFFECTS OF A39. MY ASSOCIATION WITH DOC HAS LEFT ME WITH A SENSE OF DIRECTION AND PURPOSE THAT I HADN'T REALIZED WAS MISSING.
OR WAS JUST NEVER THERE.
AND MY WEB-PUBLISHED SERIAL, "THE ADVENTURES OF DR. MIDNIGHT," HAS PROVEN A SMASH SUCCESS.
ON THE WHOLE, I FEEL WELL. BETTER THAN I EVER HAVE.
MAYBE, LIKE THE REST OF PORTSMOUTH CITY, I'M JUST RELIEVED TO KNOW THERE IS SOME CURE FOR THIS... MODERN MALAISE.
WITH THE HELP OF SOMEONE WHO TRULY CARES.

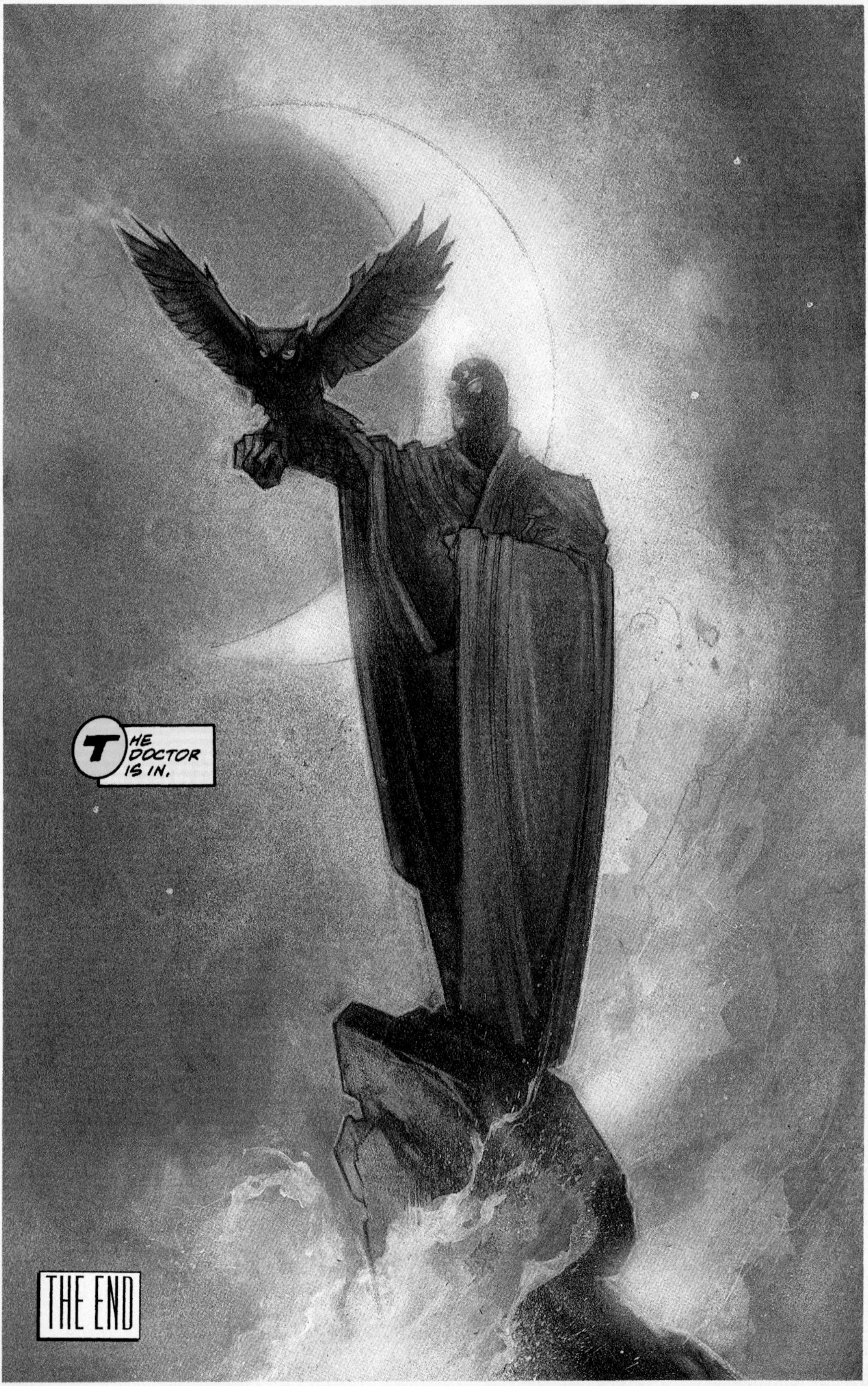
THE DOCTOR IS IN.
THE END

S K E T C H E S

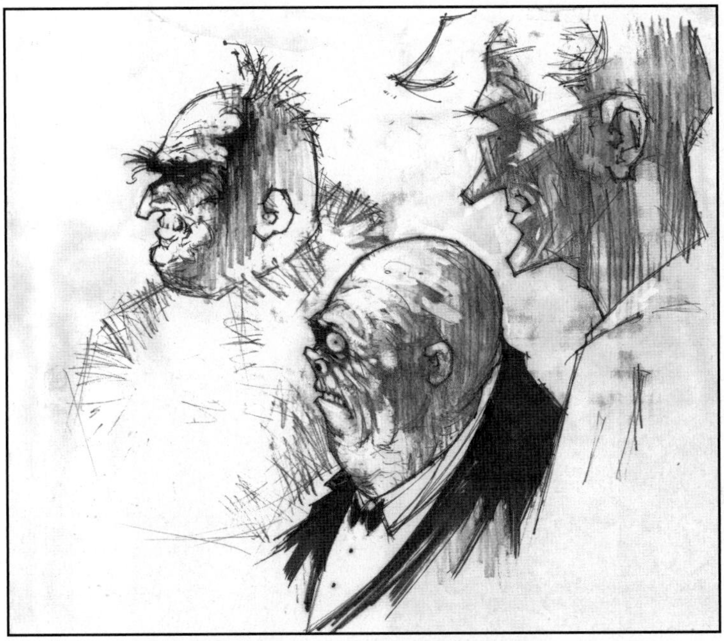

THE TERRIBLE TRIO —— THEIR FINAL UGLIFIED APPEARANCE

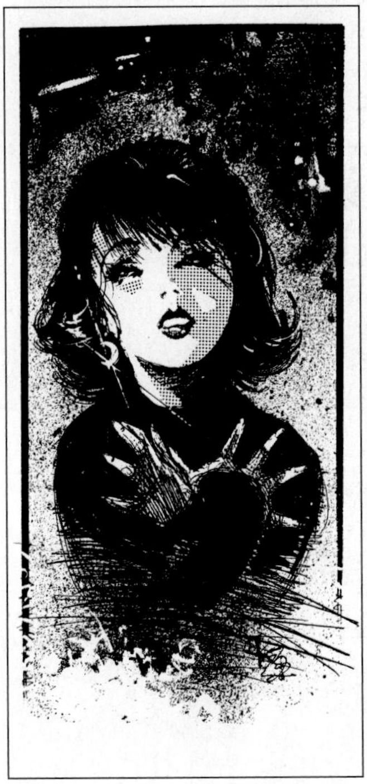

B&W STUDY OF CAMILLA MARLOWE

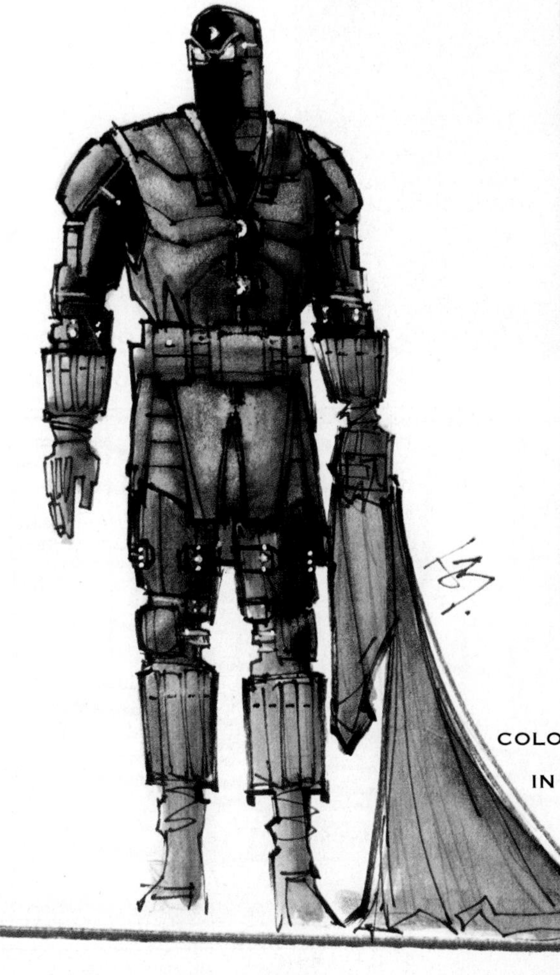

COLOR STUDY OF DOCTOR MID-NITE IN BATTLE ARMOR (DESIGNED WITH A NOD TO THE ORIGINAL GOLDEN AGE COSTUME)

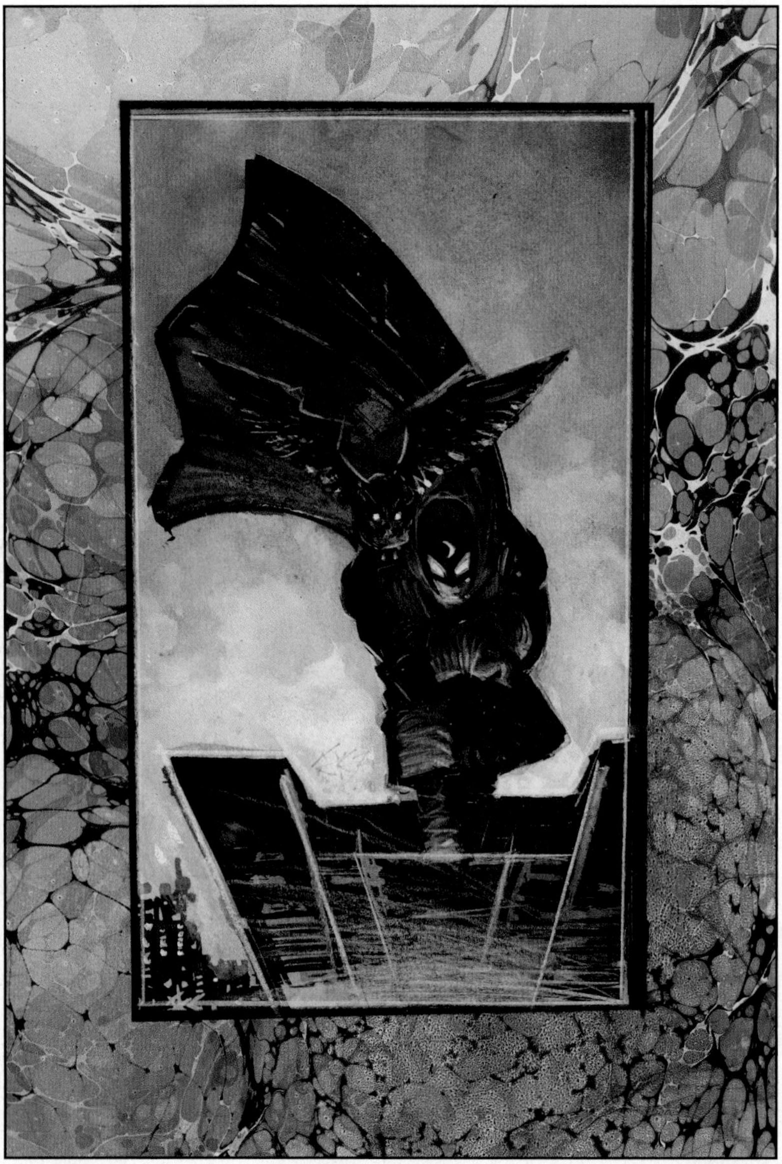

INITIAL COLOR
STUDY OF
DOCTOR MID-NITE

STUDY OF
INTERIOR OF TRIO'S
UNDERGROUND LAIR

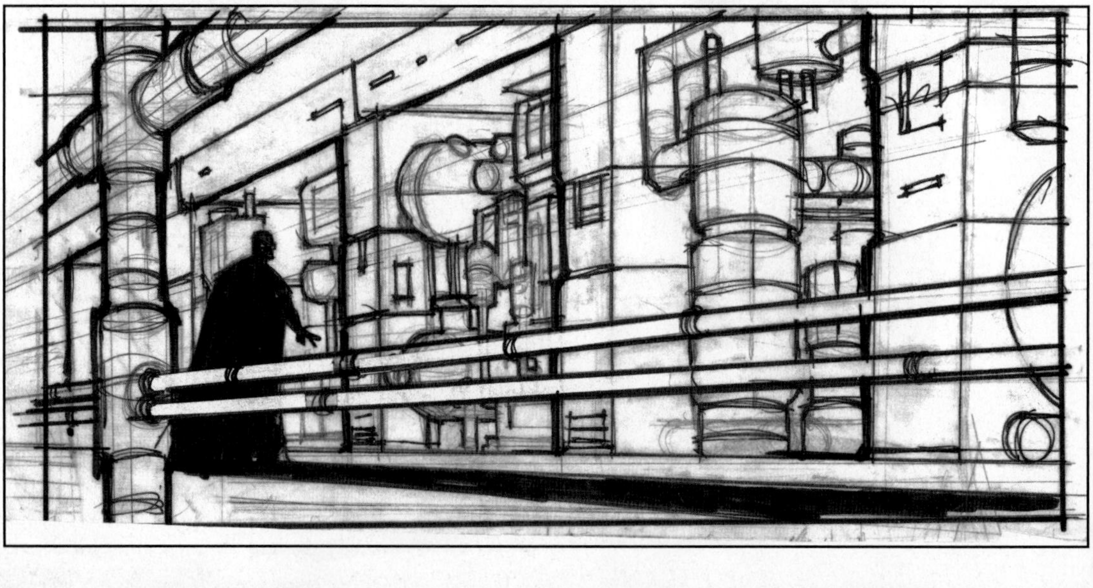

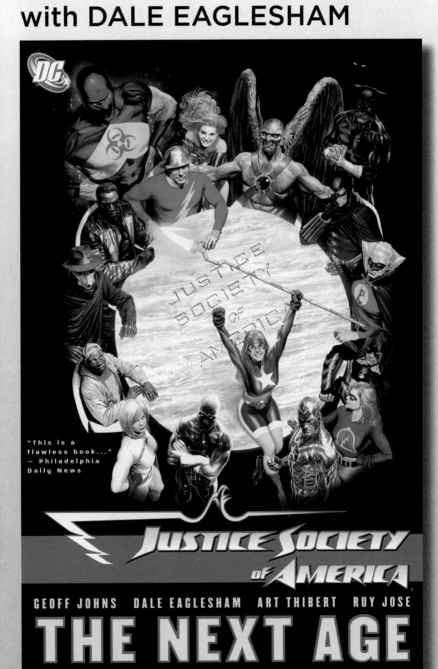

"The talk of the comic book world."
—USA WEEKEND

"Thrilling and shocking in equal measure."
—IGN

"Geoff Johns is a master storyteller."
—Newsarama

FROM THE WRITER OF *THE FLASH* & *ACTION COMICS*
GEOFF JOHNS
BLACKEST NIGHT with IVAN REIS

BLACKEST NIGHT:
GREEN LANTERN

BLACKEST NIGHT:
GREEN LANTERN CORPS

Read the Entire Epic!

BLACKEST NIGHT

BLACKEST NIGHT:
GREEN LANTERN

BLACKEST NIGHT:
GREEN LANTERN
CORPS

BLACKEST NIGHT:
BLACK LANTERN
CORPS VOL. 1

BLACKEST NIGHT:
BLACK LANTERN
CORPS VOL. 2

BLACKEST NIGHT:
RISE OF THE BLACK
LANTERNS

BLACKEST NIGHT:
TALES OF THE CORPS

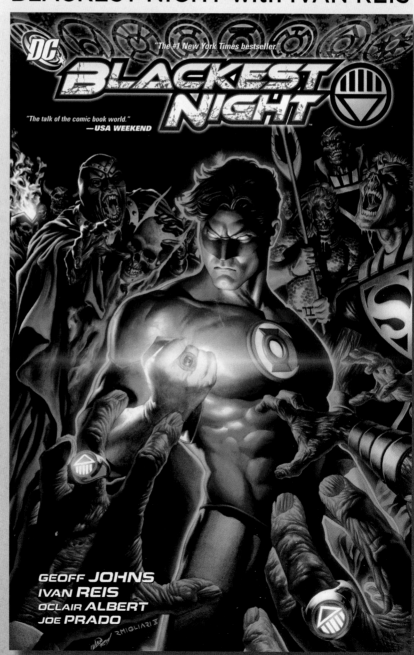

GEOFF **JOHNS**
IVAN **REIS**
OCLAIR **ALBERT**
JOE **PRADO**

"Compelling drama. A...
the literary and artist...
graph...
—SCHOOL LIBR...

FROM THE *NEW YORK TIMES* BESTSELLIN...

ED BRUBAK...
& GREG RUCK...

with MICHAEL LARK

**GOTHAM CENTRAL
BOOK TWO:
JOKERS AND MADMEN**

**GOTHAM CENTRAL
BOOK THREE:
ON THE FREAK BEAT**

**GOTHAM CENTRAL
BOOK FOUR:
CORRIGAN**

EISNER AND HARVEY AWARD-WINNING SERIES

"THE BEST BATMAN COMIC BEING PUBLISHED THESE DAYS." —Boston Phoenix

GOTHAM CENTRAL ™

BOOK ONE: IN THE LINE OF DUTY

ED
BRUBAKER
GREG
RUCKA

MICHAEL LARK

INTRODUCTION BY
LAWRENCE BLOCK

...T THE EISNER AWARD-WINNING
...TER OF *100 BULLETS*

...RIAN AZZARELLO
with LEE BERMEJO

...great example of ...c maturity of the ...novel format."
...RARY JOURNAL

...G WRITERS

with LEE BERMEJO

SUPERMAN: FOR TOMORROW

with JIM LEE

BATMAN: BROKEN CITY

...DUARDO RISSO

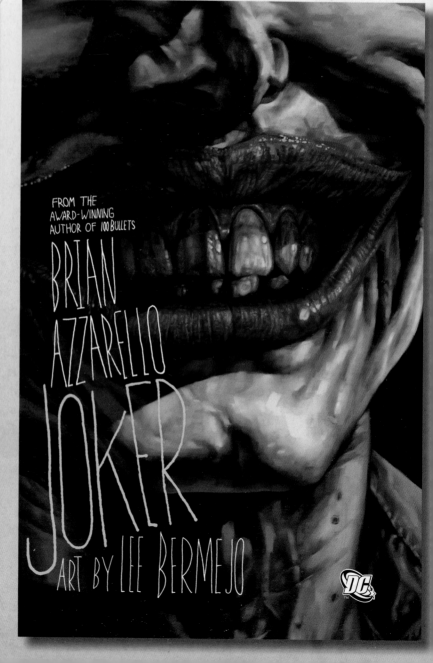

FROM THE AWARD-WINNING AUTHOR OF *100 BULLETS*

BRIAN AZZARELLO

JOKER

ART BY LEE BERMEJO

DC